Alexander Kluge

Alexander Kluge
The Last Modernist

PETER C. LUTZE

Wayne State University Press   Detroit

LIBRARY OF CONGRESS CATALOGING IN PUBLICATION DATA

Lutze, Peter C.

Alexander Kluge: The Last Modernist / Peter C. Lutze.

p.   cm. — (Contemporary film and television series)

Filmography: p.

Includes bibliographical references and index.

ISBN 0-8143-2656-0 (pbk. : alk. paper)

1. Kluge, Alexander, 1932–   —Criticism and interpretation.

I. Title.   II. Series.

PN1998.3.K598L88   1998

791.43'0233'092—dc21   97-37942

DESIGNED BY S. R. TENENBAUM

The photograph of Alexander Kluge was taken by

THOMAS MAYFRIED © Thomas Mayfried/VISUM, Hamburg, Germany.

CONTEMPORARY FILM AND TELEVISION SERIES

A complete listing of the books in this series can be found at the back of this volume.

GENERAL EDITOR

Patricia B. Erens   University of Hong Kong

ADVISORY EDITORS

Lucy Fischer   University of Pittsburgh

Barry Grant   Brock University

Peter Lehman   University of Arizona

Caren J. Deming   University of Arizona

Robert J. Burgoyne   Wayne State University

Contents

Acknowledgments

I am very grateful to Dr. Alexander Kluge for his generosity and cooperation through all the stages of development of this book. He provided me with copies of his books, films, and television programs; talked with me on numerous occasions; and allowed me to observe the production of several television programs. His assistant, Karen Petraschke, has also been most helpful in providing information and photographs.

This book was shaped in large part by the suggestions and ideas of David Bordwell. His boundless energy and dedication as both a scholar and teacher continue to serve as a model for emulation.

This book also builds on the work of a number of scholars who have done extensive work on Kluge, most notably Miriam Hansen. Her work is exemplary for its perceptive, sympathetic, and yet critical examination and interpretation of Kluge's art. She was largely responsible for introducing Kluge to American scholars, and her substantial body of articles rewards multiple readings. Hansen also edited the special Kluge issue of *New German Critique* that appeared in the winter of 1990 and coordinated the New York Kluge conference in 1988. Rainer Lewandowski's two German monographs on Kluge provide a wealth of data and insight on his films and writings. Stuart Liebman has played a significant role in broadening the information available in America about Kluge and has increased academic interest in his films by organizing the retrospective of Kluge's films that toured the United States in 1988–89. Liebman also edited and contributed to the 1988 issue of *October* devoted to Kluge, which served as the catalogue to the retrospective. The retrospective and associated events and publications were the occasion for significant scholarly reevaluations of Kluge's work. Tim Corrigan's work on Kluge and the insights of Thomas Elsaesser and Rick Rentschler have also been invaluable.

Other major influences on this book have been extensive conversations about Kluge with Meinhard Prill, Daniela Sannwald, Maximiliane Mainke, and Alexandra Kluge. I am also indebted to Ursula and Hannes Frank, and Anne Heritage and Paul Kremmel for all their support and encouragement through the years. The staffs of the Deutsche Film- und Fernsehakademie Bibliothek in Berlin and the Deutsches Institut für Filmkunde in Frankfurt have also been most helpful. I would also like to thank Friedrich Knilli, Siegfried Zielinski, and Hennig Falkenstein for their advice and support.

From my years in Wisconsin, I want to thank Tina Balio, Jim Steakley, Tom Streeter, John Fiske, J. J. Murphy, and Vance Kepley; and my colleagues Murray Smith, Mike Curtin, Rick Maxwell, Darrell Davis, Mike Myers, Jane Shattuc, and Ellen Risholm. At Boise State, Peter Wollheim, Marty Most, and especially Ellen Agler have made numerous helpful suggestions, while Bob Boren and Marvin Cox have provided fiscal and emotional support. Lastly, I want to thank Kathy, Isaac, and Solomon for their patience, sacrifices, and love.

Introduction

Although relatively unknown in the United States, Alexander Kluge has been a major figure in German culture for over thirty years. His obscurity in this country is the result of his low media profile and his rather difficult films. Compared to more flamboyant figures such as Rainer Werner Fassbinder or Werner Herzog, Kluge seems more cerebral and pedestrian. Nor are his films as readily enjoyable or comprehensible to most cinema-goers as those of Wim Wenders or Volker Schlöndorff.

Nevertheless, Kluge's contribution to New German Cinema and cultural politics in Germany would be difficult to overestimate. Since 1961, Kluge has produced almost thirty films and hundreds of television programs, written four volumes of fiction, coauthored three major works of sociocultural theory, and won almost every major literary and film prize within Germany. Perhaps even more important for the development of postwar cinema in the Federal Republic have been his tireless organizational and promotional activities as a teacher, political lobbyist, and public spokesman. As one writer has remarked, "outsider and insider, center and periphery, one who provides the impulse and at the same time is there where it is received. An impossible position. Kluge has maintained it for years and with success. He was always there where you didn't expect him, and wherever you do expect him, he's there, too."[1] Kluge has brought remarkable energy to the task of revitalizing German cinema so that it could play a more active role in culture and society.

By the early 1960s, West German cinema was much in need of such revitalization. What had been Europe's largest and most widely distributed cinema during the war years was split in the postwar era between East and West Germany—with much of the productive capacity located in the East. But the crisis in West German film was much more acute than the physical and geopolitical difficulties. On the one hand, the West German film industry faced severe pressure from Hollywood, which had been given very favorable treatment during the Allied occupation and continued to maintain a key role in distribution and at the box office. On the other hand, the wide acceptance of television had seriously begun to erode cinema attendance.

Moreover, throughout the 1950s, West German cinema had difficulty establishing its own identity. The requisite break with National Socialist cinema was being attempted by personnel who, for the most part, had been retained from that tainted era. With a few notable exceptions, the postwar films demonstrated a lack of innovative energy or a clear sense of purpose. German society at this time was anxious to forget its recent traumatic past. Most felt the Third Reich should not be publicly celebrated, lamented, or critically examined. With a few striking exceptions, the cinematic consequences of this public amnesia were optimistic films: nostalgic recreations of imaginary pasts or romantic comedies set in an idealized present.

Kluge and his cohorts proposed an alternative: relevant, contemporary films by younger filmmakers. Between 1965 and 1980, these filmmakers created a remarkable body of work that gained many of them international acclaim. Throughout that period, Kluge played a central role in nurturing, unifying, and defending this new cinema while continuing his own prodigious output.

His political activities alone would make Kluge a worthy and interesting subject of study, and they will be discussed extensively in chapter 2. However, a close examination of Kluge's media productions and writings proves even more intriguing. The conjunction of politics and aesthetics, of radical theory and innovative practice provides a particularly rich site for analysis. Kluge's work is closely related to the modernist aesthetics of Theodor Adorno and the Frankfurt School but constitutes a unique instance of that theory as program rather than simply critique. His media productions as well as his writings confront many important contemporary aesthetic issues: autonomous art and social function, the relation of author to text, collectivity versus individual action, radical form and spectatorship, the making of meaning and the taking of pleasure, the dynamic symbiosis of high and low culture, and chaos and purity of forms. This book will explore the often complex articulations of these issues within the film and television productions of Alexander Kluge.

Given the substantial body of theoretical work that Kluge has produced, it is extremely tempting to use his theory as an interpretive key to his work. The enigmatic nature of the films and the wealth of extratextual explanatory comments by Kluge tend to encourage such a practice. Both film critics and spectators have often succumbed to this temptation, treating Kluge's films as the embodiment or exemplars of his theory. The relationship between his films and his theory, however, is much more problematic. Theory is only one determinant in Kluge's cinematic practice. Accident, improvisation, economic constraints, and the particular nature of the filmic medium intervene. Moreover, Kluge's filmic and theoretical activities share an eclecticism that encourages contradiction rather than consistency. Nor should his theory be reified. His theoretical pronouncements are situational and frequently developed ex post facto to explain a result rather than a priori to obtain one. In fact, it is the contradictions and tensions within Kluge's work that are most interesting to explore.

Although one cannot overlook the explanatory power of Kluge's theory, the central chapters of this book are based primarily on a close examination of his films and television programs rather than his extratextual commentaries. This examination will explore Kluge's narrational strategies (chapter 3), stylistic techniques (chapter 4), thematic elements (chapter 5), and the modes of reception that they encourage.

Many of the issues raised by Kluge's practice have become key terms of the modernism/postmodernism debate. Kluge's productions —as well as his pronouncements—demonstrate a modernist sensibility and an appropriation of modernist formal strategies. Before looking at Kluge's work, therefore, it is necessary to first come to terms with the question of what modernism is.

1 LATE MODERNISM AND THE ARRIÈRE-GARDIST

Surveying
the Modernist
Terrain

A word of purely common origin, created out of the aston-
ishment of the majority for the latest novelties, modernism
means something different to each person who utters it.
                                              —Manuel Machado [1]

In an interview in July 1988, Kluge asserted that he
was a modernist.[2] Characteristically, he did not explain what he
meant. A year earlier, in conversations with the film scholar Stuart
Liebman, Kluge had also positioned himself within modernism, although more circumspectly: "Let me say right away that I am not
at all sure that my ideas or my practice are inconsistent with modernism." The context for this remark was a discussion of two related aesthetic concepts: the avant-garde and postmodernism. Liebman had remarked that, "Your practice [using old materials to create
new constructions] seems closer to postmodernism than to that
highly refined purism that we have come to call—unfortunately
and incorrectly—modernism."[3] In rejecting this postmodernist label, Kluge asserted that his modernism has nothing to do with purity. He cited Theodor Adorno's antipathy toward purists and to
the notion that any art can be pure. These comments reaffirmed both
his relationship to the Frankfurt School and to a particular artistic
tradition.[4] What is key in all of Kluge's work is its self-conscious

function as a critique rather than an instrument of modernity and mass culture.

As a late modernist, Kluge's approach has been eclectic. He has been able to draw on a large body of preexistent modernist art works for methods of evading or resolving what might seem insurmountable artistic difficulties posed by modern society—commodification, mass reproduction, fragmentation of experience. In particular, the aesthetic practices of Bertolt Brecht and the Russian montagists have been very influential on him. His provisional solutions are also inflected by the terms of theoretical debates in Germany between major modernist figures, especially Adorno, Brecht, and Walter Benjamin. Kluge brings a particular kind of critical or political modernism to bear on the social conditions of his time—even now when those conditions might more aptly be identified as postmodern.

To determine what modernist elements are present in Kluge's work, however, it is necessary to look at how the term "modernism" has been used in critical literature. It is also useful to briefly examine the two related terms raised in the Liebman interview with Kluge: "the avant-garde" and "postmodernism." What is at stake here is more than simply settling a label on Kluge or his work. Central to Kluge's aesthetic work is a particular conception of the social functions and responsibilities of art and the formal and thematic implications of this role.

1
The Artist
as
Activist

KLUGE AND MODERNISM

There has not been a single accomplished work of art in the last hundred years or so that was able to dodge the concept of modernism, no matter how tentative it may be. The more art tried to get away from the problematic of modernism, the sooner it perished.

—Theodor Adorno [1]

Although the terms "modern," "modernity," and "modernism" have been appropriated in many different contexts and applied to a variety of phenomena, it is perhaps most useful to trace how these terms have been used in German aesthetic criticism and in particular by Adorno, whose work stands as both a backdrop to and a resource for Kluge's artistic and theoretical work. At one time an aspiring composer and student of the musician Alban Berg, Adorno retained a keen interest in musical innovation but also wrote on contemporary literature, drama, and the visual arts. He was also an astute and impassioned critic of the modern society in which these art works were created and experienced.[2] His theory of artistic modernism and social modernization have been very influential on postwar German artists and intellectuals.

In his book *Aesthetic Theory* (1970), Adorno insists on modernism's close relationship to a particular historical and social situation: the era of monopoly capitalism. Key features of this period are domination by the bourgeoisie, industrialization, mechanization, and rationalization. The economy and most aspects of public and private life are controlled by large institutions such as corporations and the state. The dominance of the profit motive results in relentless commodification and reification of human relationships. The fetishization of "the New" undergirds the bourgeois attack on traditional institutions and fosters increased consumerism to fuel the production economy.

Adorno argues that art in modern society has been freed of its ritual (ecclesiastical) functions and has been granted a certain autonomy that also ensures that it is separated from the concerns of everyday life: art is free to be irrelevant. In this view, modern art supports the bourgeois project by negating tradition, but it also negates the administered society in which it arises. It rejects attempts to turn art into a commodity or into something useful to the aims of society. Rejecting the false harmonies and the totalitarian tendencies of modern society, art is negative, dissonant, and fragmented. Increasingly, art becomes isolated and removed from society. As it follows its own laws and principles, art becomes more complex and less accessible, something that can be appreciated only by a very sophisticated audience. Although artists attempt to preserve a sphere of autonomy that is inaccessible to most people, the culture industry manufactures products for consumption by mass audiences: movies, television and radio, magazines, pulp fiction, and popular music. All of these cultural commodities serve to affirm the status quo, to lull the audiences into acceptance of the inevitability of their condition, to ameliorate the pain of their alienated, unfulfilled, and inauthentic lives.

Adorno's writings are particularly relevant to any study of the work of Kluge, who developed a strong personal friendship with Adorno in the 1950s.[3] Much of Kluge's work is informed by and can be seen as a response to Adorno's theory. Kluge shares Adorno's interest in the relation between the individual and institutions. Most of his protagonists (in both his films and fiction) are trying to find an authentic identity in the face of impersonal, antagonistic, and invasive governmental, religious, and commercial bureaucracies. On a formal level, Kluge attempts to resolve the high culture/low culture split by utilizing the media of mass culture to create "autonomous" art. On an institutional level, Kluge tries to insulate film artists from some commercial pressures by providing alternative funding and distribution mechanisms.

Adorno's social/aesthetic analysis of modernity has at least four important features that Kluge and many other theorists have incorporated into their critical theory. First, Adorno consistently emphasizes the close connection between modernity (late capitalist society) and modern art. The latter derives its themes, formal structures, materials, and much of its creative force from industrialized, urban capitalism. As Andreas Huyssen has noted: "Modernism and the avantgarde were always closely related to social and industrial modernization. They were related to it as an adversary culture, yes, but they drew their energies . . . from their proximity to the crises brought about by modernization and progress."[4]

For Kluge, too, all cultural artifacts are products of their historical context, and it is the duty of the artist to critique the structures and assumptions of contemporary society: "Either social history will narrate its reality novel with no consideration for human beings, or human beings will narrate their own counter-history. They cannot do this, however, unless at the same degree of complexity as reality. This requires in the most literal sense the 'art object,' an aggregate of art objects."[5] Some suggest that all art in this period inevitably reflects dominant economic and social conditions, while others discern a more mediated and complex interrelationship. Adorno's analysis suggests that many different kinds of art are practiced during this period, and only the most advanced will fully realize the contradictions of the society in which they come to be. This is often an unconscious rather than conscious synchronicity. Other commentators stress the ways in which contemporary social phenomena are thematized in modern works (the city, the machine, war) and the ways in which inventions and mechanization in general have altered perceptions of distance and time.[6]

Adorno's emphasis on the social context of modernism leads to a second point, which has also been raised by a number of other theorists: modernism connotes more than just certain formal or stylistic affinities. That is, modernists can be said to share a certain sensibility or attitude, and this is a largely negative or critical one.[7] Lionel Trilling has referred to modernism as the "adversary culture."[8] The modern element is "a bitter line of hostility to civilization," a "disenchantment with culture itself."[9] This negativity manifests itself both in content (the bleakness of subject in absurdist theater or expressionist antiwar painting) and in formal principles (fragmentation, lack of closure, dissonance).[10] Dissonance is for Adorno "the trademark of modern art," and it indicates the problematized convergence of artistic autonomy and external reality.[11] For Kluge, this negativity is expressed in his cinema—a *cinema impur*[12]—which utilizes the dissonance of montage as a resistance to the fatalism of social reality.

In other eras, new aesthetic tendencies gradually transformed dominant artistic styles and practices, but "modernism negates tradition itself," thereby adapting a radical notion of progress to the aesthetic sphere.[13] This is a third aspect of Adorno's critique that is widely accepted: modernism's emphatic break with the old and valorization of the new. Tradition, whether centuries or weeks old, is rejected in favor of innovation. Movements and styles develop and disappear quickly and when gone are as useless as yesterday's newspaper. Both art and art criticism become normative and intolerant, although these norms are constantly shifting (but always facing forward, never back). Art changes like fashions, artists are spurred to find new methods, new materials, and new stimulation. The new is thrilling, abstract, and cryptic. As in modern society at large, the new offers both the hope of something completely different and the threat of more of the same: "Art has appropriated the economic category [of novelty]. The new in art is the aesthetic counterpart of the expanding reproduction of capital in society. Both hold out the promise of undiminished plenitude."[14] Underlying this antitraditionalism is a sense that universal values and meanings have disappeared, resulting in a historical relativism.[15]

Although Kluge's cinematic career is characterized by narrative, stylistic, and thematic iconoclasm, he nevertheless maintains a more ambivalent attitude toward tradition than some modernists. He overturns conventional forms while critiquing relativism and insisting on a historical perspective. He appropriates and transforms traditional materials, techniques, and subjects in the construction of relevant contemporary works. For Kluge, such modernist application of cultural fragments works dialectically: neither tradition nor modernity is valorized, but the present is forced to confront the past. In addition, as a *late* modernist, Kluge can draw on various strains of modernism as an antitraditional tradition, which can also be quoted and reworked.

Fourth, Adorno's distinction between high culture and mass culture is especially important for modernists. Mass culture is one of the most pernicious and insidious tools of the "other modernity," of "contemporaneity."[16] Although sometimes drawing on mass culture as source material, modernism has felt threatened with inundation by these popular products of capitalism. It is only in the era of mass production and distribution of art that popular culture begins to constitute a serious threat to art. Clement Greenberg has argued that the development of a large urban working class, the increase in leisure time, and the spread of universal literacy throughout Western Europe and North America led to a demand for more cultural products but by a less sophisticated audience. "To fill the demand of the new market, a new commodity was devised: ersatz culture, kitsch, destined for those who, insensible to the values of genuine culture, are hungry nevertheless for the diversion that only culture of some sort can provide. Kitsch, using for raw material the debased and academicized simulacra of genuine culture, welcomes and cultivates this insensibility. It is the source of its profits. Kitsch is mechanical and operates by formula. Kitsch is vicarious experience and faked sensations."[17]

The giant centralized machinery for manufacturing kitsch—for diverting and manipulating the masses—makes artisanal, autonomous art difficult if not anachronistic. The modernist critique of mass culture is aimed at both institutions and individual products. Although some products of mass culture may evade their affirmative mission, most fulfill it. Even escapist productions serve as a controlled but unreal and unrealizable alternative to the horrors of everyday life.[18] Although sensitive to the real human need for escape from modern life, Kluge has repeatedly attacked Hollywood-style cinema: "Pleasure as a corrective should not be taken to mean that the entertainment principle of television shows or Hollywood hits is a better corrective than a critical consciousness. But not much else remains. All mass loyalty to repressive entertainment can be attributed to realistic pleasure interest inherent in it."[19] Entertainment cinema is not merely a waste of time, it functions to disguise reality and repress human resistance to inhuman conditions.

Because of mass culture's production and distribution conditions, because of the function that mass culture artifacts are produced to serve, they must be condemned and resisted. Thus modern art wages a cultural war on two fronts: against the oppressiveness of the past and its established cultural traditions and against the onslaught of mass culture. Modern art, in the face of these assaults, insists more vehemently on its autonomy.[20] But as it retreats ever further from the corruption of commercial mass culture, it becomes even less accessible to the uninitiated. Adorno comments: "Just as the nonexpert has trouble grasping the most recent developments in modern physics, so the nonexpert cannot understand the complexities of modern painting or music."[21] As a high culture of an intellectual aristocracy, modernism makes ever-increasing demands on its recipients. It posits an active, sophisticated audience. Kluge's films have often been criticized as difficult, a charge only partially answered by Kluge's insistence on the central role of the spectator: "Film is not a thing of authors, but a dialogue between author and spectator. That is a very high conflict step, because the spectator through all of his previous experience with the cinema is preprogrammed . . . and the film is realized for me, not on the screen but in the head of the spectator." [22] By shifting the locus of control from the artist to the viewer, Kluge's films place a heavier burden on the audience than do more conventional works. Kluge comments: "I am always being asked, Can't you make it a little cheaper? Can't you make it somehow friendlier for the spectator? . . . I cannot do so. Just like a respectable physicist, we don't give discounts." [23]

Audience response to difficult and esoteric modern art typically takes two forms: shock or cerebral appreciation. For most recipients, the radical break with traditional art is wrenching and disturbing. Anti-illusionist, antirepresentational, and fragmentary works cannot be understood or made to fit into the recipients' notions of what art should be. This sort of art does not make them feel good or provide a sense of wholeness and harmony that is lacking in their everyday lives. It is the quest for fulfillment that frequently draws people to the aesthetic realm, but modern art often frustrates these needs and desires. Many modernists refused to give audiences what they wanted or would enjoy. In fact, the intent to shock philistines constituted a significant impulse in the program of many modernist artists. [24]

For the few sophisticated recipients who understand the nature of the modernist project and who are no longer shocked, modern art offers substantial rewards. Not the least of these is membership in an elite group of *cognoscenti*. Another is the sense of personal courage manifest in the face of cultural shock: not being offended like the philistines. There is also the challenge and amusement of the sport. As each new art work invents its own internal rules and purposes, the recipient must discern what these might be: is this work allegorical or psychological, is it concerned with the material and if so what aspect, or is it a comment on its social context? [25] In any case, the recipient is constantly stimulated and challenged by new works, by new ways of seeing, by new materials. The recipient is invited to participate in the construction of meaning, to fill in the blanks, and to make difficult connections. Kluge seems to have collected a dedicated group of *cognoscenti* who derive varied pleasures from his films, television programs, and books: mental challenge and stimulation, visual pleasure, intellectual status, and connections and insights to their own lived experience.

The modernist work's formal strategies for differentiating itself from both the past and mass culture are manifold. Formal innovation is highly prized by modernists. Adorno claims that "artists are compelled by force of circumstance to experiment," and that in fact "art today is virtually impossible unless it is engaged in experimentation."[26] Without a radical style, he suggests, no artwork can function critically. Indeed modernism has been disparaged as the "fetishism of form."[27] As the aesthetic media and individual artists search for originality and novelty, a broad spectrum of stylistic techniques is employed. Many of these formal techniques contradict one another. Despite the fact that modernism is often reduced to a category of style, any purely stylistic account of modernism can be overturned by counterexamples, exceptions, and contrary trends. Nevertheless, it is possible to hazard a few observations about certain formal structures that occur in many, if not all, modernist works across the lines of particular genres and media. These include: self-consciousness, reflexivity, a concern with process and materials, a refusal to obscure the constructedness of the work, the use of montage and collage, an invention of personal styles and standards, the insistence on fragmentation over unity or coherence, a preference of abstraction over illusionism, and the maintenance of an ironic tone. Any referentiality to the external world is minimized, and art itself becomes the subject matter: "Content is to be dissolved so completely into form that the work of art or literature cannot be reduced in whole or in part to anything not itself."[28] In its quest for stylistic novelty, modernism constantly puts on display the vivid, the striking, and the incongruous. The unexpected comes to be expected.

Based on these varied usages of the word modernism, it is possible to synthesize a working definition that would be useful in discussing Kluge's work. Modernism is an artistic sensibility originating in late capitalist society (early twentieth century) that attacks previous art traditions and their modes of representation. It rejects harmony, totality, and coherence for dissonance, process, and fragmentation, and calls for an active and sophisticated mode of reception.

As indicated earlier, however, modernism manifests itself differently in different artistic media. What might constitute a modernist film practice? Two mutually contradictory objections have been raised regarding cinematic works as modernist. The first, based on Adorno's thought, asserts that as a mass medium, film cannot be autonomous art and if not art, then not modernist. The second objection is that the

term "modernist" is meaningless as a category for distinguishing between films because all films are modernist. Critics like Arnold Hauser
have argued that the cinema is a product of the modern period and
has modernity stamped on it. Its production, reproduction, and dissemination are all mechanical, its material is a seriality of image
frames, its essence is collage—juxtaposition of one image with another. Thus it is impossible to speak of a film that is not modern.[29]

This latter argument, based strictly on the mechanical apparatus, is
unconvincing and seems based on a confusion of "modern" with
"modernist." Printed literature is equally mechanical in its production
and distribution and is equally serial. Yet few would argue that all
literature is equally modernist.

The first objection—that film is a mass medium, not an art—contains several related, but distinct assumptions: 1) it is aimed at a mass,
uneducated audience and therefore must be of low quality; 2) it is
fundamentally commercial, and thus obeys the laws of the marketplace rather than its own internal aesthetic principles; 3) it is a means
of social control and thus has been instrumentalized (as in the previous assumption, it has lost its autonomy and integrity); and 4) it is
not produced by an individual but by a group or corporation and
therefore has no coherence and lacks any personal expression. Most
films, it is true, have such characteristics that might disqualify them
from consideration as art and thus as modernist art. Nevertheless, the
film medium has been utilized by any number of artists for different
purposes and in different ways. These range from experimental projects often undertaken by established visual artists such as Salvador
Dali, Man Ray, Hans Richter, Maya Deren, or Andy Warhol to more
commercial "art films" by directors such as Abel Gance or Jean-Luc
Godard. Such films show strong traces of the personality of an individual creator (even if she or he collaborated with others). For some,
there is virtually no prospect of any financial return; for most, the
choice of subject, style, and mode of distribution precludes any possibility of substantial financial success. Rather than functioning as le-
gitimators of prevailing social structures and norms, these filmmakers
were often highly critical of their social environment and particularly
of the conventions of mainstream cinema. If artistic autonomy, non-
commodification, and critical negativity constitute the criteria of authentic art, then at least some of these films have as much right to
claim artistic standing as works in any other medium. If certain films
are or might be art, then presumably some of these may also be modernist art.

What then are the characteristics that would constitute a modernist film practice? In the first place, such films are often self-conscious about the medium and its uses. They may display a negativism, a critical attitude toward society. Most are suspicious of traditional narrative and particularly of closure. They reject or critique melodrama and expect an active participation of the viewer. They prize innovation and experimentation in shooting and editing. Stylistically they may prefer abstraction to representation, montage to linearity, fragmentation over coherence, dissonance over harmony. They resist the subordination of aesthetic considerations to the demands of commerce or functionality. As in other artistic media, a broad range of works fits some, if not all of these criteria: the abstract filmic experiments of Hans Richter or Norman McLaren; the surrealism of *Entr'acte;* the spatial and temporal ambiguities of *Last Year at Marienbad;* the emphatic montage of Sergei Eisenstein or Dziga Vertov.

Kluge, coming late in the modernist era, had at his disposal a wide variety of modernist styles and practices to draw on, both cinematic and noncinematic, a whole modern tradition that he could imitate, transform, and transcend in the search for his own new style. His films have appropriated diverse materials and styles, montage/collage organization, and voice-over authorial narration. He regards film as a construction site both for filmmaker and spectator, rejects Hollywood illusionism and closure, and employs an insistently ironic tone. Metaphor and visual essay are employed to examine art, cinema, history, and contemporary society. In his media work from 1960 to the present, he has refined his eclectic, associational style, while constantly searching for new subjects and techniques. In some cases, this has led to forays outside his own style and the modernist tradition, and has ultimately resulted in his participation in a new medium: television.

Yet Kluge, more than many modernists, is profoundly traditional. The modernist movement's rejection of the past is echoed in Kluge's commitment to an innovative filmic style, but his attitude toward both the modernist and the premodernist aesthetic traditions is one of admiration and nostalgia rather than disgust and rejection. Although he bows to the common understanding that totalizing productions of the past are no longer feasible, he repeatedly returns to these productions as a source of material and inspiration. A noteworthy instance is the prominent role of opera, the *Gesamtkunstwerk* of the nineteenth century, throughout his work, but particularly in his film *Die Macht der Gefühle (The Power of Emotion,* 1983).[30]

Kluge's attitudes toward innovation and tradition as well as his emphatic conjunction of artistic and political practice compel us to examine a second concept raised in the Liebman interview, the avant-garde and its relationship to modernism.

THE AVANT-GARDE

The notion of the avant-garde is intricately connected to that of modernism. Not infrequently the two words have been used interchangeably.[31] "Avant-garde," however, carries more militant connotations (in part because its etymology has military origins) than does "modernist." These connotations have helped blur a significant problem in twentieth-century aesthetics: the relationship between revolutionary art and militant politics.[32]

Too often the aesthetic avant-garde has been taken—by itself and others—as a political avant-garde. This conflation is especially tempting when artists have strong political beliefs or even undertake to support political struggles through their art. When artists such as Eisenstein, Brecht, or John Heartfield make intentionally political art, utilizing the most advanced materials and techniques available, the assumption of identity between these two species of avant-gardes becomes virtually irresistible. Nevertheless, it is important for analytical purposes to consider the aesthetic and political avant-gardes as two distinct concepts, even while observing their frequent interaction.[33] A radical aesthetic style need not have a radical political effect and politically radical art may not be stylistically innovative.

As Matei Calinescu points out, when the aesthetic avant-garde associates with the left-wing political avant-garde, elitism becomes a central concern: "To be a member of the avant-garde is to be a part of an elite—although this elite, unlike the ruling classes or groups of the past, is committed to a totally antielitist program, whose final utopian aim is the equal sharing by all people of all the benefits of life."[34] But these artists frequently insist on radically innovative forms that are often not accessible to mass audiences.[35]

Adorno does not consider the aesthetic avant-garde to be coextensive with modernism. Rather, he sees the avant-garde as the extreme, and perhaps purest, case of modernism. Peter Bürger, however, sees an opposition between modernism and the avant-garde. For Bürger, the term "avant-garde" is not merely a descriptive adjective that can be applied to formally radical works whenever they arise. Rather, he speaks of a "historical avant-garde" that existed between 1910 and 1930, whose identifying characteristic was its attempt to destroy the institution of art, not just previous artistic styles. Groups like the Surrealists and Dadaists rejected the bourgeois notion of autonomous art, of which the highest expression was the Aestheticists' program of "art for art's sake."[36] The historical avant-garde attempted to break out of this hermetically sealed compartment, to integrate art into life, and thereby to transform both art and life. For the most part, however, this effort failed: the art became contaminated and corrupted by the same real world that it hoped to redeem. The art institutions did not crumble, but rather the avant-garde movement petrified. The anti-art of the Dadaists (e.g., Marcel Duchamp's and Man Ray's "ready-mades") was transformed into art—objects bought and sold and displayed in museums. In Bürger's view, no subsequent avant-garde has existed or can exist in the wake of this failure: no matter how radical, any work of art is still produced and consumed as art, and thus any subversive intent it might have is recuperated.[37]

Although this conception of the avant-garde as a particular historical phenomenon may be attractive because of its narrowness, it does not correspond to the more common descriptive usage of the term. In particular, the term has been widely used in reference to certain experimental filmmaking of the 1960s. Although sometimes politically radical, these films are almost always stylistically radical.[38]

Andreas Huyssen suggests that the avant-garde can be seen as one form of modern art but that it differs from modernism in one significant way. The avant-garde rejects the elitist assumptions of modernism, and in particular its "hostility to mass culture." Huyssen points out that modernism's "radical separation from the culture of everyday life and its programmatic distance from political, economic and social concerns was always challenged as soon as it arose," most importantly by the historical avant-garde.[39] Huyssen suggests that the high culture/low culture split—which he refers to as "the Great Divide"—is more important than that between modernism and its predecessors or successors. Like Bürger, he believes that the historical avant-garde was not successful in eliminating this chasm, but he insists that the gap must be bridged: "The high modernist dogma has become sterile and prevents us from grasping current cultural phenomena. The boundaries between high art and mass culture have become increasingly blurred, and we should begin to see that process as one of opportunity, rather than lamenting loss of quality and failure of nerve."[40]

Although these distinctions are important, the connections and similarities between the historical avant-garde (however inclusive this category might be) and other modernist artists and tendencies are much stronger than these differences. Indeed, as will become evident in the case of Kluge, the elitist/antielitist contradiction often arises within the works of a single artist. It also seems useful to accede to common usage and employ the term "avant-garde" as a transhistorical attitude to art and art institutions. For Kluge this has meant a position on the periphery of, but still within, the commercial production and distribution system. Most of his films have opened in small commercial theaters, but also played in underground venues: communal theaters, film clubs, and cafes.[41] His work is neither completely popular nor purely esoteric.[42]

The twin questions of elitism/antielitism and the transformation of art and art institutions are central in the work of Alexander Kluge. His overall project might well be regarded as the attempt to create modernist art works in a popular medium: to create space for artistic autonomy by reshaping both the cinematic institutions and critical-theoretical cultural discourse by forcing it to consider cinema seriously. One important strategy has involved incorporating traditional art—literature, opera, music—into his cinema. He has, in fact, claimed that the only reason that he turned to cinema was because it offered him the opportunity to combine literature and music.[43] As a late modernist, however, Kluge finds it difficult to be avant-garde:

> After literature has developed and tested all the possibilities to express human experiences, after music has had such a huge, rich development from Bach and Schütz through the late romantics, Schoenberg and the Vienna School, you can't establish a new music. There is no avant-garde when the avant-garde has done everything. . . . If we have to lead something, we lead it both as the avant-garde and the *arrière-garde* [rearguard]. The avant-garde is a concept valid for the early bourgeois period, but not for the end of the bourgeoisie. At this time it may be necessary to be behind and to bring everything forward.[44]

This quotation indicates that for Kluge the notion of avant-garde is connected to the history and aims of modernism. By bringing forward all the materials, styles, and techniques of modernism—as well as of premodernist arts—into the contemporary context of media institutions, he is able to innovate, to challenge radically both the aesthetics and the affirmative complicity of the media in supporting the status quo.

Characteristic of Kluge's best work is the conjunction of both avant-gardes: a radical aesthetics and a radical politics. This critical or political modernism avoids lapsing into pure formalism even as it self-reflexively explores the conditions and modes of its representations.[45] The term "political modernism" has been used with opprobrium by Fredric Jameson and Sylvia Harvey to designate the tendency to assume that radical political effects flow inevitably from radical aesthetics. Their critique is extremely persuasive and could in certain instances be leveled at Kluge's work. At times his aesthetic practice becomes so complex, fragmented, or even dazzling that it obscures or distracts from any political impact. Whether clear or oblique, however, all of Kluge's work is informed by a critical engagement with social reality on both an institutional and personal level—even if it largely avoids political statement in the narrow sense of party politics or program. The interaction of social critique and formal innovation is often problematic but always evident in Kluge's films. It is in this sense and without opprobrium that Kluge's cinematic work is here described as "political modernism."

D. N. Rodowick has also used this term to designate certain cinematic and theoretical practices of the 1960s and 1970s in which concerns of representation, ideology, and subjectivity were paramount.[46] Most of the writers and filmmakers that he discussed, however, were working in a French and Anglo-American theoretical tradition. Kluge's work, although contemporaneous and engaged with similar concerns, was largely independent of the work of Lacan, Barthes, and Foucault, drawing more heavily on the German theoreticians previously discussed. Although also interested in epistemology, Kluge's theory focused primarily on the effects of representation, materiality, and deconstruction on an active spectator and did not incorporate semiotics or psycholinguistics.

Rodowick argues that French/Anglo political modernism reached a crisis for two reasons. First, it became trapped in a modernist aesthetic of rupture and anti-illusionism: "the starkness of the opposition between realism and modernism . . . seemed to foreclose any interest in popular cinema as irredeemably compromised by the 'dominant ideology' in content and form."[47] Secondly, films were considered "autonomous and self-contained formal systems identical to themselves, and problems of spectatorship and meaning were considered as constructed or determined by this internal dynamics of form."[48] Kluge's work on both the theoretical and practical level incorporated elements that avoided, or at least minimized, this impasse. Kluge has always insisted on realism—on real experience—in his work. On a theoretical level, this involved a notion of realism as human protest against oppressive reality. In his practice, documentary and quasi-documentary material was always juxtaposed and often integrated with fictional material. Secondly, Kluge viewed texts as open to the play of the spectator's fantasy and his films always contained a great deal of indeterminacy.

Although Kluge's theory of viewership is never fully developed, his films show a concern for the range of interests and desires of a relatively broad audience. Not only did Kluge, like Brecht and Benjamin, seek to appropriate mass distribution technologies, his formal and narrational strategies tended to avoid esoteric extremes. To bridge the gap between high culture and low culture, Kluge's modernism was never ascetic, minimalist, or sadistic toward his audience, but rather offered the viewer pleasures as well as challenges. He always retained some fictional, representational narrative; provided visual and aural—especially musical—diversity; and constantly surprised the viewer with his ironic comic touch. Like Brecht, Kluge believed that audiences must enjoy as well as think. Both artists shared an attitude toward social reality that unites learning and pleasure. As Jameson observed of Brecht, "The spirit of realism designates an active, curious, experimental, subversive—in a word, *scientific*—attitude toward social institutions and the world. . . ." This "reunion of 'science' and practical, change-oriented activity," according to Jameson, "transforms the process of 'knowing' the world into a source of delight or pleasure in its own right. . . ."[49] Although many viewers may understand only parts of a Kluge film, most experience at least some pleasures in seeing the world in new ways and making new associations.

The modernist questions of the role of art in social transformation and the relation between high culture and mass culture cannot be avoided in any investigation of Kluge's work. Kluge's aesthetic and theoretical productions are highly influenced by modernist sensibilities and, on a formal level, employ a variety of devices and strategies that draw their inspiration from other modernist artists and theorists. The questions that Kluge poses have been inherited from other modernists, and the solutions he proposes are developments consonant with their manner of thinking. This is not to say that Kluge's productions are not distinctive and in many ways original. Kluge also has much in common with avant-garde artists, both those of the 1920s and those of the 1960s, particularly in his concerns about relating art to everyday life. In addition, it can be argued that the momentum and development of his work leads him, perhaps unwillingly, to the brink of postmodernism, particularly in his television work. In Kluge's case, this development does not present a rupture in the continuity of his artistic production, but it does force an adjustment in his theoretical position. Although considerable differences can be discerned between his first and last films, and even more so between his early film work and his later television programming, these changes have been accomplished in small, easy steps, almost imperceptible as they occur.

Nevertheless, Kluge maintains modernism's critical negativity toward current social conditions in all his film and television work. The term "political modernism" is employed to distinguish Kluge's work from the more institutionalized and affirmative manifestations of high modernism as well as similar tendencies in postmodernism. Even if his films have sometimes played a role in legitimizing German culture and its liberal democracy, these works have always contained a critical dimension. Indeed it could be argued that the negativity and even melancholy of his works has increased over time. Not only do they avoid endorsing partisan politics or concrete social programs, they have rarely even presented positive models of social engagement.

Despite many affinities in style and subject matter to postmodernism, Kluge maintains a modernist sensibility: a respect for high art, an indifference to contemporary popular or mass art, an ironic rather than blasé attitude, a commitment to aesthetic standards and social change, and, perhaps most important, a fundamental assumption that meaning exists beneath the play of surfaces. Kluge holds that rationality (and enlightenment) can be utilized, and that utopia, although perhaps unrealizable, is an invaluable guide in making real choices in everyday life.

Before analyzing these modernist elements in Kluge's cinematic and television productions, however, it is necessary to first examine what is arguably his most important and complex construction, the public figure of Alexander Kluge. The artist in the age of late capitalism has realized the possibilities/necessities for self-promotion that stem from the conceptual difficulties of modern art: the artist has become the main interpretive coherence and validation for his or her art. Kluge has taken this one step further by using his artistic status to promote new institutions, which in turn foster his own productivity and that of his colleagues. In Kluge's terminology, he was able to utilize the bourgeois public sphere to create or expand an oppositional one. The construction of the public Alexander Kluge was the precondition and context for his feature film and television work.

2

The Armed Filmmaker

DONNING THE AUTOR ARMOR

There was almost no money available. So in order to make their films, they first had to create the necessary conditions. The Autorenfilm is inseparably bound up with Autorenpolitik.

—Klaus Eder[1]

In a 1976 interview, Alexander Kluge was asked about his activities in film politics in West Germany.[2] He recalled a Goethe quotation that referred to Friedrich Schiller as an "armed poet" ("bewaffneter Poet"). In this era, Kluge suggests, every artist must be ready for political combat: "I believe that armaments and poetry are related these days. That is, if I make films, I must also concern myself with the circumstances of production. I must be active in the legal and political arenas, if I have aesthetic and poetic ideas."[3] For Kluge, this intersection of art and politics, of the aesthetic and the social, is both the precondition and the subject of art. The conjunction of radical politics and radical aesthetic form that characterizes much of twentieth-century art is transformed by Kluge into a unique form of political modernism. Kluge's modernism goes beyond a "materialist theory" of film practice to engage both theoretically and politically with the social formations that are the preconditions for and the reception context of his aesthetic work. He is not just interested in changing ideas, he wants to change the material relations of production. This aesthetic practice and the economic, political, and social conditions of its production are for Kluge inextricably intertwined and warrant more detailed examination. How did Kluge make space for his distinctive, autonomous aesthetic practice within and against a postwar German cinema that was both politically and aesthetically conservative?

In the modern era, much of the interest in art has been transferred from the artifact to the artist. The public prominence of the creative personality behind the art work is in part a remnant of Romanticism's notion of the inspired genius, boldly oblivious to institutional or market constraints. This notion stubbornly survives in much popular and scholarly literature and has been augmented by two convergent contemporary phenomena. First, the cult of personality in the media is a key promotional tactic for selling the product, be it a motion picture, television show, or mass-circulation periodical. Social theorists may argue about the causes of this public appetite for personality (and the underlying needs that are being so incompletely met), but the ubiquity of these star images is undeniable. The second phenomenon is a response to the increasingly esoteric nature of modern art. In order to comprehend the meaning and mode of organization of these fragmented and unconventional creations, the recipient often looks outside the individual art work. By examining other works by the same artist, certain patterns may begin to emerge. Even more helpful is any interpretive or biographical information that the creator intentionally or involuntarily provides in interviews, writings, or public appearances. As works become more complex and incoherent, coherence seems embodied in the figure of the artist, whose psychology provides a key to intelligibility and organization of difficult works. The question of intentionality is foregrounded and the artist's cult status is heightened.

Rather than resisting or passively acceding to the demands of mass media publicity, Kluge saw a unique opportunity. The contradictions between the economic imperatives of the mass media and the anachronistic figure of the autonomous artist could be exploited to change the social conditions for aesthetic production. Kluge armed himself with all the cultural and intellectual credentials available to him, banded together with other artists, and created alliances with intellectuals, politicians, and administrators. Like Adorno, who gave press and radio interviews, Kluge used the mass media to attack the institutions of modern administered society and to create counterinstitutions.

Kluge's implicit identification of himself as an "armed poet" is a key instance of his self-construction as a public figure. Recurrent military metaphors in his writings and interviews have accentuated this notion of struggle necessary to create conditions for a filmmaker to produce a new kind of cinema—in Kluge's case, a politically modernist film.[4] This chapter will discuss how Kluge armed himself, what strategies he employed, and what victories and defeats he experienced in his struggle to create what he later came to call an "oppositional public sphere" ("Gegenöffentlichkeit").[5]

Although not always successful, Kluge's efforts bore much greater fruit than even he might have anticipated in the early 1960s. The New German Cinema became a phenomenon of international proportions, rivaling the French New Wave and superseding most other non-Hollywood national cinemas in the 1970s. The films of Rainer Werner Fassbinder, Werner Herzog, Wim Wenders, and Volker Schlöndorff moved beyond the circles of cinephiles to reach wide audiences in many countries. Film became West Germany's best-known cultural export, a symbol of a revitalized, self-critical society. Beneath this most visible stratum of internationally acclaimed directors, hundreds of lesser-known filmmakers also learned the craft, producing a wide spectrum of fictional and documentary films.

In describing Kluge's role in the development of postwar German cinema, it is tempting to lapse into a "great man" account. It can be argued that no single individual has done as much as Alexander Kluge to create and sustain the internationally acclaimed New German Cinema. Although some of its films would no doubt have been produced even without his efforts, the broad achievements of the movement as a whole would probably not have been possible without Kluge's organizing and creative energies. His role has been many-faceted: filmmaker, theoretician, film teacher, literary figure, and, above all, public spokesperson and organizer. He has demonstrated extraordinary energy, persuasiveness, and pragmatism in dealing with governmental and media institutions.

Nevertheless, it would be wrong to regard Kluge as a genius whose talent and charisma have allowed him to impose his will on contemporary German cultural history. He is sensitive to the social and economic formations of his era and thus has been able to inflect and utilize them, rather than completely reshape them. His canny sense of timing and analytical intelligence have allowed him in many instances to find a successful course of action. He has been able to marshal the resources available to him, both personally and in society at large, to influence social institutions and accomplish many of his ends.

Realizing that single actions by isolated individuals are often ineffectual in achieving or maintaining new conditions, Kluge set out to
create new institutions and, in a sense, to construct *himself* as a public
institution, as a public persona, whose characteristics included intelligence, creativity, and sophisticated charm. Modestly, he has never
seemed to be promoting himself, but simply representing the interests
of various colleagues and constituencies as an unofficial spokesman.
In most instances avoiding leadership titles, he has preferred to exercise his influence more informally and to share credit.

This modesty has caused some commentators, such as Timothy
Corrigan, to describe Kluge as a "reluctant" auteur.[6] However, Kluge's
public career was not passive or inadvertent, but rather was decisive
and deliberate. His specific appropriation of the artist's role has consistently intertwined both a political and an interpretive aspect. His
status as keeper of meaning (as partially revealed in interviews) gives
him authority that has been transformed into political influence.[7]

The main objective in Kluge's overall project has been the creation
of a new kind of cinema in Germany, one that would be politically
relevant and stylistically innovative. By the 1960s, modernist aesthetic
models were available to him in various artistic media—literature,
drama, music, the graphic arts, as well as cinema. In the latter field,
Soviet silent film was being rediscovered and combined with a re-
newed interest in Brecht. These models had gained wider intellectual
respectability while still retaining some radical impact. To upgrade
German cinema from embarrassingly bad movies to internationally
respected art required both an economic and an aesthetic transformation of major proportion. Allies would not be found within the
German film industry. Rather, they would come from the ranks of
intellectuals who accepted many of modernism's basic assumptions
and commitments, and from among young people eager for experimental forms, contemporary subjects, and a political/social commentary in art.

THE PREPUBLIC KLUGE

Perhaps the two most salient qualities that Kluge has
demonstrated through the years are a keen analytic intelligence and a
pragmatism that borders on frugality when it comes to maximizing
available resources. This shrewd productivity is nowhere more evi-

dent than in his construction of himself as a public figure. Kluge utilizes most of his talents and qualities to create a uniquely effective media persona. Kluge's public image is not radically different from his private personality. Rather, he has been able to exploit his qualities and accomplishments publicly in a way that is consonant with his personality.

One element in this construction is Kluge's limiting and shaping of his own biographical data. Although very interested in documenting the lives of others in books and films, Kluge has been reticent about revealing his own biography. The few autobiographical elements that do appear in his media work are often obscure. Although he has filmed many of his family members, especially in his short films, they are often presented in fictive contexts and rarely is any specific factual or emotional information provided.[8] The few facts available about him have become almost mythic through repeated incantations and can be briefly summarized.

Ernst Alexander Kluge was born on February 14, 1932, in Halberstadt, a city of about 50,000 inhabitants located in Saxony-Anhalt in the Harz Mountains.[9] He was the first child of Ernst Kluge, a doctor of medicine, and his wife Alice née Hausdorf.[10] A sister, Alexandra Karen Kluge, was born in 1939. Alexander was educated at the Volksschule and Domgymnasium (the cathedral high school) in Halberstadt. Perhaps the most significant event in Kluge's early years occurred on April 8, 1945, less than a month before the end of World War II. On that date a massive allied air attack on Halberstadt destroyed over 80 percent of the city, leveling Kluge's home. This incident has been the most directly represented personal experience to recur in Kluge's films and stories.[11] The bombing has also had some influence on his theoretical notions of "strategies from above" (the exercise of power by political, military, and corporate authorities) and "strategies from below" (the organization and resistance of ordinary people).

In 1943 his parents divorced, and in 1946 Kluge moved to West Berlin to live with his mother, who remarried an attorney.[12] Alexander was enrolled in the Charlottenburg Gymnasium, from which he received his diploma in 1949.[13] Alexandra remained with her father in Halberstadt, studied medicine in the German Democratic Republic and then moved in 1959 to West Germany where she finished her medical degree.[14] She starred in two of Kluge's feature films, *Abschied von gestern* (*Yesterday Girl*, 1965–66) and *Gelegenheitsarbeit einer*

Sklavin (*Occasional Work of a Female Slave,* 1973) and played a minor role in a third film, *The Power of Emotion.*

The house in which Kluge grew up prior to the war was full of music and culture. The elder Kluge was *Theaterarzt,* the theater doctor, in Halberstadt and counted many actors and musicians among his patients and friends. The father himself played the violin, and social gatherings at the house included concerts and impromptu group participation in musical performance.[15] Alexander played the piano and later studied organ and church music as well as modern history at the Universities of Marburg and Freiburg.[16] Although he went on to study law, his strong interest in music and especially opera is evident throughout his film and television work.

Of his adult personal life, very little has been written. Kluge remained a bachelor for many years, living in Munich, Ulm, and Frankfurt. In 1981, at the age of forty-nine, he married Dagmar Steurer, a fact commemorated at the time in an ironic essay by Fassbinder.[17] Subsequently, two children were born, Sophie Alexandra in 1982 and Leonard in 1984.

His adult public life is better known. Kluge received his Doctor Juris degree in 1956 with a dissertation entitled *Die Universitäts-Selbstverwaltung* (University Self-Management), a study of institutional organization.[18] In 1953, he began working part-time in the legal practice of Hellmut Becker and then in the Kuratorium of the Johann Wolfgang Goethe University in Frankfurt. Together, Kluge and Becker wrote a book entitled *Kulturpolitik und Ausgabenkontrolle* (Cultural Politics and Financial Control, 1961), the first of many collaborative intellectual and artistic enterprises in which Kluge was to engage.[19] The book also anticipated some of the central cultural concerns that were to engage Kluge over the next twenty-five years.

Soon after graduation, Kluge began to realize that law was much less attractive to him than literature and film, although he had no training in these latter areas. Through his friend and mentor Theodor Adorno, Kluge became acquainted with the filmmaker Fritz Lang and worked briefly as an intern on Lang's film, *Das indische Grabmal* (*Journey to the Lost City*), in 1958–59.[20]

Perhaps the most striking aspect of this experience for Kluge was observing how the world-renowned director's authority was undercut by the whims of producer Artur Brauner.[21] Learning from this experience, Kluge was later always careful to maintain artistic autonomy by producing his own films. For Kluge, the studio production routine quickly lost its appeal, and he spent much of his time in the canteen, writing the stories that were to become his first book, *Lebensläufe* (*Attendance List for a Funeral*, 1962).[22] He later characterized this literary production as a rechanneling of creative energies for which he could find no outlet in film at the time.[23] Although Kluge's first public notoriety actually resulted from his film work, the interplay between literary and filmic activity was artistically stimulating throughout his career. Kluge has described himself as first and foremost a writer. What drew him to film was the opportunity to combine literature and music. This dual status as author and filmmaker was to serve him well in the sphere of cultural politics.

KLUGE AS FILMMAKER: THE SHORT FILMS

The prevailing conditions within the German film industry in the late 1950s were not propitious for aspiring young filmmakers like Kluge. The industry was not receptive to new ideas and approaches to cinema such as those beginning to take hold in France at this time. Unwilling to become a cog in a film factory, Kluge, like many of his contemporaries, turned to an alternative mode of cinematic production: the independent short film. His first film venture, undertaken in 1959, is exemplary in its pragmatism. Unskilled in film craft and without extensive financial resources, he collaborated with more experienced filmmakers, Peter Schamoni and Wolf Wirth, on the production of a short, documentary film.[24] The subject chosen was technically manageable and politically provocative. *Brutalität in Stein* (Brutality in Stone, 1960) combined archival material with new footage of the Nazi architectural ruins in Nürnberg. Although a collaborative work, this film, on both formal and thematic levels, contained elements that would be more fully developed in Kluge's subsequent works.

Politically, the film demonstrates an approach that was to serve Kluge well. It addresses a serious German social issue from a critical, controversial, and leftist position, but without endorsing any political program. At a time when the "economic miracle" was attempting to build a new future and leave behind the nagging legacy of the war years, a film about the Nazi past was provocative, but it expressed the concerns of many young postwar intellectuals who believed it was time to end the collective amnesia. Kluge and Schamoni approached the historical abstraction by focusing on specific details, the architectural remnants of the Nazi regime. These take on larger, metaphoric implications through the sound-track words of Hitler and Rudolf Hoess. Interspersed with shots of the abandoned and partially destroyed ruins are shots of the architectural models that Hitler oversaw in planning his city of the future. Zooms, pans, and tracking shots give a sense of the overpowering and inhuman dimensions of the buildings, the rigid lines, the unyielding materials.

This early collaborative project already contains two central elements of Kluge's political modernism: a social critique and an innovative style based on principles of montage. *Brutalität in Stein* avoids the didactic expository style of traditional documentaries. The viewer does not get an initial establishing shot, a coherent sense of space, or an informational narration. Shots are composed and combined not to tell a story, but to dispel preconceived notions through a confrontation with the reality of the subject. Obtrusive camera mannerisms and the contrapuntal use of sound as an independent element emphasize the process of the film's production. *Brutalität in Stein* won a main prize at the Oberhausen Short Film Festival in 1961 and first prize at the Prague Film Festival.[25] Here, as later in his career, festivals and prizes were very useful for legitimizing Kluge's status as filmmaker.

Kluge continued to work in the short film format throughout the 1960s and into the 1970s, producing documentaries, quasi-documentaries, and some pseudodocumentaries.[26] Kluge regarded this medium as ideal for experimentation and training. Many of the aspects of his mature cinematic style were developed in these films: the use of intertitles, quotations, and voice-over narration; the minimalizing of synchronous sound; the utilization of archival footage and still photos; the fictionalization of documentaries; and the juxtaposition of apparently incongruous materials. He emphasized the constructed quality of his productions by the use of fast-action footage, slowed-down music, and jump cuts. Kluge's short films are like his minishort stories and have a curious status: they seem at once authentic and false. Their construction and ironic tone call into question the authority and assumptions of both documentary and fictional genres.

Kluge's work in short film gave him an opportunity to explore the medium and develop his own uses for it. It also gave him a certain legitimacy as a clever and at least mildly successful filmmaker, as he won several other awards at Oberhausen. Moreover, the associations that he was able to develop with other young filmmakers, both in production and in more informal social relations, led to the development of strategies for governmental funding.

KLUGE AS PROSE WRITER

Film is for me a literary medium of expression, which, however, compared to literature and theater, offers wholly new possibilities for expression.[27]

—Alexander Kluge

Kluge's commitment to the film medium was never exclusive. Throughout his career, he has found that literary and cinematic work can be complementary and mutually enriching. Moreover, his strategy has been to borrow some of the established legitimacy of the older medium to promote the possibilities of the younger.[28] Although the scope of this book precludes any substantive discussion of his literary production, an overview of this work is necessary to understand Kluge's unique authority as a respected producer in both high culture and mass culture spheres.

The literary production that Kluge had begun in 1958 was continued concurrently with his short film productions. When his first book, *Lebensläufe*, was published in 1962, it was well received and soon translated into several languages. It won the Berlin Art Prize—Young Generation and brought Kluge some notoriety in literary circles.[29] Throughout his career, he has continued to publish works of fiction, although they soon became overshadowed by his films, theoretical writings, and activities in film politics. Nevertheless, the fictional work was important initially in establishing his reputation, and it was instrumental in the development of stories and techniques that could be utilized in his films.

Attendance List for a Funeral, the 1966 English translation of *Lebensläufe,* is a collection of short stories based on real case histories and told in a mock bureaucratic style. Kluge is interested in the everyday lives of ordinary people caught in circumstances—often involving official bureaucracies—which they cannot comprehend, let alone control. Although the stories are perhaps not very inventive, they have a relish for contradictions and anomalies. Implicit is a Frankfurt School critique of institutional inhumanity. The techniques employed anticipate some of the stylistics of Kluge's filmic work. The narration is distanced and ironic, while the episodic, fragmented nature of the tales suggests his cinematic montage.

Schlachtbeschreibung (*The Battle*, 1964) added to Kluge's reputation as a literatus and gained him the Bavarian State Prize for Literature in 1966. *The Battle* is a description of various aspects of the 1943 defeat of the German army at Stalingrad. Like *Attendance List for a Funeral*, it is not a novel; it presents no straightforward narrative that features one or several protagonists. Many different stories and situations are described, both outside and inside the besieged city. It is neither psychologically realistic, nor does it employ any first-person narration. Rather, its seemingly objective description is ironic, sympathetic yet distanced. The book is both an analytical investigation of the causes of this disaster to the German army and a glimpse of individual behavior in a time of extreme duress. Memos, letters, and reports are inserted into the text so that it becomes difficult to distinguish document from fiction, history from story. Although *Attendance List for a Funeral* is the prototype for *Yesterday Girl* (and for most of Kluge's early fictional films that focus on one or several protagonists), *The Battle* is the prototype for his collaborative films that use many different kinds of material to investigate a broader social subject. Both prototypes contain a modernist mixture of documentary and fictional elements, and these two prototypes tend to converge in Kluge's later films.

Kluge published two larger volumes of short stories in the 1970s and 1980s: *Lernprozesse mit tödlichem Ausgang* (*Learning Processes with a Deadly Outcome*, 1973) and *Neue Geschichten, Hefte 1–18: Unheimlichkeit der Zeit* (New Stories, Books 1–18: The Uncanniness of Time, 1977). Similar in style to his earlier writings, these also have provided subject matter for his films. Like these books, Kluge's later feature films can be considered cinematic collections of short stories, loosely connected by shared themes and Kluge's distinctive style. Increasingly, Kluge's literary work has incorporated photographs, illustrations, maps, and diagrams, as well as boxed inserts, moving toward a more visual, almost collage style of layout.

Kluge's strictly literary production has been supplemented by the publication of six books containing various versions of his screenplays and additional explanatory, fictional, and theoretical material. In 1987, he published *Theodor Fontane, Heinrich von Kleist und Anna Wilde*, based on his Fontane and Kleist Prize speeches. His active participation in the literary world has included membership in Group 47;[30] writing reviews and commentary in periodicals; performing numerous public readings of his fiction; and interviewing many prominent literary figures on his television programs. In addition, together with the sociologist Oskar Negt, Kluge has written three books of social theory: *Öffentlichkeit und Erfahrung: Zur Organisationsanalyse von bürgerlicher und proletarischer Öffentlichkeit* (*The Public Sphere and Experience*, 1972); *Geschichte und Eigensinn* (History and Obstinacy, 1981); and *Maßverhältnisse des Politischen: 15 Vorschläge zum Unterscheidungsvermögen* (Proportional Measure of the Political: 15 Proposals for Discernment, 1992). These broadened the scope of his reputation as a social critic and man of letters. He has also collaborated on four books of media theory and contributed to others: *Filmwirtschaft in der BRD und Europa* (The Film Industry in the Federal Republic of Germany and Europe, 1973); *Ulmer Dramaturgien: Reibungsverluste* (Ulm Dramaturgy: Frictional Losses, 1980); *Bestandsaufnahme: Utopie Film* (Stock-taking: Utopia Film, 1983); and *Industrialisierung des Bewußtseins: Eine kritische Auseinandersetzung mit den "neuen" Medien* (Industrialization of Consciousness: A Critical Debate with the "New" Media, 1985). Most recently, he has published three volumes of interviews and conversations that were recorded for his television broadcasts. *Interview mit dem Jahrhundert* (Interview with the Century, 1995) contains interviews with Valentin Falin, Russian diplomat and close advisor to Gorbachev. *"Ich schulde der Welt einen Toten": Gespräche* (I Owe the World a Fatality, 1995) and *"Ich bin ein Landvermesser": Gespräche mit Heiner Müller, neue Folge* ("I Am a Surveyer": Conversations with Heiner Müller, New Installment, 1996) consist of a series of conversations with the former East German playwright and friend of Kluge's, Heiner Müller. *Die Wächter der Sarkophags* (The Watchmen of the Sarcophagus, 1996) includes interviews with scientists, journalists, and military officers who entered the Chernobyl area immediately after the disaster.

The last two volumes prompted a reappraisal of his status as a literary figure and garnered him a number of prestigious awards: the Bremen Prize (1978); the Berlin Fontane-Prize (1979);[31] and the first postwar Kleist Prize (1985), whose prewar recipients included Bertolt Brecht. Kluge has also been awarded the Munich Culture Prize (1986), the Lessing Prize (1990), Cologne's Heinrich Böll Prize (1993), and the Darmstadt Ricarda Huth Prize (1996). All of these literary activities, publications, and awards have contributed to the authority of Kluge as an artist and intellectual and helped make him a formidable adversary in the struggles of cultural politics.

AUTEUR/AUTOR

The combination of literary and cinematic credentials was extremely useful for Kluge in developing a strategy for creating a new kind of cinema in West Germany. The same modernist sensibility that he employed in his stories and short films he wished to bring to the production of feature films. In order to elevate German films to the status of art, however, Kluge felt that the filmmaker needed to have artistic control over all phases of production. He argued that serious cinematic production should be organized analogously to literary production. A key support for this position came from recent developments in the French cinema. The theoretical formulations of the *politique des auteurs* ("policy of the authors" or "*auteur* theory") and their successful implementation in French New Wave films was transformed in Germany into the *Autorenfilm* ("authors' cinema").[32]

The problems facing young filmmakers in France and Germany in the 1950s and 1960s had their roots in the early history of cinema. From its inception, the motion picture has had to justify its claims for consideration as a serious art form. Art was often defined by its distance from mass-produced and mass-consumed culture, which cinema seemed to epitomize. One of cinema's most effective legitimizing strategies has been to associate itself with more established narrative arts—literature, drama, and even opera—and thereby obtain a certain respectability among the educated classes.

In the postwar era, a more sophisticated application of the literary model was applied in France: the *auteur* theory. The notion that all good films, like all good books, have an author was an important step in rejecting the model of film as an impersonal product of a factory system.[33] This legitimating move was more subtle and flexible than previous attempts and paid more attention to cinematic rather than literary elements. Proponents of the *politique des auteurs* did not insist on any direct relation to literature (adaptation) or literariness (imitation). In fact, much of their polemic was directed against what they considered the overly conservative, literary, and uncinematic productions of the so-called "cinema of quality." Turning away from adaptations of nineteenth-century narratives, the young French critics emphasized the unique capacity of cinema for addressing contemporary issues in a contemporary way. For this cinema to function, it needed fresh, energetic directors who could free themselves from the shackles of a sterile production system and who would be able to stamp their own personalities on truly innovative and relevant films.

Not only did this *auteur* criticism serve to legitimate film as an art form analogous rather than subservient to literature, it also elevated the director as the creative personality behind the film. The young French critics shifted the focus of criticism away from stars, producers, or screenwriters to the director as controlling artist.

The French New Wave was an important influence on German cinema in the 1960s. Several directors, such as Schlöndorff and Jean-Marie Straub, received their training by working on French films.[34] Kluge's early writings and interviews are full of references to the New Wave French directors—many of them former critics at the journal *Cahiers du Cinéma*—as important influences. He has claimed, for example, that it was Jean-Luc Godard's *A bout de souffle* (*Breathless*, 1959) that convinced him to become a filmmaker.[35] More important than the individual films of François Truffaut, Eric Rohmer, or Robert Bresson, however, was the *politique des auteurs,* which offered Kluge and other young German filmmakers an important model for dealing with a moribund national film industry.

Unlike the French New Wave directors who came into feature film production from film criticism, Kluge brought credentials that were much more varied culturally and intellectually. Not only was Kluge already a short-film auteur and literary author, but he combined real-world experience and more academic interests. Among politicians and businessmen, he was respected for his legal background. Among intellectuals, he was a friend of Adorno and was interested in questions of cultural theory.[36] This multisided persona made it difficult to categorize or dismiss Kluge and gave him an arsenal of weapons for dealing with a variety of situations and institutions.

Learning from the achievements of the French New Wave, Kluge developed a complex strategy for revitalizing German film. Facets of this strategy included publicly promoting his multidimensional and authoritative persona; utilizing the German reverence for high culture against the established film industry; emphasizing innovation and youth as opposed to outmoded institutions and traditions; and collaborating with others to organize new institutions. Although the first three facets reflect basic modernist tenets, the last, artistic coalition-building, constitutes a political strategy and commitment that was often true of modernist and especially of avant-garde groups and was also particularly adapted to a mood of cooperative labor and participatory democracy in the 1960s. Kluge's career demonstrates an uncanny capacity to gain the credibility necessary to achieve his objectives by maximally utilizing his diverse qualifications and connections. One early instance of this was his pivotal role in the formulation of the Oberhausen Manifesto and the practical realization of its goals.

FILM POLITICS I:
THE INSTITUTIONALIZATION OF OBERHAUSEN

Prior to the Eighth West German Short Film Days at Oberhausen in 1962, several young filmmakers held a series of meetings in Munich bars and cafes. The group that gathered represented a number of smaller circles of friends, whose members had all made independent short films, some of them achieving national and even international attention. They shared a desire to make longer films of "artistic and political distinction" such as those being produced in France, Italy, and Eastern Europe.[37] Doing so, however, required significant changes in the German film system, an institution that had locked them out. In early 1962, the time seemed ripe for such changes. The industry was bankrupt—aesthetically as well as financially—and the young filmmakers could present themselves as a legitimate alternative.[38] Their strategizing led to the production of a manifesto to be delivered during the Oberhausen festival on February 28, 1962. Alexander Kluge, because of his background as an attorney, was designated to respond to questions from the press.[39]

The manifesto was short and bold. It proclaimed the old cinema dead: "The collapse of the conventional German film finally removes the economic basis for a mode of filmmaking whose attitude and practice we reject. With it the new film has a chance to come to life."[40] The filmmakers able to create this new film would be those who had already won "a large number of prizes at international festivals and gained the recognition of international critics" for their short films. They "speak a new film language." To succeed, the new film would require "freedom from the conventions of the established industry," from commercial controls, and from limitations by interest groups. "We have concrete, intellectual, formal, and economic ideas for the production of the new German Film." The manifesto was signed by twenty-six young filmmakers.[41] Although only four paragraphs long, the manifesto was to have a significant impact on the course of German film.[42]

As Raymond Williams has pointed out, the aesthetic manifesto is a characteristic promotional device of modernism, "the badge of self-conscious and self-advertising schools" of art. It boldly attacks commercialism and orthodoxy, to proclaim its own "passionate and scorn-ful vision."[43] The Oberhausen Manifesto, despite its almost evasive brevity, garnered substantial attention in the press and provided the focus for an ensuing debate. In a series of subsequent articles and in-terviews, Kluge served as group spokesman, expanding the Oberhau-sen critique and expounding a program for change. The manifesto was not a plea for admission into the current system, it was a denunciation of the system and a demand for an alternative. The critique was lev-eled both at the poor quality of current German films and at their lack of relevance to contemporary life. Implicit in this two-pronged attack are the twin assumptions of political modernism: that cultural prod-ucts should constitute serious, quality art and be socially relevant. The solution was to make film more publicly responsible, by "seeking out themes appropriate to this responsibility." Kluge promised a more po-litical, educational cinema that would concern itself with contempo-rary social reality.[44]

For the young filmmakers, the enemy was the old commercial cine-ma, referred to variously as "Papa's cinema," the industry (*die Bran-che*), and the entertainment film. It included the older generation of producers and distributors, the theater owners, and especially Holly-wood's German branches, which played an important role in postwar German cinema. Kluge's criticism of the old industry was aimed both at the films themselves and at the mode of production that fostered such products. Although some outstanding German films were pro-duced in the 1950s, most were of poor quality and artistically un-ambitious: formulaic imitations of Hollywood; kitsch, not high art. Such films were often referred to as "Zutatenkino" ("ingredient cine-ma") because of their reliance on conventional elements of story, style, and stars to attract audiences. Corroborating these charges of aes-thetic bankruptcy was the decision of the federal government to award no film prizes for the year 1961.[45]

At the same time, these films were felt to be out of touch with con-temporary reality and the real needs of the audiences. Like the *Cahiers* critics of the 1950s, Kluge often in the early 1960s mentions the lack of "reality" ("Wirklichkeit") in mainstream films.[46] They were not dealing with contemporary settings or contemporary issues in a seri-ous way. The most popular genre of the 1950s was the *Heimatfilm* ("homeland film"), which suggests that German audiences possessed a nostalgic and nationalistic yearning for a mythic past.[47] The Sissi films starring Romy Schneider were also a romantic evocation of the past, in this case, court society of the nineteenth-century Austro-Hungarian empire. Other popular films transformed contemporary social conditions into mindless comedies, musicals, and melodramas full of improbable coincidence and bubbling optimism.

According to the young directors, these commercial films were irrelevant because they were based on a false or limited notion of cinema, and they stemmed from an outmoded production system that relied on formulaic genres in an attempt to compete with Hollywood, but on a much impoverished scale. The industrial mode of production ensured that all but a few prominent directors were interchangeable operatives, exactly like the other technicians employed in production. Predictable profits were sought through replication of successful products. Such strategies had run their course by the early 1960s, and an increasing number of Germans preferred to remain at home and watch television rather than attend the movies. Attendance fell to the lowest point since prior to the war. In 1961, UFA, the giant production company that had survived both the war and subsequent attempts by the Allies to dismantle it, was forced into bankruptcy. The old system simply didn't work.

In addition, one further level of antagonism existed between the old industry and the young filmmakers. The framework, organization, and, most important, the personnel of the old industry had been inherited from the Nazi era.[48] The decision makers were now allied with other capitalist interests in support of the Christian Democrat and Christian Socialist parties. Although some notable films were made about the war—such as *Des Teufels General* (*The Devil's General,* 1954) or *Die Brücke* (*The Bridge,* 1960)—most films on the subject dealt less with the policies and atrocities of the Third Reich than with more generalized antiwar themes. The younger filmmakers, who grew up in the postwar era, were more critical of the Nazi past and more willing to address it in their work. As the 1960s wore on, their politics were influenced by the growing student movement.[49] Given the polarization and institutionalization of the political parties in cultural affairs, these alignments were both necessary and crucial to the struggle that would take place over the next twenty years.

In an article entitled "What do the Oberhauseners want?" published a month after the manifesto, Kluge set forth three proposals for an alternative film culture. First, he called for an organization to finance feature productions by first-time filmmakers. Second, he demanded support for short films as a training ground. Third, he sought the establishment of an "intellectual center" for the study of film.[50]

Of these goals, the first and third were realized, but the second was not. Although short films have continued to find support at several festivals, and Kluge himself has sometimes run his shorts as complements to his feature films, no regular nationwide subsidization system has been established, and perhaps more importantly, no consistent exhibition forum has been found.

Although Kluge and the other "Oberhauseners" were not the first to criticize the condition of the postwar German film industry, their critique was the most effective in arousing public opinion. The use of a manifesto was a well-conceived and well-timed publicity maneuver, one that reverberated with both political (*The Communist Manifesto*) and modernist (*The Futurist Manifesto*) associations. They supplemented the manifesto with specific proposals for building an alternative film culture and followed up with political lobbying activities to achieve these goals.

All three of Kluge's proposals were envisioned as taking place outside the commercial industry. Private enterprise had not been able to achieve these goals, so public institutions would have to be established. Kluge and others were able to convince the Federal Minister of the Interior, Hermann Höcherl, that public funding was as appropriate for film authors as for novelists, musicians, and other cultural creators.[51] The Kuratorium junger deutscher Film (Board of Young German Film) was established by the federal government in 1965, allotting five million DM to twenty novice directors over a three-year period. Kluge became one of the members of the Kuratorium board and was among the first to receive funding for his initial feature film *Yesterday Girl*.[52] Since only twenty of the fifty proposed projects could be funded, this led to some dissension and envy among the young directors. Nevertheless, the emphasis on film as culture rather than as an industry, on the auteur rather than the production studio, had created a public space and initial funding for a new generation of feature filmmakers.

Kluge's third goal, the establishment of a cinema production academy, was realized much sooner. On October 1, 1962, West Germany's first film school opened as a department of the Hochschule für Gestaltung (College of Design) in Ulm.[53] The Ulm college had been founded as a postwar successor to the Bauhaus. It was established as a private, anti-Nazi institution offering a critical approach to higher education in four areas, Architecture, Industrial Design, Visual Communication, and Information.

The college's tradition of educational and aesthetic innovation and social criticism made it an attractive site for Germany's first film academy. Although film courses had been taught there prior to the

Oberhausen Manifesto, a permanent department was set up in 1962 under the leadership of Detten Schleiermacher, Edgar Reitz, and Alexander Kluge, despite Kluge's minimal practical experience in the medium at the time.[54] In keeping with the principles of the college, the program emphasized the creation of film designers, filmmakers with an all-around background in liberal arts as well as in the technical aspects of filmmaking. Strongly influenced by the Frankfurt School, the curriculum would develop critical thinkers, auteurs rather than technicians. In 1964, the film department became semiautonomous Institut für Filmgestaltung (Institute for Film Design), which had three functional areas: the film school, for instruction and training; the development studio, to solve problems of film form and film organization through small development groups; and research projects, to work through theoretical, technical, formal, and historical questions.[55]

The curriculum stressed both theoretical lectures (in politics, sociology, economics, cybernetics, and literature, as well as film history and theory) and practical instruction and exercises (camera, sound, and editing).[56] It attempted to build the students' capacities for both adaptation and resistance to social circumstances. However, less emphasis was placed on cinematic history and analysis than in developing a new kind of cinema. In keeping with principles of the *Autorenfilm*, the program looked to literature and New Music—high modernist art—for models rather than contemporary German or Hollywood cinema. Given the strong influence of critical thought on the college as a whole—with its connections to the Frankfurt School, the Bauhaus, and Group 47—students saw film not as a tradition of mass entertainment but as a tool of enlightenment and self-expression. "A well-rounded education does not mean the accumulation of knowledge, but rather the capacity to create experiences, and the capacity to transform those experiences once they have occurred."[57] Students were encouraged to know their own interests and desires and to film the world around them.

In 1964, as plans developed for additional film schools in Berlin and Munich, Kluge suggested a differentiation of curricular goals: Berlin would produce film critics and experts in various film specialties, Munich was to turn out television people, and Ulm would develop film authors.[58] Filmmaking at Ulm was experimental and, whether fictional or documentary, tied to representing reality. The dramaturgy was later summarized as: "radical shorts, discoveries which permit greater lengths and degrees of intensity."[59] These miniatures were regarded as the best mode for exploring the parameters of the medium, small units that could include both found and new footage and could later be combined into larger works. Students were not, however, taught to subordinate word to picture, but to regard film as a communicative medium in which content (life experience) was as important as form.[60]

The Ulm Institute functioned for only a few years as a school, with less than twenty-five graduates. The rise of radical movements in the 1960s led to a factionalization of the students at the college, right-wing criticism in the press, and ultimately a withdrawal of funding.[61] When the college closed in 1968, there seemed no further reason for the Institute to continue as a film school. Berlin and Munich now filled this need, the former emphasizing independent, socially engaged filmmaking and the latter focusing on technical and industrial aspects.

Nevertheless, the Institute could provide Kluge and his associates minimal financial support and a haven from the social storms of the 1960s. The earlier insistence on a three-fold mission for the Film Department meant that it could drop the instructional component and continue its development and research functions. According to its constitution, the mission of the Institute since 1970 has been "Research and Discovery in the Area of Film."[62] It continued to receive funding from the state of Baden-Württemburg until 1994, moneys which were utilized for a number of books, films, and television programs by Kluge and Ulm graduates.[63]

Kluge's status as a film expert and as an academic was enhanced by the Ulm Institute, which also offered him certain material resources for his productions. Furthermore, it allowed him to develop and propagate his ideas by working closely with young filmmakers, several of whom have gained some reputation within Germany. Ula Stöckl has directed several well-received feature-length fictional films. Others, including Maximiliane Mainka, Peter Schubert, and Reinhard Kahn, continue to make films, for the most part documentaries and shorts. A number of Ulm graduates now teach media production. In terms of its overall impact, however, the Ulm Institute has been at best marginal, producing no major filmmakers and having little effect on either commercial or auteur cinema in Germany.[64] In part this is due to the Institute's bias against traditional entertainment cinema and its emphasis on documentary and experimental production, spheres in which Ulm graduates have made a more substantial impact.[65] Kluge asserts, however, that while Ulm graduates have not directed any of the most successful films of the New German Cinema, the "roots of these successes lie, however, in its offshoots. The Institute has been seriously working on these offshoots from 1962 to 1980." [66] Kluge's position as an academic was further enhanced in the 1970s when he was appointed Professor of Film at the prestigious Johann Wolfgang von Goethe University of Frankfurt, where he teaches occasional short seminars on film.

KLUGE AS JURIST

The implementation of two of the three Oberhausen objectives was due in no small part to Kluge's energy and skills. In the sphere of film politics, his perceived legal expertise thrust him into a leadership role in negotiation and public relations. His understanding of institutions, particularly government and politics, enabled him to grasp clearly what was actually happening and to analyze how it could be altered. It encouraged him to think of structural, institutional solutions to problems such as the Kuratorium and the Ulm Institute. His background enabled him to draft and lobby for legislation, to set up companies and other organizations, and to negotiate contracts. On occasion, the legal credential could serve as an offensive weapon as well. [67] In several newspaper articles, he is said to have a continuing legal practice, but if so, such practice has been of a very limited scope, for he has little time to devote to it. More likely, Kluge has felt it important to stress that these legal armaments have not grown rusty through desuetude.

COUNTERINSTITUTIONS

The Kuratorium and the Ulm Institute were not the only institutions that Kluge helped organize. From early on, Kluge sought to strengthen his hand politically by finding allies and collaborators. He understood that group activity or even the appearance of group consensus had more impact on the public sphere than an individual acting alone.

Beginning with Oberhausen and continuing until the present time, Kluge's habit has been to speak most often in the first person plural:

we believe, *we* demand, *we* think, *we* are working on. The referent of the pronoun "we" is often unclear. Sometimes it seems a rhetorical device to include the interviewer, the reader, indeed humanity at large. At other times, all young filmmakers, his close associates, or his staff seem designated. Often the referent seems to be simply Kluge himself. In most instances, however, this mode of speech seems related to Kluge's modesty, but it remains a flexible tool, especially useful because of its vagueness. Using the first person plural suggests that the opinions he states are widely held and the listener is invited, as a reasonable, intelligent person, to hold them too. Kluge is a master at using the middle ground of ambiguity in his operations. People agree with him in principle, thereby providing him with license for maneuvering in specific details.

Kluge's mode of operation does not depend merely on such linguistic manipulations. Like the members of the Frankfurt School, he was convinced of the centrality and dehumanizing potential of social institutions in modern life. At the same time, his own analytical studies of institutional behavior suggested that institutions can also provide more power and stability than any individual's isolated acts. If institutions could be designed more democratically, they might function as servants of human needs rather than their masters. A crucial part of his political, economic, and aesthetic strategy involved the establishment of counterinstitutions that could be used to organize and wield collective power.[68] The Oberhausen Manifesto constituted the first attempt at organizing the disparate and sometimes mutually antagonistic young filmmakers. It was not all-inclusive, however, nor did it have any lasting formal structures.

One of the first durable structures that Kluge set up was not collective. In 1963, he established his own film company, aptly named Kairos. The Greek word *kairos* means time, not time as a continuum (*chronos*), but time as a particular opportune moment at which something important occurs.[69] For Kluge, the notion of *kairos* is fundamental: observe the unique conjunction of events, and then act decisively on this perception. As a legal entity, Kairos made Kluge a true auteur: both a director and his own producer. Kluge encouraged other filmmakers to follow suit; only by controlling their own finances could they ensure artistic control as well.[70] This is one significant difference between the *auteur* directors in France and the *Autoren* in Germany. Most of the latter were not content just to write and direct their films, but also functioned as producers. Kluge attributed the rise of the New

German filmmakers to the development of lightweight and relatively inexpensive equipment, which allowed them to set up their own production companies with little capital investment. "This is the *Kino der Autoren:* the Nagra tape recorder, an Arriflex, your own cutting table, a knowledge of bookkeeping, and the idea that this was a process of enlightenment."[71]

Despite the availability of some public financing, the resources available to these young producers/directors were minuscule compared to those of most commercial producers. Yet the young filmmakers were sufficiently eager to get their films produced that they improvised, invented, and cut corners. They borrowed low-budget techniques from the Italian neorealists and the French New Wave: location shooting, small crews, available light, nonprofessional actors, black and white stock, etc. These became the aesthetic currency of the Young German Cinema, the badge of their authenticity. The established industry referred to them derisively as the "rucksack" producers.[72] According to Kluge, the main thing these filmmakers had in common was not any particular content in their films, but this mode of production, "a way of making films, low budget films, that translate highly personal experiences."[73]

In 1966, forty-two of these new production companies joined together to form the Arbeitsgemeinschaft Neuer Deutscher Spielfilmproduzenten (Association of New German Feature Film Producers), and Kluge took a leading role in the organization.[74] Kluge's influence did not result from complex internal maneuvering so much as from the minimal interest of most filmmakers in film politics. In fact, Kluge complained in the 1970s that the prevalent attitude had too long been: "Let Kluge do it."[75] The Arbeitsgemeinschaft was established as a counterweight to SPIO, Spitzenorganisation der deutschen Filmwirtschaft (Association of the German Film Industry), and was useful for lobbying and representation on film subsidy boards.

In 1970, a Syndicate of Filmmakers was formed, representing over three hundred film and television directors, and Kluge again became its spokesman.[76] The political and cultural pluralism of the Federal Republic required representation of all relevant groups, and their formalization ensured the inclusion of the young filmmakers' points of view in the decision-making process. The other major organization of the New German filmmakers was the Filmverlag der Autoren (Film Distribution Company of the Authors), which provided an urgently needed distribution system for young filmmakers. Kluge was not one of the founding members of this organization, but most of his later films were handled by Filmverlag. More recently, Kluge has set up a variety of new institutions to facilitate his television work.[77]

FEATURE FILMS: INTERNATIONAL RECOGNITION

By 1966, the offensive of the young filmmakers seemed relatively successful. In addition to achieving some of the institutional goals they had set (the Kuratorium and the Ulm Institute), they managed to produce a group of feature films that were favorably received both at home and abroad. Part of the legitimation strategy of these young directors was to achieve international recognition through participation in film festivals throughout Europe. This seemed a natural tactic because it was this broader European film culture that had inspired their efforts and had served as a standard for the development of a German film culture. Films such as Kluge's *Yesterday Girl* shared many features of the international art cinema of that time. They were in fact constructed with some attention to possible reception outside of Germany.[78] *Yesterday Girl* won the Silver Prize at Venice in 1966, while *Der junge Törless* (*Young Torless*) by Schlöndorff won prizes at Cannes and Berlin. Straub's *Nicht versöhnt* (*Not Reconciled*) was also well received at festivals. The German critics were quite enthusiastic about this wave of new films, and theater attendance improved. *Es* (*It,* Ulrich Schamoni), *Schonzeit für Füchse* (*Closed Season for Foxes,* Peter Schamoni), and *Yesterday Girl* were all West German box office hits for these filmmakers.[79] For Kluge, as for several other filmmakers, this was only the start of a long career. Kluge has directed fifteen feature films over the course of twenty years and has in the process garnered much critical praise as well as numerous awards at international festivals.[80]

FILM POLITICS II: THE INDUSTRY STRIKES BACK

Busy with production or basking in their successes, the young filmmakers were unprepared for the counteroffensive from the established industry. The formation of the Arbeitsgemeinschaft in 1966 was insufficient to defeat or significantly amend the Film Subsidy Law (Filmförderungsgesetz, known as FFG), which was passed in 1967. This federal law provided producers (rather than directors) with funding for new films on the basis of a previous film ("Referenz-film"), which was financially successful.[81] This law, pushed by SPIO and conservative politicians, constituted a de facto subsidization of established film production companies. Meanwhile, funding for first-time filmmakers was reduced when the Kuratorium was turned over to state governments.

Whether due to the Oberhauseners' harsh rhetoric or the intransigence of the old guard, an adversarial relationship had become entrenched. Unlike the French New Wave, which found space within or in conjunction with the established film industry, the New German Cinema was conceived as an alternative to the established German film companies. Despite the considerable successes and excitement generated by these young filmmakers, they were not embraced by the established industry.[82] In fact, the animosity resulted not only in unfavorable legislation for the young directors, but also contributed to the distribution/exhibition crisis that blocked most of their productions from achieving any commercial distribution.[83] Buoyed by subsidies and an international market for soft-core pornography, the old industry continued to wield substantial political and economic power.

FILM POLITICS III: THE RETURN OF KLUGE

In the late 1960s, Kluge withdrew somewhat from the public arena. Despite its Golden Lion award at Venice, his second feature film, *Die Artisten in der Zirkuskuppel: ratlos (Artistes at the Top of the Big Top: Disoriented,* 1967), failed to achieve much commercial success. His failure to block the new Film Subsidy Law was also demoralizing. Kluge returned to Ulm where he worked with associates and former students on several low-budget science fiction projects and spent time on literary and theoretical writing.

After this period of personal retreat and reevaluation, Kluge returned to the attack in the early 1970s. Together with Michael Dost and Florian Hopf, he compiled a book entitled *Filmwirtschaft in der BRD und Europa* (The Film Industry in the Federal Republic of Germany and Europe, 1973), a white paper criticizing current conditions. This became the platform for an assault in the media and for a lobbying campaign to revise the first Film Subsidy Law.

When the new law was adopted in 1974, it reflected many of the concerns that Kluge and others had raised in the book and in the media. Not only were moneys allotted for script development and for subsidies independent of the box office, but a landmark agreement with German public television was created. Kluge became active in negotiations that created the Film und Fernsehen Rahmenabkommen (Film and Television Framework Accord) of 1974, which allotted thirty-four million DM to German filmmakers over a period of four years.[84]

Once these new funding institutions were set up, Kluge continued to participate in their implementation. He served as a member of several boards: the Presidium of the Filmförderungsanstalt (Film Subsidy Board) or FFA, the Film-TV Accord's Parity Commission; the Film-Television Negotiations Group; and the Achter Commission (for Film and Television Joint Productions).[85] In addition, his public pronouncements served to maintain a pressure on the decision-making of these boards.[86]

FILM POLITICS IV: BLURRED BATTLE LINES

Although most accounts of the New German Cinema have stressed the assault on the "old German Cinema" in the 1960s and early 1970s, such discussions have served primarily to set the stage for accounts of the emergence and ultimate international triumphs of the younger filmmakers. As a matter of fact, the old cinema did not wither away in the face of the new; it continued to survive. Although the relationship between the new and the old became more complex, with shifting alliances, crossovers, and compromises, the struggles continued throughout the 1970s and into the 1980s. The terms and personnel of the battles shifted and the battle lines blurred, but a tension and hostility between the more and less commercial approaches to filmmaking continued.

Underlying this struggle was the historical tension between notions of cinema as artistic expression and as commercial activity. The cinema of the *author*—the director—fought to maintain its independence from the cinema of the *producer*. Thomas Elsaesser makes the useful distinction between the cultural mode of production and the industrial mode of production.[87] The former is purportedly concerned not with profits, but with art. But these cultural products are not without their use value. Cultural artifacts are important both as reflections and inflections of the society in which they arise. The New German Cinema was such a cultural mode of production. These films provided graphic images and pointed commentary on contemporary West German life. They lent their society a certain self-respect and dignity even as they attacked its social ills. In fact, the measure of postwar Germany's maturity and transformation from the National Socialist era was its capacity for self-criticism. Central to this critique, especially as the 1970s wore on, was the cinematic examination of the Nazi era, which had for so long been taboo. Moreover, the thematic presence of Nazism in these New German films contributed greatly to their success abroad. The international art cinema audiences demanded sophisticated techniques and style combined with a distinctive national flavor. This combination of universal and particular qualities, resulting in a contained exoticism, seemed epitomized in such films as *Die Blechtrommel (The Tin Drum)* or *Die Ehe der Maria Braun (The Marriage of Maria Braun)*.

Success in this cultural mode of production depended in the first place on festival screenings; ultimately, however, international distribution was needed. In the late 1970s, many of the projects of Herzog, Fassbinder, and Schlöndorff were produced with high production values in order to tap this market. As such films became very successful financially, the distinction between the *auteur* cinema and the commercial cinema was more difficult to maintain. With Hollywood providing not only international distribution but even some production financing, issues of nationalism, creative control, and intended audience became increasingly complex. For many of the emerging filmmakers, Hollywood became less the enemy than the model.

Kluge, however, continued to argue for a more cultural mode of production. His films were still produced on relatively low budgets. With the exception of *Der starke Ferdinand (Strongman Ferdinand, 1975–76)*, Kluge's films resisted any tendency toward popularization or simplification. Although hesitant to denounce other New German directors for their commercialism and their affinities to the "cinema of illusion," Kluge nevertheless tried to provide theoretical and practical support for a more radical, modernist style. He collaborated on films with Fassbinder, Schlöndorff, Margarethe von Trotta, and others, integrating their segments into a filmic collage that bore many of the marks of his own films.

Kluge also continued to work collaboratively in film politics, asserting that market forces alone should not control film production. When the Film Subsidy Law came up for renewal in 1979, he led an attack once more on what he described as the "unholy alliance be-

tween CSU [Christian Socialist Union] leaders, the bureaucratic kill-
ers, and the foreign interests present in the FFA."[88] He has pointed out
that funding agencies constitute the "modern form of censorship."[89]
As long as the money is going for commercial films, they are getting
an extra advantage in competing against less commercial films. The
only way to realize the goals of the 1974 law, according to Kluge, is to
pay more attention to the viewer, and to make smaller, less pretentious films.[90]

Nevertheless, Kluge was forced to adapt to the changing times. In
the 1980s, he shifted the bulk of his energies from film to television,
even though this entailed an abandonment of his relationship with
public television for an uneasy interaction with right-wing publishers
and elements of the commercial film and television industries.

PUBLIC PERSONA

Kluge has been active in film politics now for almost
thirty years. Since 1962, he has given hundreds of print interviews,
appeared on television and radio, and often participated in discussions
following screenings of his films. He has constructed a public persona
that is unique among German filmmakers and that has made him remarkably effective in creating opportunities for his own film work as
well as that of his colleagues.

One important aspect of any public persona in this visually oriented age is physical appearance. Kluge's is quite unimposing (Fassbinder referred to him as "The Little Doctor"). With whitish gray hair,
he affects neither stylish nor flamboyant attire, preferring more conservative garb. He speaks softly and his demeanor is thoughtful and
restrained, more like an academic than a film director. He is charming,
witty, and articulate.[91] Although reticent to speak of himself or his
family, he is curious about others and is a good listener. An interviewer can easily find her/himself the interviewee, as Kluge flatters,
charms, interrogates, evades, and probes. Unlike Fassbinder or Herzog, Kluge was never the kind of media star whose exploits could sell
tabloids.[92]

This modesty and ordinariness have undoubtedly contributed to
his relative nonrecognition outside Germany. Even in Germany he
seems almost like an anti-auteur. Yet one cannot conclude that he has
no public persona at all, nor that it is not carefully shaped. One measure of this is the degree to which Kluge, despite his apparent mod-

esty, has put himself into the limelight. The sheer number of interviews and public appearances that he has made is astonishing. Often
these have very specific objectives: providing interpretive keys to his
films, maneuvering for certain political goals, or promoting particular
projects.[93] But the types and amount of information dispensed are
carefully controlled. The paucity of personal information revealed in
this massive public exposure is a measure of Kluge's manipulation of
this constructed persona.

Through the years, many reporters have noted Kluge's intelligence,
his diffidence, and his frankness.[94] They have frequently been baffled,
however, by his comments. This stems not only from Kluge's penchant for elusiveness, but also from his mode of thought. Kluge's conversation, like his films and writings, is frequently more associational
than logically coherent. He often speaks elliptically, using verbal shorthand that is not always clear to the listener. He will speak, for example,
of a "Robinson" mentality, leaving the listener to identify this reference
to Robinson Crusoe and to puzzle out what aspect of Crusoe is relevant
and whether the reference is positive or negative. By this time Kluge's
stream of thought has raced into a different channel. Kluge presents
specific examples almost like parables, but often without a clarifying
final axiom. Indeed, closure seems antithetical to Kluge. His thoughts
and creations seem provisional. Kluge has referred to his films as essays. In its original sense, the word "essay"—meaning "trial" or "attempt"—is possibly the most apt description of his entire oeuvre.[95]
Such a mode of expression has functioned remarkably well, providing
journalists with vivid metaphors and catchy phrases, while still allowing Kluge enough ambiguity for maneuvering.

Most of the early newspaper articles about his work refer to him as
"Dr. Kluge" and mention that he is a jurist.[96] Although such references
might seem excessively formal in American culture, academic titles
are more prominent in German society, indicating the higher prestige
that they are accorded there. Particularly in his early film career,
Kluge obviously did not want his academic degree nor his legal training to be overlooked by the journalists who interviewed him.

How then did Kluge construct himself as a public figure? He presented himself as reasonable and affable but also intelligent, critical,
and innovative. His public role is much more that of an Enlightenment figure—statesman, man of letters, philosopher—than a Romantic figure—moody, passionate, eccentric poet. Those Romantic traits
that were present in the early years—his emphatic youthfulness and
rebellion against the cinematic status quo—were contained within a
larger context of rationality and apparent self-effacement.

Timothy Corrigan has argued that the multiplicity of Kluge's credentials, and the elusiveness, ambiguity, and contradictions evident in Kluge's films and public activities create a "fortuitous instability" in his auteur image: "his expressive agency through most of these tactics achieves a 'prismatic effect' which tends to assert and then disperse its own authority."[97] This is absolutely correct if one does not construe this dispersal as some sort of weakness or diffusion of energy. Rather, to return to military metaphors, Kluge's strategy seems modeled on principles of guerilla warfare. Kluge's strength is his ability to gather forces for important assaults and then to slip away from counterassaults. "I'm a Robinson Crusoe. If I'm an artist, I am alone, and individually I can work only this way. I'm esoteric like Adorno is, like every artist is. But I would like to have camouflage, mimicry. I think it is important not to show one is an artist nowadays, because it's a very dangerous status."[98] This shifting, contradictory voice does not deprive it of authority, however, but enhances its aura of uniqueness, authenticity, and complexity. As Corrigan says, Kluge uses a broadened notion of auteurism "to initiate a modernist critique of contemporary cynicism and vacancy, a way of reorganizing a devalued and emptied auteurism as a critical subjectivity."[99] Kluge's reasonableness and intellectual style have served to legitimize both his own projects and those of many other directors as well.[100] Kluge in turn has benefited from the antics of the more bohemian and colorful directors. Not only did they provide broader publicity for the New German films, but they allowed Kluge to serve as a mediator, as a rational voice who could converse with both the institutions and these outsiders.

Kluge has been and continues to be one of the central personalities in West German media politics. His activities were never directed solely for the benefit of his own film work, but were always aimed at creating a larger public space—room for a whole group or movement. Nevertheless, his own productions repeatedly benefited from his activities in film politics. He received some sort of public funding for almost all of his projects: *Yesterday Girl* was funded by the Kuratorium, and most of his projects of the 1970s and 1980s received money from the Film and Television Accord.[101] Kluge used his considerable talents, training, and credentials as lawyer, cultural theorist, educator, and award-winning author and filmmaker to create a variety of institutions—both within and outside government—to support a wide range of filmmaking.

3
Telling, Condensing, Interrupting

NARRATIVE/ANTINARRATIVE

I would make no films if it were not for the film history of the twenties, the silent film. Since I make films, I make them in connection with this classical tradition. According to my conception, the narrative cinema is exactly this, namely, to tell stories, and what is the history of a country other than the broadest story plane. Not one story, but many stories.
—Alexander Kluge [1]

Indeed, few filmmakers and writers have told more stories than Kluge. Yet, like many modernists, Kluge has an attitude toward narration that is both ambivalent and innovative: he is fascinated by the storytelling process, but at the same time rejects traditional models of narration. Over the course of his career as a filmmaker, Kluge has employed a broad range of narrative structures and techniques, many of them questioning the very concept of narration and exploring its limits.

There is a general movement in Kluge's work from fairly straightforward narratives centering on a single protagonist toward increasingly complex films with multiple narratives. Even in his early films, however, Kluge tends toward episodic stories with interruptions rather than linear narratives unified by clear causality and spatial/temporal continuity. His later films take this process even farther by eliminating any overarching narrative and embedding several shorter narratives within other nonnarrative material. A similar development occurs on the level of narrative techniques, where Kluge finds new

63

ways to tell stories using a variety of visual and aural material. In the later films, Kluge's own voice becomes increasingly important as a source of narrative information and as a guide to interpretation. This oral storytelling foregrounds both the role of the director and the process of narration.

For Kluge, the stories themselves and their characters are less important than the ideas, feelings, and experience that can be culled from them. As Benjamin has pointed out, storytelling is neither a matter of communicating information (like most documentaries), nor of providing sensations (like most feature films). "It is not the object of the story to convey a happening *per se*, which is the purpose of information; rather it embeds it in the life of the storyteller in order to pass it on as experience to those listening. Thus it bears the marks of the storyteller much as the earthen vessel bears the marks of the potter's hand." [2] Kluge's distinctive shaping hand is everywhere evident in his narrational practice. Like Kafka, Kluge is a fabulist, a teller of parables. But unlike classical fables, Kluge's stories contain no explicit moral. Kluge's spectators must fill in this gap and draw their own conclusions. Although the subjects of most of these stories are ordinary people and everyday events, verisimilitude and psychological realism often yield to other narrative strategies and styles. Often Kluge's stories are fragmentary, elliptical, and brief. Many tales are told rather than enacted, summarized rather than spun out.

Kluge's narrative approach must always be seen as influenced by, but opposed to, most commercial film practice. Kluge's modernism is self-consciously iconoclastic. His rejection of classical Hollywood's psychological realism, coherent story world or diegesis, and character identification (as well as logical causality and suspense) constitute only a portion of his rebellion. Perhaps even more important is the way in which Kluge foregrounds and problematizes narration itself, questioning the centrality and coherence of narrative in the motion picture. Perhaps no filmmaker tells more stories per film than Kluge, yet few directors seem more detached from their narratives. The very abundance of these tales diminishes the relative weight of each. The story seems to be merely a vehicle for Kluge's ideas, an illustration of the interaction of human passions and needs. [3]

Nevertheless, Kluge's films never abandon story altogether. Although an iconoclast who has positioned himself at the very edge of commercial cinema, Kluge does not want to withdraw from this arena completely. He does not want his work exiled to the limited venues of avant-garde art films or political documentaries. As the opening quotation indicates, Kluge understands that to remain in the commercial theaters, he must continue to tell stories. As a modernist, however, he bears a fundamental mistrust of any illusionistic narrative that attempts to hide its constructed nature. Modernism, Adorno claimed,

> rebelled against the misperception of art without illusion. This is the aim of all efforts to pierce the hermetically closed texture of works by means of unabashed intervention, to release production in the product, thus putting, within limits, the productive process in the place of its result. . . . The dialectic of modern art to a large extent is such that it seeks to shake off its illusory character, as an animal sometimes seems to want to shake off its antlers.[4]

Thus, interruption, lack of closure, and reflexivity become key strategies for problematizing narrative illusion. Moreover, Kluge often subordinates the stories to other considerations—thematic or formal. This places less emphasis on script, acting, and character identification, and thereby gives the filmmaker many more creative—and cost-saving—options.

NARRATIVE STRUCTURE IN KLUGE'S FILMS

The broad range of narrative structures in Kluge's films spans two extremes: 1) the traditional Hollywood model of narration with its straightforward, linear plot development; and 2) a modernist collage model with a more fragmented assortment of short narratives whose only interconnections are thematic and stylistic, offering no unified story world or diegesis. Most of Kluge's earlier films—*Yesterday Girl* (1965–66), *Artistes at the Top of the Big Top: Disoriented* (1967), *Willi Tobler und der Untergang der 6. Flotte* (*Willi Tobler and the Wreck of the Sixth Fleet,* 1969–71), and *Occasional Work of a Female Slave* (1973)—fall closer to the Hollywood end of the spectrum;[5] while the later films—*The Power of Emotion* (1983), *Der Angriff der Gegenwart auf die übrige Zeit* (*The Blind Director,* 1985), and *Vermischte Nachrichten* (*Odds and Ends,* 1986)—increasingly come to exemplify the second extreme. Two films from the middle to late 1970s—*In Gefahr und größer Not bringt der Mittelweg den Tod* (*The Middle of the Road Is a Very Dead End,* 1974) and *Die Patriotin* (*The Patriot,* 1977–79)—fall between these extremes. The most striking exception, however, to this rather neat historical progression is the 1975–76 film *Strongman Ferdinand*. Of all Kluge's films, *Strongman Ferdinand* comes closest to a pure instance of Hollywood-style narration.

The Classical Hollywood Model

After making several films in the early 1970s that achieved little box office success, Kluge undertook one of his most radical experiments: he abandoned his own distinctive style and

I *Der starke Ferdinand* (*Strongman Ferdinand*): Always on duty

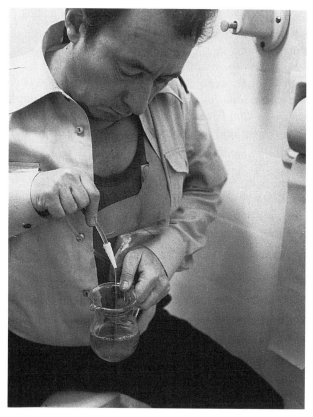

I *Der starke Ferdinand* (*Strongman Ferdinand*): Ferdinand delivers
a urine sample

storytelling approaches in order to create a classical feature film.[6]
Strongman Ferdinand is certainly the most straightforward and accessible of his narratives. Despite some episodic tendencies, the film employs traditional narrative causality to interlock most incidents into a
coherent story. The actions of the protagonist Ferdinand Rieche, a
company security chief, become increasingly obsessive and extreme
until they culminate in his attempt to assassinate a government official. This climax is set up through the use of a definite time deadline:
Rieche has a six-month contract, during which he must prove himself. His chief adversary is a company director who announces his
opposition to him at the beginning and ultimately succeeds in firing
him. The tale ends with Rieche's arrest and his explanation of the motives behind the assassination attempt. No nonnarrative sequences are

introduced to disrupt the story and most of the episodes are logically linked to increase the emotional effect.

In addition, Kluge introduces a classic secondary romantic plot-line, which closely parallels the main storyline. As Rieche's behavior at work becomes increasingly erratic and obsessive, so too does his homelife. His paranoia and idiosyncracies (such as a November camping trip to practice celebrating Christmas) finally force his girlfriend, Gertie, out of his apartment and out of his life in the same way that they are forcing him out of his job.

This film is also notable as the first Kluge venture to employ a well-established star. Heinz Schubert had become one of Germany's most familiar personalities, starring as *ekel Alfred* (disgusting Alfred), an Archie Bunker figure on a popular television series.[7] This combination of a straightforward, action-oriented plot, a bankable star, romance, and a rather controversial topical subject—terrorism, security, and constitutionalism—seemed to have all the ingredients (*Zutaten*) for box-office success. Unfortunately for Kluge, two factors intervened to prevent this success. Conservative theater owners disliked the film's subject matter and tone and were reluctant to exhibit it. In addition, a national newspaper strike coincided with the premiere of the film, leaving Kluge without publicity and hence without spectators.[8]

The Episodic Narrative

Kluge's first five features (*Yesterday Girl, Artistes at the Top of the Big Top: Disoriented, Der grosse Verhau* [*The Big Mess*, 1969–70], *Willi Tobler and the Wreck of the Sixth Fleet,* and *Occasional Work of a Female Slave*) constitute significant, if limited, departures from the narrative model exemplified by *Strongman Ferdinand*. The most striking structural features of these narratives are their episodic and cyclical qualities. In each case, the narrative could be characterized as a quest, but the vague or unarticulated nature of the goal, the confusion and indecision of the protagonists, and the injection of nondramatic incidents and material from outside the story world or diegesis, all serve to reduce the linearity, coherence, and momentum of the plot. The typical trajectory of conventional cinematic narration involves disruption of harmony, increasing conflict leading to a climax, and a resolution that restores harmony. Characters and incidents depicted in the drama should contribute to this climax and resolution. Events are linked in a causal chain leading to this denouement. In his early films, Kluge is already beginning to challenge or eliminate many of these elements of traditional narrative structure and effect.

I *Abschied von gestern (Yesterday Girl)*: Anita moves on

Yesterday Girl, like several other early Kluge films, features a single, female protagonist, who is present in almost every scene and whose story is apparently told in chronological order.[9] The tale of Anita G., a refugee from East Germany, involves a quest for her own place within West German society. The film is a documentation of her various unsuccessful efforts to fit in. Because of her confusion and inarticulateness, this goal is unstated and assumes various guises. Her encounters with the legal system, the business world, educational institutions, and various lovers are all discouraging and unproductive. Each different attempt at integration becomes a separate, relatively autonomous episode. The episodes often begin on an optimistic note, then misunderstanding, ill-will, or misconduct lead to failure and flight.[10] Each cycle serves as simply another variation on the theme. Most of the episodes are logically and chronologically interchangeable. Only two pairs of episodes are causally interdependent. Her release from prison in one episode is conditioned upon her cooperation with a sanctimonious social worker in the next. Her affair with a married bureaucrat results in a pregnancy, forcing her in the subsequent episode to seek prenatal shelter by returning to prison.

Causal, temporal, and spatial connections between episodes (as within episodes) are often blurred by ellipses and by limited narrative information. The viewer is uncertain exactly where Anita's odyssey leads her and how many stops she makes along the way. Similarly, it is unclear whether the film takes place over a period of one year, five years, or some period in between. The only firm temporal clue is the pregnancy, and even this is elliptically told so as to be overlooked or misunderstood.[11] The parallel between the beginning and the end of the film, with Anita imprisoned and wearing the same prison clothes, emphasizes the circularity of the plot. No lesson is learned, no climax endured, no resolution achieved.

Leni Peickert's goal in *Artistes at the Top of the Big Top: Disoriented* is to establish a reform circus. As in *Yesterday Girl*, this goal is vague, and it is defined largely in negative terms—as something different from the normal circus. Leni wants to innovate, to create new experiences in the circus, but has no clear concept of such a utopian circus. The goal is pursued rather stubbornly but, perhaps because it is so vague, with a certain lack of efficacy and intensity. Hence the audience

❙ *Abschied von gestern* (*Yesterday Girl*): Anita in prison

▌*Die Artisten in der Zirkuskuppel: ratlos* (*Artistes at the Top of the Big Top: Disoriented*): Leni buys an elephant

is not encouraged to identify with the protagonist, but rather to watch her critically. The spectator becomes detached from the story world—in Brecht's terms, distanced or alienated.

Again in this narrative, Kluge minimizes causal and temporal connections. The story seems to be told in a chronological fashion, but the sequence of incidents is not logically necessary. There is, however, a general progression in the film from vague dream to partial realization to abrupt termination. This cycle is repeated three times within the course of the film. She sets up the circus, then runs out of money, allowing the creditors to take it over. She goes into television, starts to make headway, and then decides to give it up. She inherits money and starts up her circus again, only to abandon it for another try at television. Although this last cycle is merely referred to, it serves to keep the narrative ending open and to indicate the ongoing circularity of the film.

Kluge's third film was a venture into science fiction that is aptly named: *The Big Mess.* Like *Strongman Ferdinand,* this film's narrative course escapes the overarching trajectory of narrative development in

Kluge's films. However, unlike *Strongman Ferdinand,* this is not a classical Hollywood narrative, but rather a strange concoction of shorter stories which are juxtaposed and intercut, anticipating Kluge's later narrative strategies of miniaturization and fragmentation. Less evident here is any coherent authorial control or intention.[12] The film tells several different stories all set in 2034 A.D., but otherwise not interrelated: two families try to escape the control of a capitalist corporation that is rapidly expanding through the whole galaxy; a middle-aged Bavarian couple lives by plundering spaceships; and an untrained pilot flies spaceships while waiting to get into the flight academy. All of these tales have an open ending. At the end of the film a new character is introduced, the last American (a millionaire), and he is mistakenly killed when his ship is shot down.

The treadmill-like circularity of *Yesterday Girl* and *Artistes at the Top of the Big Top: Disoriented* (and present to a lesser extent in *The Big Mess*) is also repeated in the other two early films, *Willi Tobler* and *Occasional Work of a Female Slave. Willi Tobler,* Kluge's second venture into science fiction, features a careerist protagonist seeking access to the centers of power. But each opportunistic move of Tobler toward power and security seems to result in further insecurity, as the forces of civil war keep turning things upside down. His ready betrayal of

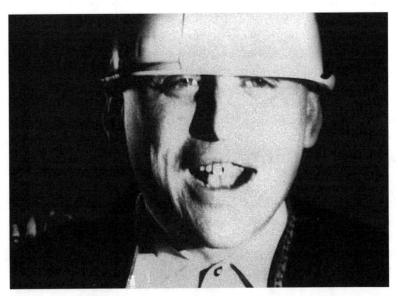

I *Willi Tobler und der Untergang der 6. Flotte* (*Willi Tobler and the Wreck of the Sixth Fleet*): Willi Tobler

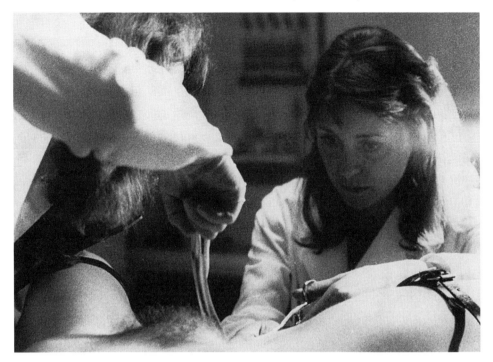

▌*Gelegenheitsarbeit einer Sklavin (Occasional Work of a Female Slave)*: Roswitha performs an abortion

allegiances (to profession, family, and country) prevents him from maintaining stability for very long. Tobler tumbles through each cycle of revolution and counterrevolution, trying to land on his feet. The film has no definite resolution, but does suggest at the end that he has been caught by a social and political maelstrom and may not be able to escape.

In contrast to Tobler's mercenary ways, the socially conscious Roswitha Bronski in *Occasional Work of a Female Slave* is looking for a way to make her life meaningful and take care of her children's future. At first this means working as an abortionist; later she becomes involved in various forms of political organizing activities. Although her motives and goals remain somewhat obscure even to herself, an inner compulsion drives her to action. However, her inexperience, urgency, and unclarified goals contribute to a certain incompetence in the execution of her actions.

The film falls into roughly two parts: her attempts to earn money as an abortionist and, later, her decision to take on responsibility outside

I *Gelegenheitsarbeit einer Sklavin* (*Occasional Work of a Female Slave*): Children playing in the snow

the domestic sphere, in society at large. In each part, her energetic and committed attempts to achieve these ends come to naught. She reaches a stand off with the police and the rival who informed on her, but then abandons her abortion practice. Her random and tentative political activities culminate in action against the company for which her husband works. The only consequence of her activities is that her husband is fired. The film ends with her working in a fast-food stand where she wraps hot dogs in political leaflets: a new cycle begins.

In all five films, the vague, ephemeral, or shifting nature of the characters' goals makes their quests seem much less important to the spectator than they might in more conventionally structured films, where the establishment of and emphasis on concrete goals—getting the money, the crook, or the romantic object—propel the plot and bind the episodes. In Kluge's films, the episodes threaten to break off and become independent elements. They are not constructed as building blocks of dramatic tension. Many scenes have the nonteleological feel of everyday life.

In each of these films, Kluge denies the viewer any dramatic or emotional climax. Not only is there no happy ending, there is virtually no narrative closure. Instead, there is a cyclical, Sisyphean quality to each of the narratives: Anita G. is imprisoned again; Leni continues her work as a reformer; the pirates and small business people of *The Big Mess* continue to glean a living from the leavings of the galactic monopolies; Tobler's chameleon character is unaltered; and Roswitha carries on her ineffectual organizing. Life goes on. The filmmaker has arbitrarily selected moments from these lives for the film, but other moments and episodes would have shown similar actions and reactions.

The narrative line in each of these films is further weakened by the introduction of nonnarrative material into the middle of the story. In *Yesterday Girl,* a hotel manager talks directly to the camera about his experiences during the war; a noted jurist confesses inhumane behavior and proposes a utopian courtroom. Although both characters are placed within, or in proximity to, the diegetic world, the quasi-documentary style and obliquely relevant content interrupt the narrative. In *Artistes at the Top of the Big Top: Disoriented,* old newsreel footage of a National Socialist "Day of Culture" is introduced under the caption "The Incapacity to Mourn." The relevance of these documentary interjections, either spatially, temporally, or thematically, is not easily ascertainable. Their effect on the spectator is to break up the narrative coherence and dissipate the accumulation of plot interest and tension.

The extremely loose narrative in *The Big Mess* often makes it difficult to ascertain whether certain footage is diegetically motivated or not. Among the clearer cases of nonnarrative material is an insert of a toy monkey playing a drum and a documentary sequence of crowds, military vehicles, women sitting around a table, and several shots of plasterwork renovation (apparently outtakes from *Yesterday Girl*). Other obtrusive instances of materials with only tenuous relations to the narrative include drawings and still photos of soldiers from World War II and old newsreel footage. These seem to illustrate elements of the story, but, given the futuristic diegesis, are markedly anachronistic.

Willi Tobler and the Wreck of the Sixth Fleet could be regarded as the other half of *The Big Mess.* Many of the same actors, characters, and actual shots recur, as do the anachronistic interruptions to a chaotic plot: World War II air attacks illustrating intergalactic battles and still photos of grotesquely wounded soldiers.[13] *Willi Tobler* also includes several sequences of drawings ("skating on thin ice" and "the life of an elephant") that are only metaphorically related to the story.

In *Occasional Work of a Female Slave,* most of the interruptions are quasi-diegetic. On several occasions, shots from the Soviet film *Chapayev* are inserted. One such interruption occurs after the narrator asserts that Roswitha knows about power from films she has seen. Later clips are introduced by her staring into space, as if she is remembering them. A long sequence documenting a tour of Frankfurt by government officials is incorporated into the narrative by having Roswitha accompany them on the bus trip. The trip does nothing to advance the plot nor is there any explanation for her presence on this official tour. Two sequences, however, are more clearly nondiegetic: a children's rhyme accompanying shots from a book and a brief montage of nineteenth-century illustrations of families, villages, and mermaids. Neither of these sequences is set up as Roswitha's memory or stream of consciousness.

Thus, in his early films, Kluge is making significant departures from traditional narration. These less goal-oriented, less dramatic narratives are often interrupted by nondiegetic elements that serve as counterpoint to or commentary on the events of the storyline. His first two films were particularly successful in international festivals, indicating that they had considerable appeal for contemporary art cinema audiences. Precisely those elements that are vague or confusing to traditional audiences may be prized by art cinema audiences as subtle, complex, and challenging.

Yet none of these five films is so radical as to stray from the ambit of the art film. They employ a level of metaphoric representation and the abrupt editing techniques that appeal mainly to sophisticated audiences, but they remain largely comprehensible fictional films. For the most part they address topical subjects, do not overstep middle-class boundaries of good taste, and are delivered in the standard 90–120 minute format. These are not avant-garde, underground, or subversive films, but were photographed in 35 mm and intended for commercial distribution. They bear the differentiating marks of their national origin without becoming too parochial or esoteric. Particularly the first two films, *Yesterday Girl* and *Artistes at the Top of the Big Top: Disoriented,* speak the aesthetic language of other international art films of their period. As Kluge's films became more narratively fragmented, more specifically Germanic in content, and more difficult to understand, they were less attractive to juries at international film festivals and to international distributors.[14]

The Transitional Films

In his 1974 film *The Middle of the Road Is a Very Dead End,* done in collaboration with Edgar Reitz, Kluge attempted a more ambitious narrative strategy. He set out to tell two stories in one film. As in *The Big Mess,* the two protagonists were linked only in general spatial and temporal terms. Both resided in Frankfurt during a time of social unrest: protests, house occupations, and police evictions. The two main characters, a prostitute/thief and an Eastern bloc spy, never meet one another, nor do their stories intersect or overlap. Both are outsiders, both seem to be vaguely seeking something; but again, any strong plotline is absent. No crisis is reached, no arrests are made, no changes of heart or lifestyle are accomplished. The addition of a second plot line gives Kluge more possibilities for fragmenting the narrative (by alternating sequences from each story). In addition, Kluge makes extensive use of documentary footage—fragments of an extra-diegetic reality. These shots of student protests and house demolitions further interrupt the narrative flow and segment the film. Like the previous films, there is little dramatic intensification or closure in these slices of fictional lives.

After the anti-experiment, *Strongman Ferdinand* in 1976, Kluge's next projects reverted to the more fragmented, multiple-narrative approaches that he had been developing. He was pushed further in this direction by his participation in an important collaborative film in 1977, *Deutschland im Herbst (Germany in Autumn).* This film was a reflection on the controversy surrounding the deaths of the industrialist Hanns Martin Schleyer and members of the Red Army Faction in Stammheim prison. Kluge coordinated this topical project, which involved eight teams of filmmakers, writers, and technicians.[15] Each team contributed at least one autonomous segment, either fictive, documentary, or, in Fassbinder's case, an apparently autobiographical docudrama. Kluge's blue intertitles and softly probing voice-over commentary provided the cohesion necessary to bind these extremely heterogenous elements together. The tremendous box-office success of this film not only encouraged other similar collaborative films, it also pointed Kluge toward even more innovative narrative structures.[16] No longer did it seem so necessary to shape the thematic material into one narrative. Rather, the film could be structured almost like an anthology: a grouping of shorter, more autonomous segments of documentary and fictional material. This freed Kluge from what he perceived as the arbitrary tyranny of commercial film distri-

I *In Gefahr und größer Not bringt der Mittleweg den Tod* (*The Middle of the Road Is a Very Dead End*): Rita conducts espionage

bution: all films must be fictional narratives lasting about two hours. In the past, he had argued that such requirements do not necessarily reflect the internal demands of the material nor the interests of the viewer. Now he had demonstrated that looser, more fragmented narrative structures could be both comprehensible and attractive to audiences.

The first of Kluge's feature productions influenced by this new experimentation in fragmented narrative is his 1979 film *The Patriot*. This film contains one overarching narrative, the story of the history teacher Gabi Teichert, but it is interrupted repeatedly by a variety of nondiegetic materials. Three miniature narratives are dramatized, each set in the period between 1939 and 1945: three expert bomb defusers discuss their craft, a grave digger hops into a grave to nap during an air raid, and a German officer and his wife take their first trip to Italy. None of these is diegetically motivated as a story within the main story. In addition, many small stories and excursuses occur that are not acted out.

Documentary material is also introduced, including footage of a disruption of Christmas shopping by demonstrators at a department store and interviews with a doll salesman and a fairy-tale expert. Although the interviews are unrelated narratively to the main story, the first sequence, the disruptive demonstration, is placed in peripheral relation to the main story: Gabi Teichert observes some of the commotion from outside the store. Fiction and documentary are combined more thoroughly in the long sequence where Gabi Teichert attends the Social Democrat (SPD) convention. There she becomes a more active participant in a real event as she lobbies (in character) for social changes that she hopes will result in a better German history. In *The Patriot,* like the earlier films, there is no strong narrative trajectory and no sense of culmination at the end. Moreover, the interrup-

❙ In Gefahr und größer Not bringt der Mittleweg den Tod (*The Middle of the Road Is a Very Dead End*): Street fighting over house occupations

tions in the narrative line distract from any sense of development and disperse any tension.

The Late Films: Miniature Narratives

In his last three feature films, Kluge dispenses with any overarching narrative and structures each film as a collection of shorter narratives, documentaries, and other elements. Miriam Hansen and other commentators have compared Kluge's later work to the heterogeneity of early cinematic and precinematic entertainment: the variety show, the revue, and the circus.[17] Enacted narratives still constitute the majority of the material in these films, and often one narrative is longer and has a privileged position within the film. In two films, this results from its location at the conclusion of the film; in the other, the major narrative is the only one which is presented in two parts.

According to Kluge, his 1983 film *The Power of Emotion* contains twenty-six stories and, like the films of D. W. Griffith, belongs to the epic genre.[18] Although many of these stories consist of preexistent footage with added narration, the film does contain eight dramatized narratives.[19] Most are short or interrupted by nonnarrative sequences. Some of them pose as documentary footage, such as a mock interview with an opera singer. Nevertheless, dramatization maintains its preeminent position. The last and most prolonged segment of the film is the twenty-minute story of a crime and its unmaking. This is broken into parts by intertitles and really consists of three intertwined crime stories involving prostitution, robbery, near murder, and resuscitation. Although this last tale finishes on an ironic note, the couple is at least united by their unpaid hard work. Its position at the end of the film gives the whole film an apparent retrospective meaning and closure that is not fully warranted. Viewers may forget about the earlier segments of the film whose meanings and interconnections were not fully comprehended.

The Blind Director, completed in 1985, has a structure similar to *The Power of Emotion,* although it is a bit more intricate. This film consists of six dramatized stories, set in varied locales and periods. Again, the primary narrative is a relatively long final sequence (twenty minutes) that serves as a culmination of the foregoing shorter narratives and nonnarrative material. The structure of this final narrative is more complex than most of Kluge's short film stories. The tale begins with a monk having sex with the corpse of a young woman for whom

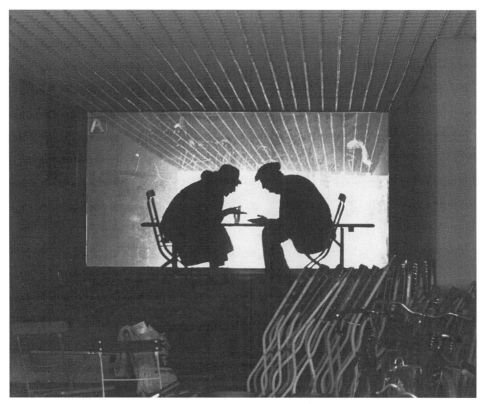

❚ *Die Macht der Gefühle* (*The Power of Emotion*): "She has engaged a detective, whose job it is to find out the reason for world-wide divisiveness."

he is supposed to be praying. His sexual stimulation apparently revives her. At the conclusion of this dramatization, a wider shot reveals a production crew filming these scenes. The framing story, which actually constitutes the bulk of this narrative, concerns the director of this film crew, a man who is going blind. This film within a film not only heightens the narrative reflexivity, but provides a new way for Kluge to organize narratives: not just serially or through cross-cutting, but now through layering of tales inside tales.[20]

Odds and Ends (1986) is, as its title suggests, the most atomized of all Kluge's films, with a great variety of narrative and nonnarrative segments. The title itself is a reference to the last page of a newspaper where little assorted tidbits of news and human interest are gathered together. Not only does Kluge avoid any overarching narrative, he de-

I *Vermischte Nachrichten (Odd and Ends)*: Frozen soldier, Stalingrad

nies the longest story a position at the end of the film, which would have contributed a sense of partial closure. The film consists of eight dramatizations, five documentary pieces, three condensed old movies, parts of a civil defense instructional film, eight short montage sequences, and an on-screen announcer, Sabine Trooger, who introduces many of the segments. The program introducer is a unifying device borrowed from German television, and Trooger has served this function in several Kluge television broadcasts. Although many of these segments deal with death and war, only two of the dramatized pieces feature the same protagonists. This bifurcated tale, about an African prostitute and a waiter, lasts about twenty minutes, only one-fifth of the film's running time.

It is important to distinguish between interruption of narrative (which characterized Kluge's earlier films) and atomization into smaller narratives (which characterized his later productions). The former technique can often serve to heighten narrative effect by increasing suspense. Although Kluge's films have a relatively low level of dramatic tension, the delaying and interruption of narrative in his earlier films does sometimes serve to increase the sense of anticipation. In the later films, this spectator response is transformed. At the beginning of the film, the viewer wonders how long each story will last and whether it will be continued after the interruption. As the pattern of atomization becomes established, however, one no longer feels this expectation of a delayed payoff. Instead one is either slightly curious about what new material will come next or, more often, is too busy trying to work out associations retroactively even to attempt to anticipate.

In summary, the history of Kluge's narrative structures, with the exception of *Strongman Ferdinand* and to a lesser extent *The Big Mess,* demonstrates a pattern of development from relatively simple episodic narratives, to increasingly fragmented, shortened, and proliferated narratives in the later films. His storytelling becomes more modernist, moving him farther from the narrative structure of classical Hollywood cinema.

NARRATIVE TECHNIQUE

Kluge's modernist film practice is evident not only in his divergence from and critique of classical narrative *structure*, but also in his departure from classical narrative *techniques.* The most salient narrational technique in Kluge's films is his utilization of extradiegetic commentary through intertitles and off-screen narration. Although these devices are not unknown in mainstream cinema, for Kluge they become the key expository, unifying, and explanatory elements in his films.

In his early feature films, Kluge employed several kinds of external commentary on narrative events. The most important of these was visual rather than aural: the intertitle. Some of Kluge's intertitles seemed to function analogously to literary chapter titles and were influenced by silent film practice. In Kluge's films, such segmenting titles provide a general, if often vague, clue as to what may happen in the subsequent segment; or they may suggest a level of abstraction from which to interpret the specific events that will follow. Although implicitly the product of the author's subjectivity, these titles take on a certain concrete and objective quality, stemming from their apparent omniscience.

Other intertitles owe their authority not to any objective or omniscient status but to their sources. Kluge is fond of quotations from
literary figures. These accord the films a certain cultural dignity and
seriousness and provide interpretive clues and generalizations. An example in *Yesterday Girl* is the final quotation: "Every person is to
blame in all things, but if everyone knew that, we would have paradise
on earth." Kluge puts quotation marks around the citation, but does
not attribute it to Dostoyevsky.[21] The source of the quotation becomes
yet another puzzle for the spectator's speculation. As Miriam Hansen
comments: "Kluge's obsessive use of quotation marks, figuratively
speaking, foregrounds the act of enunciation itself, suspending and
simultaneously provoking the question of authorship: a discourse in
search of spectators who can remember and revise."[22]

In *Willi Tobler,* intertitles are extremely frequent and essential to
the intelligibility of the episodic and rambling plot. Kluge has continued to use intertitles throughout his career: they appear in all of his
films (even *Strongman Ferdinand* has one near the end) and in most of
his television programs. In addition to their narrative function, these
titles have a stylistic function of visual contrast and repetition that will
be discussed in the next chapter.

In *Yesterday Girl,* Kluge employed another type of extradiegetic
commentary that has proven even more flexible than intertitles: voice-
over narration. Although such narration also occurs in classical Hollywood cinema, its use is kept to a minimum and is normally reserved
for introductory or transitional purposes. Kluge's more extensive em-
ployment of such voice-overs violates a cardinal rule of Hollywood
screenwriters: "show, don't tell." A classical Hollywood film relies
primarily on visual elements of the story world—gestures, objects,
setting, and action—to reveal character, mood, and information.
Kluge inverts this hierarchy by emphasizing the words. Telling often
takes precedence over showing in Kluge's films. Although such oral
storytelling is in fact the oldest narrational technique, Kluge's application of it in the film medium is an important aspect of his modernist
practice. According to B. Ruby Rich, "In such a recognized, if vaguely
defined, area as contemporary modernist cinema, certain assumptions
are operative. The tenets hold that a self-interruptive text provides the
appropriate rupture with linear narrative or transparent narrativity."[23]
Voice-over narration not only alters the relation of the spectator to
the film, but allows Kluge a great deal of latitude for experimenting
with the relation of sound and image in various kinds of storytelling.
This technique gives Kluge another level of narration, another way

of interrupting as well as connecting story segments, and is a chief factor in the films' reflexivity. Moreover, its usefulness—particularly during the postproduction process—as a bridging and expository device is important to Kluge's strategy of producing films on very low budgets.

Kluge's use of voice-over narration differs in several respects from classical cinema. In mainstream cinema such voice-overs occur rather infrequently, and often these instances are diegetically motivated as the memory or point of view of one of the story's characters. Such narrations serve as a commentary on the events depicted, provide links between different places and times, and convey the mood and thoughts of the character. Like the point-of-view shot, this type of voice-over can be effective in conveying subjectivity and encouraging audience identification with a particular character. Sometimes the narrators are not the main protagonists of the action, but have a privileged position of knowledge or a restricted knowledge that increases dramatic suspense. Occasionally, the classical cinema borrows another type of voice-over narration from documentary and newsreel films: the objective narrator. Sometimes this may be a recognizable news reporter or other authoritative personality. At other times, it may be an unidentifiable voice that adopts the confident tone of authority and dispenses apparently reliable information from a position of omniscience.

Kluge's oral narration is a unique combination of these two tendencies, which would appear, at first, to be mutually exclusive. After early experiments with character voice-overs in *Yesterday Girl* and *Artistes at the Top of the Big Top: Disoriented,* Kluge developed a technique more effective for his aesthetic project and more suited to his mode of production. In his 1973 film *Occasional Work of a Female Slave,* Kluge himself took over the role of narrator. This move eliminated problems of actor availability during the editing process and allowed him more control over intonation and inflection. Kluge's voice has a very distinctive warmth and intelligence. He is often ironic, but in a gentle rather than sarcastic way. He creates an omniscient narrator, but also a personal one, who does not preach or compel, but rather almost whispers to the audience. This new mode of narration thus combined the omniscience of an objective narrator with the subjectivity of a narrating character. Kluge stands outside the narrative but is still intimately related to the story and characters.

Although Kluge's identity as narrator is never announced or credited, most viewers will recognize his distinctive voice from other public forums. This recognition significantly, if subtly, alters the spectator's relation to the film and foregrounds the process of narration. Moreover, this recognition means that the voice has a privileged access to information and meaning, a personal stake in the proceedings, and offers the spectator the possibility of direct contact with the author, unmediated by characters and story. In fact, the presence of Kluge as narrator does more than promise the revelation of meaning within the story; it insists that there must be a meaning beyond the events of the story, even if his comments are enigmatic.

Many commentators have observed the prominent role that voice-over narration plays in Kluge's films. While acknowledging its importance, Miriam Hansen has questioned the degree of authority that resides in the narrator. She argues that Kluge's narration "shifts its stance and mode of articulation, deconstructing itself as it goes along."[24] This, she argues, encourages viewers to make their own meanings instead of relying on an unstable narrator.

Although her observations about the complexity, ambiguity, and shifting tone of the narration are accurate, the effects of this kind of narration on other spectators may be quite different. Even if the information that Kluge provides, as both narrator and filmmaker, is inadequate or puzzling, the voice-over narration remains the spectator's best hope for making sense of the film. Kluge's confident and often superior attitude reinforces the notion that he understands what is significant about the images flowing past. This technique sets up a tension between two levels of expression: the images and the commentary. As Hansen has remarked, although Kluge "maintains the basically narrative function of cinema," his techniques result in an "emphasis on the act of narration, not story."[25] This emphasis on process and construction is a modernist alternative to the classical attempt to absorb the spectator into the diegetic world.

Kluge's modernist use of voice-over narration not only creates a more complex position for the spectator, it is also a very practical tool for Kluge as a filmmaker. In Hollywood filmmaking, narrative cohesion is achieved through spatial and temporal continuity. Any significant shifts in time or space must be clarified to the viewer, either through technical conventions (fades, montage sequences), visual clues (city limits signs, calendar pages, or, more subtly, different clothing fashions), or expository dialogue. For Kluge, any lapses in narrative continuity can be easily handled in the voice-over. In Kluge's films, such discontinuities abound. Voice-over narration does not eliminate the sense of discontinuity altogether, but it keeps the films from disintegrating completely. In *The Patriot*, for example, Kluge sets up several segments by telling us the date and a little information about the character: "Gabi Teichert, a history teacher"; "1943. A mother and two children"; "Two Bomb Experts"; "A grave digger, 1945." Although such information could have been carried in an intertitle or in a superimposed title, the voice-over contains a more personal tone and foregrounds the process of storytelling.

The voice-over also offers other advantages to Kluge's strategy of low-budget filmmaking. In Hollywood films, every important event must be shown, and any significant motivation or thought process must be revealed by action or dialogue. Kluge has no such constraints. If an event is too difficult or expensive to film (e.g., a crowd scene, an exotic location, a special effect), he can summarize it in a few sentences. Characters' subjectivities can also be succinctly revealed without dialogue or action, simplifying both rehearsal and the shooting process. High-quality location sound is not essential. In postproduction, continuity problems can be bridged or material substantially reshaped through voice-overs.

In addition to these pragmatic advantages, voice-over narration substantially alters and augments the types of storytelling available to Kluge. Along with more traditional cinematic enactments, Kluge often uses three types of preexisting visual elements: a) old film footage, either from documentary or fiction films; b) still photographs, from archives, books, magazines, and sometimes from films; and c) drawings, paintings, and other illustrations. Combinations of these three types of material are utilized in three different modes of storytelling: condensation, illustration, and excerpt.

Perhaps the most interesting of these is condensation. In this mode, Kluge reduces a long and complex tale to a short story. For example, in *The Power of Emotion*, Kluge tells the story of the opera *Aida*—a two-hour work—in about three minutes. The plot, character motivations, and a commentary are all combined in the voice-over narration, while the visuals show selected scenes from a silent film version of the opera. Kluge's abridged version emphasizes plot twists and themes of love, patriotism, and mass psychology, but still retains some traces of the original operatic spectacle in both the visuals and the music. The exoticism of costume and landscape are felt despite the relatively low production values of the early film. The musical passages, although shortened (often abruptly), still retain the tempo, sonority, and some of the emotional impact of an operatic performance. Like a good modernist, Kluge foregrounds this process of collage and the differences between the media by using slow motion, freeze frames, and iris framing.

Although this condensation into miniatures is, like Kluge's dramatized sequences, heavily dependent on voice-over narration, it is in some respects diametrically opposed to Kluge's usual dramatizations. Much of Kluge's normal dramaturgy consists of nonactions, nonevents, and quotidian reality, but the miniatures condense time and eliminate the details and the specificity of real life for the schematic plotline of extremely emotional, dramatic events: passion, war, and death. While these dramatic events are told by the narrator, they are also shown in the visual clips. The viewer sees Aida and Radames being stoned by a crowd, giant battle scenes, cities set afire: images that Kluge has neither the means nor the inclination to direct on his own.

What interests Kluge about stories is the emotions they contain: how people respond to difficult situations.[26] He is less interested in giving the spectator the vicarious experience of these emotions— through psychological identification with the characters—than he is in making the spectator understand these conflicts of force and passion. His condensations are often synopses of plots, and these schemata are then juxtaposed with other similar stories. An opera plot can, for example, shed light on parallel aspects of a contemporary political situation.

The second nonacted storytelling approach that Kluge uses is illustration. He invents a tale or retells a preexisting story, often a poem or nursery rhyme, and finds still photos, drawings, and occasionally motion picture footage to illustrate it. In *Yesterday Girl,* he narrates an illustrated children's book about an ice-age mammoth who thaws out in modern times. In *The Patriot,* he reads the Christian Morgenstern poem, "Das Knie," and uses old paintings, drawings, still photos, and archive footage to illustrate moments of German history and literature. He then tells a story about the knee of a soldier killed at Stalingrad, with a rich montage of visual images that sometimes closely parallel the oral text (e.g., "our beautiful Germany" accompanies shots of fields and flowering meadows). This technique allows Kluge to take literary material, oral traditions, or original material and visualize it without enacting it.

The third technique is to excerpt a part of a visual performance (often a clip from a film or a scene from an opera) and use the narration to provide the context and to explain the action. In this instance, Kluge does not recount the entire story from the original tale, only one part or episode. For example, in *The Blind Director,* Kluge excerpts a sequence from the opera *Tosca* and comments on the action in voice-over. Although pure instances of excerpts, condensation, and illustration can be found in Kluge's work, it is more common to find him combining these techniques in montage sequences.

This oral storytelling allows Kluge to tell many more stories in a much shorter time, and to present many more parallels and inter-connections, than he could using standard narrative techniques in standard ways. Through these alternative narrative techniques, Kluge can also introduce a variety of thematically related material—both visual and aural—that is of interest to him, but that could not be die-getically motivated. They also allow him to reduce the amount of en-acted, dramatized material. This not only reduces production costs, but diminishes the centrality of an illusionistic narrative line. The film can become a more flexible site for essays, allusions, quotations, and association. All of these nonillusionistic techniques contribute to the modernist effect by increasing the fragmentation and complexity of the film, foregrounding the storytelling process, and inscribing the artist himself within the work of art.

Characterization and Identification

Kluge's method of oral storytelling intervenes between the viewer and the character to alter or obstruct certain processes that are central to classical cinematic practice. Hansen remarks that "the status of character in Kluge's films is inseparable from its rela-tion to the voice-over, the absent narrator who intervenes, seem-ingly, to mediate the character for the spectator." [27] Although Hansen goes on to question the degree of narrator authority, there is no doubt that the narration changes our relation to the characters, con-trols most of our knowledge of the characters, and provides a new position for the spectator. This, too, B. Ruby Rich has observed, is a central belief of cinematic modernism: "an uninflected voice-over provides the distantiation necessary to prevent an unmediated iden-tification with a character that is not a 'character' at all. . . ." [28] The tone in Kluge's books and also in his filmic narration is detached, sympathetic, and ironic. In his written stories, he often both mocks and imitates the objective style of bureaucratic reports in recounting the lives of his characters. He refers to some of his stories as case his-tories, and they are indeed more like case files than biographies. A certain facticity also is present in his exposition of characters. For Kluge, much can be learned about people from their jobs, their edu-cation, their family circumstances, and the particular situations in which they currently find themselves. This approach corresponds to

Brecht's analysis of cinema's distinctive potential. "[Film] gives life to its people, whom it classes solely according to their function, simply adopting available types that occur in given situations and are able to adopt given attitudes in them. Character is never used as a source of motivation; these people's inner life is never the principle cause of the action and seldom its principle result; the individual is seen from the outside." [29] Kluge's characters often seem like "types" and especially in his later films are often introduced that way in voice-overs, intertitles, or credits. In *Odds and Ends,* Kluge includes the following characters: "The African," "The Restless One," "The Threatened Woman," and "The Successful Type." Frequently these descriptions serve as substitutes for names.

Very little information about these characters is revealed through their actions or conversations. Most comes directly from Kluge's narration. There is rarely much interaction between characters and very little dialogue or direct conflict. Much of the visual action involves ordinary activities: walking, driving, putting on make up, drinking coffee. Perhaps the most typical Kluge shot is of a character staring vacantly into space, sometimes looking at the camera, but often not. Her (or occasionally, his) thoughts can only be guessed unless Kluge reveals them. For the most part, however, Kluge does not delve very deeply into their dreams, thoughts, or motivations; he recounts instead facts, events, or conversations that we have not seen. Although he may move into a character's mind (e.g., "Leni Peickert believes . . . "), in the next breath he will make some judgment or comment on the character that reestablishes a distanced position. Anton Kaes has commented on how Kluge's narration filters information about the characters resulting in the modernist goal of viewer detachment:

> The voice-over commentary provides a counterpoint to the images and has the function of both engaging and distancing the viewer. . . . Even a viewer who is unaware that the voice is Kluge's could reasonably relate the off-screen voice to an authorial consciousness that selects the images, controls what is shown, tries out experimental arrangements and tests new combinations. This running commentary, a didactic gesture which is sometimes parodied through exaggeration, creates a distance from the fictional space of the film and thus undercuts identification. [30]

One can contrast this with several Hollywood devices for narrowing the distance between spectator and character. It is not uncommon in classical films for the viewer to hear sounds and to see images that occur only in a character's mind. For example, in Hitchcock's *Strangers on a Train,* we see in Ann's glasses her hallucination of flames; we hear the carnival music that fills Bruno's head as he is overtaken by the urge to kill. Such clear instances of mental point of view are almost totally absent in Kluge's films.[31] Although certain montage sequences could be taken as dreams, memory, or stream of consciousness, they need not be understood in this way. The absence in most cases of conventional markers of interiority (e.g., a preceding shot of someone thinking or sleeping followed by a dissolve), and Kluge's established patterns of nonnarrative interruptions, lend these sequences an ambiguous status. The strong presence of an extradiegetic narrator accentuates the possibility that these sequences need not be understood as an element of the story world.[32]

Optical point of view is another common classical device for increasing the viewer's involvement with characters. Typically, a shot of a character looking off screen is followed by a shot from the character's position showing what she or he is looking at. The camera and, ultimately, the spectator step into the character's shoes for a moment. This technique is also rare in Kluge's work.

A third technique used to encourage identification with a character has been labeled "attachment point of view" by David Bordwell. Attachment describes shots in which the spectator sees the activities and surroundings of a particular character, but without necessarily being given an optical point of view. The more time one spends with a character, the more information one gets about his or her world. In Kluge's early films, attachment to the protagonist occurs in almost every scene. In later films, however, with multiple narratives and large amounts of nonnarrative material, this attachment is greatly reduced. Even in those early films where attachment is consistent, the amount of information provided and the detached method of providing it tend to minimize involvement with the character.

When characters do speak or act in Kluge's films, they often do so in a way that serves to further distance the viewer from the character. Their dialogue is often nonsensical or metaphorical. One of the apparent attractions of the recurrent actor Alfred Edel (who appeared in *Yesterday Girl, Artistes at the Top of the Big Top: Disoriented, Willi Tobler and the Wreck of the Sixth Fleet, The Patriot,* and others) is his capacity for improvising torrents of almost-plausible idiocy. Other Kluge actors also seem to be chosen for their ability to improvise extended dialogues, in which their self-preoccupations and monomanias generate comic effects. For example, Edgar Böhlke and Michael

❙ *Die Patriotin* (*The Patriot*): Gabi digs up German history

Rehberg have the capacity for uttering stubborn and earnest inanities in the face of repeated cross-examination by interviewers. Hannelore Hoger also has this capacity for seriocomic dialogue (two instances in *The Power of Emotion* are the trial sequence and the marriage-broker interview). However, Kluge often utilizes her almost as a comic mime, directing her to embody certain ideas through the literal enactment of metaphorical rhetoric. For example, in *The Patriot,* she sets out with shovel in hand to dig up German history and attempts to change history by attacking textbooks with saw, drill, hammer, and sickle. Although such words and actions are amusing, they make the character seem less plausible and more remote from the viewer.

In general, two types of characters predominate in Kluge's films: obnoxiously self-absorbed males and generally incompetent females. Sometimes the incompetent women are comic; other times they are more tragic. Occasionally, the obnoxious males seem almost pitiable rather than disgusting. Increasingly in Kluge's later films, the ironic seems to verge on pathos. In any case, whether sardonic or sympathetic, Kluge the commentator is superior to his characters, who seem oblivious or at least confused. Andreas Huyssen has pointed out that Kluge's stories often present "events and situations whose meaning is somehow not available to the participants."[33] What meaning is provided comes from the narrator/filmmaker. He sees their faults and illogic, understands their limitations and failures, and finds it all sadly ironic. He communicates this attitude to the viewer.[34] This superiority tends to increase the apparent reliability of the narrator, even though he often chooses to provide less information than the spectator might wish.

The limited information about these character types, their lack of most positive qualities, and the distance at which Kluge keeps them, all discourage the viewer from that type of emotional engagement that has been called identification. The characters are not psychologically realistic or fully developed. They seem rather more like Kluge's puppets, controlled and manipulated by his directorial whim. They resemble characters in fairy tales, whose purposes, psychology, and individuality are scarcely known. Only a few things are known about them—mostly their limitations and inadequacies. Stuart Liebman observes: "In many of the films, the characters are allegorical ciphers, not 'three-dimensional' figures; it is their (or rather Kluge's) projects, rather than any psychological motivation or causal logic, that provide the fragile tentative links between incidents."[35]

Although agreeing that these characters are often allegorical, Miriam Hansen has pointed out that what is interesting is their complex status as more than simple rhetorical constructions: "Since when, to return to Gabi Teichert, does an allegory take a hot bath to warm her frozen feet?"[36] Nevertheless, neither these realistic touches nor even the occasional ad-libbed dialogues suffice to create identification with these constructed characters.[37] In Brecht's terms, the audience is not "worked up" or "swept away" by the actors: "in short, no attempt was made to put [the audience] into a trance and give it the illusion of watching an ordinary unrehearsed event. . . . The audience's tendency to plunge into such illusions has to be checked by specific artistic means."[38]

In his later films, Kluge develops several new techniques for reducing identification. The most interesting and obvious occurs in *The Power of Emotion* and in *The Blind Director,* where Kluge has several characters played by the same actors. In the earlier film, Hannelore Hoger plays a defendant accused of shooting her husband and, in an unrelated narrative, the marriage broker Frau Bärlamm. In the second film, an actor and an actress play a romantic couple in Poland during World War II and later a monk and a rape victim in the filming of a thirteenth-century story. Also in this film, several actors appear in different scenes that may or may not be narratively related—but the contexts suggest that they cannot possibly be the same character. Andre Jung, for example, plays Max, the chauffeur, but also plays a suitor to a woman who lives in another city. No narrative motivation is provided to explain this apparent difficulty. It almost seems as if Kluge does not care how we interpret this.

A similar carelessness or intentional disruption takes place in *Odds and Ends,* where one of the main characters is an African prostitute. Rather than using an African actress, Kluge employs a German actress in blackface. Every time she appears, her false status is noticeable. A perhaps less intentional and certainly less visible instance occurs in *The Patriot,* where the actor playing a German officer has his long hair gathered back into a bun. In any case, these instances break down the narrative illusion and distance the audience from the characters on screen.

This distantiation, which Brecht and Benjamin advocated, has been frequently endorsed by Kluge as well. He believes that films should be seen by disinterested spectators. He also believes that spectators should be given as much freedom as possible to use both their fantasies and their intellects in creating the film in their heads. This undermining of character identification is crucial to the success and failure of Kluge's work. It is this distantiation that lends his work much of its aesthetic radicalness and high-art legitimacy, and it is precisely this that deprives it of a mass audience. Although this narrative identification is not required of highly topical nonfiction films (such as *Germany in Autumn*),[39] it is fundamental to mass audience expectations in the realm of fictional films. As Huyssen has commented with regard to Kluge's literary work, Kluge's narratives "consistently and programmatically disappoint readers' expectations. . . . [They] systematically prevent reader identification and frustrate the pleasures of literariness."[40]

As suggested earlier, the rejection of identification is not only proof of Kluge's serious aesthetic purposes (film as art, not just entertainment), it is also a key component in his strategy of producing inexpensive films. By not always needing synchronized sound, he can shoot more quickly and in locations with undesirable ambient sound. By describing key scenes, Kluge does not need to pay for experienced actors who can give subtly nuanced performances. Less often will he

need multiple takes to correct muffed lines, false intonation, or in-
correct emphases. In addition, his postproduction costs can be substantially reduced: postdubbing, foley work, and extensive sound-
track manipulation are avoided. Again, modernist practice provides
Kluge with aesthetic alternatives to Hollywood that can be achieved
on much smaller budgets.

Kluge's narrational techniques and structures are an important part
of his modernist strategy. Particularly in his later films, they have
yielded him significant pragmatic and aesthetic dividends. They have
allowed him to produce films on very modest budgets while giving
him maximum artistic flexibility. Fragmented, schematized, and condensed narratives allow him much more extensive use of montage,
not just as a principle for connecting shots within sequences, but as a
device for connecting many more narrative and nonnarrative units to
one another. On a higher aesthetic level, this allows his work to reflect
the discontinuities, the contradictions, and the increased segmentation of modern life, while suggesting new relationships between these
seemingly diverse experiences. His dismantling and subversion of
classical film narrative echoes the modernist critique of realism, totality, and closure as deceptions that cover up the reality of contemporary society. The trajectory of this (anti)narrative development in
Kluge's work indicates no sudden shift or rupture, but rather traces a
gradual movement toward disintegration of narrative.

Throughout his career, Kluge's narrative approach breaks with standard conventions and transcends temporal and subject constraints
while remaining within the general framework of the feature-length,
fiction film—virtually the only format with the possibility of wide-
spread theatrical distribution. Kluge embraces many of the techniques
and certainly the radical intentions of the avant-garde: to outrage and
shock, to bury the old institutions, to experiment and innovate. His
rejection of traditional cinema and its forms leads him to the brink of
an alternative distribution system and an esoteric audience. Indeed,
his older films are now resurrected in cafes and video clubs. But Kluge
does not want to take that final step. He prefers the contradictions
and possibilities of the middle ground over an extremist position.
Narrative remains a central element in his cinema, and the narrative
segments—despite their idiosyncracies—are not incomprehensible.
This has kept his films within the commercial distribution network,
albeit at the very fringe. As his later films have become more narratively fragmented, this marginality has increased. The minimal distribution and poor box-office showing for *Odds and Ends* may be one

factor that has kept Kluge from producing any feature films since 1986.[41] His films have finally deconstructed into fragments that are now suitable only for the small screen. Before examining Kluge's television programs, however, the style and themes of Kluge's film work must be examined.

4

Cinema
Impure

AN ECLECTIC MODERNIST STYLE

Here we have a man who has to gather the day's refuse in the capital city. Everything that the big city threw away, everything it lost, everything it despised, everything it crushed underfoot, he catalogs and collects.

— Charles Baudelaire [1]

Baudelaire's description of the Parisian ragpicker is, as Walter Benjamin points out, also an apt description of the French poet and his production technique.[2] And it is no less apposite to two twentieth-century collectors—to Benjamin himself and to the filmmaker Alexander Kluge.

Indeed the ragpicker image is a powerful metaphor for one major aspect of the modernist aesthetic project: searching through the detritus of modern society for valuable fragments which, detached from their original context, can be mounted with other fragments and thereby invested with new meanings. Russell Berman refers to such montage as the "desublimization" of art by the "incorporation of elements of life."[3] One calls to mind immediately the collage works of Georges Braque and Pablo Picasso, which, according to one critic, "demonstrated that discards and irrelevant materials—junk—could result in something pictorially artistic, and that the artist could synthesize from unlikely sources."[4] No less characteristic of this approach were the stagings of Brecht's plays, the novels of John Dos Passos, or even the writings of Benjamin himself, who dreamed of creating a work that would consist of nothing but quotations. The associations and contrasts between the various fragments in these art works are often not logical, hierarchical, or unified. Rather, the relationships tend to be complex, shifting, and subtle.

It is this modernist style of collection and montage that has characterized much of the work of Alexander Kluge. Like other modernists, he does not regard style as merely an incidental flourish or an authorial signature, subordinated to a work's theme or message. On the contrary, for modernist artists, formal experimentation and innovation are often of primary importance. Modernity has presented them not only with new themes and subjects, but with new media as well. Each new medium has its own materiality, a range of aesthetic possibilities that distinguishes it from other media. New themes and new media demand new forms, new modes of expression.

For many modernist filmmakers, montage—the sequential juxtaposition of diverse images—constitutes the distinctive capacity of the film medium, a capacity only partially explored in mainstream cinema. The combination of heterogeneous materials and styles is particularly characteristic of Kluge's filmic work. In his view, the essence of cinema is its eclecticism. As a late modernist, Kluge can borrow from both modernist and older art forms (painting, opera, classical music) for his projects. He collects and mounts these, together with fragments of popular culture, into challenging filmic texts.

This mixing of materials from various sources has caused several critics to remark on Kluge's affinities with postmodernist art. In the latter, bricolage and pastiche have come to be regarded as primary techniques of construction. In his use of quotations from popular film and music of the 1920s and 1930s, Kluge can be seen as a bridge to a postmodern aesthetic. Like many postmodernists, he is recycling images and sounds, copying and recontextualizing fragments of pre-existent culture. However, the uses and objectives of Kluge's heterogenous style derive less from a postmodernist than from a modernist sensibility, one which is critical of modernity and especially of the mass media. Kluge's formal strategies represent a development of certain earlier modernist styles, which Kluge appropriates in an eclectic fashion.

The previous discussion of Kluge's narration techniques traced a historical development from relatively straightforward tales to more complex and fragmented compilations. A similarly historical approach to the other formal elements in his work would reveal a parallel development toward increasing stylistic complexity. The organization of this chapter, however, is not chronological. Instead, it consists of three parts: Collection, Montage, and Analysis. The first section catalogs the wide range of material collected by Kluge. His dramatizations as well as his documentary material can be regarded more as discoveries than creations, images and sounds that Kluge manipulates and juxtaposes to achieve a modernist distantiation effect. The second section argues that Kluge's montage serves to heighten an anti-illusionist dissonance among these diverse fragments. Editing, in this sense, cannot be considered merely a routine postproduction assembly in Kluge's films. The last section will examine a thirteen-minute segment from his 1983 film *The Power of Emotion* to see how these stylistic elements function together in one of his later, more complex productions.

COLLECTION: A DIVERSITY OF MATERIALS

> Alexander Kluge is an accumulator and a pirate. He combines the found and the strange with his own documentary observations, his pseudodocumentaries and dramatizations. He seizes others' material freely, alters it, reshapes it and thereby discovers something new.
>
> —Peter Kremski[5]

Some artists and critics have taken the modernist concern for the materiality of the medium as a process of limitation and refinement, not expansion. Rather than explore the limits of the film medium, they want a "pure cinema" that does only that which no other medium can. Liebman has cited Paul Sharits, Malcolm LeGrice, and Wilhelm and Birgit Hein as "orthodox modernists," who sought to "articulate cinema's autonomy as an artistic medium."[6] Within the entire canon of modernist art, however, this purism constitutes but one strain. More heterogenous approaches have been championed by modernist montagists in many media, including film.

Working in this latter tradition, Kluge rejects the notion of a pure cinema. He believes cinema should be pushed as far as possible in the opposite direction: Whatever the eye sees can be incorporated in the cinema. There are no purely cinematic images because there are no noncinematic images. In a 1982 interview, Kluge stated: "Everything which the fantasy of a person can depict—that is, the mirror-reflex camera in the human head—can be shown on the movie screen. There are no aesthetic rules."[7] This theoretical emphasis on inclusion reflects Kluge's own aesthetic practice. More than most other collage filmmakers—such as Dziga Vertov, Sergei Eisenstein, or Jean-Luc Godard—Kluge uses an extremely wide range of materials for his montage. Kluge collects both fictional and documentary fragments from old motion pictures, still photos, paintings, drawings, and musical scraps of both popular and classical origin.

The variety of found materials in Kluge's work lends it a rich visual diversity, particularly when juxtaposed with the diverse new material that he himself directs. By appropriating found footage, Kluge is relinquishing some control over production, while still retaining, of course, the powers of selection and contextualization. The aleatory characteristic present in all found art struggles against authorial control and lends a spontaneity and unpredictability to his work. Like the found objects in Picasso's collage, Kluge's found footage provides a variety of cinematic styles and textures, while insisting on its status as artifact. The found image can never be completely subsumed into Kluge's film, but stubbornly maintains its own particularity. This is very different from the effect that Kluge would derive if he attempted to imitate these various styles of filming. As with the Dadaists and Surrealists, this approach allows the artist to incorporate any object or experience into his work, not just the beautiful and the dramatic, but also the ordinary and the trivial.

Much of Kluge's found footage consists of old feature films. Visually and acoustically they differ from the contemporary footage that Kluge directs. The lighting styles, costumes, acting, and more primitive sound quality all reflect an earlier era. They are usually shot in black and white, although sometimes they are tinted—either in the original print or by Kluge. Such narrative film fragments serve as fantasy and memory, illusion and document. Kluge often chooses excerpts from romantic or sentimental scenes, but his abrupt method of uprooting only a few shots from their original context undermines the nostalgic mood they would otherwise evoke.

Archival documentary footage is also an important part of the visual texture of Kluge's films. Much of this footage depicts the National Socialist era: Nazi rallies and war footage. Like the fictional footage, this material is also mostly in black and white; because it was shot with available light, however, it has a more raw, unprocessed feel to it than the images from the studio-shot fiction films. It has a grainier texture, a more impromptu shooting style, and an insistent subject

I *Die Macht der Gefühle* (*The Power of Emotion*): Underworld sea with Lucifer in the background and Dante and Virgil observing

matter. Kluge has also used news footage, informational films, and television footage. Each has a distinct image quality deriving from the original subjects and shooting conditions, the editing style, and, most importantly, from the material itself: the characteristics of the original medium, its transformation through several generations of reproduction, and the physical deterioration of the actual copy available to Kluge. The poor quality of the video material is especially striking, particularly when it has been reshot off of a television screen and then inserted into a 35mm film. The juxtaposition of these contrasting visual textures emphasizes the materiality of Kluge's films.

In addition to such varied archival motion picture footage, Kluge also appropriates still photos and drawings into his films. Many of these are illustrations from old books. The range of styles and colors —from the bright but crude drawings in children's books to more sophisticated etchings—increases the films' visual diversity. Although it may be difficult to identify the exact period in which these pictures originated, most are clearly not contemporary. These images are rarely situated as objects within the diegesis and hence insist on their historical difference.

Still photographs constitute yet another type of found material occurring frequently in Kluge's films. Many are personal, although they are rarely identified as such. *Yesterday Girl,* for example, contains photographs of his father playing the violin, his mother with his baby sister, and the family home. These seem at once documentary, intimate, and anonymous. Most photos are black and white and proclaim themselves historical remnants of a previous era. Both the illustrations and the photographs, as static images, conflict with the dominant cinematic emphasis on action and movement. Sometimes Kluge pans or zooms within these static images, but most often such animating techniques are absent. Although Kluge is by no means averse to tinkering with or transforming an image, he does not find it necessary to hide its static quality.[8]

Found material is well suited to Kluge's economic as well as aesthetic needs.[9] Most of it is free, so it reduces production costs. It allows him a range of illustrative material that would be difficult for him to create with actors. For example, the *Aida* footage in *The Power of Emotion* would require immense sets, elaborate costumes, and many extras. Using found material, Kluge is able to present the spectator with visual diversity and contrasts that constantly surprise. These visual quotations, aside from their complex meanings, stimulate and often irritate the viewer by their disjunctive particularity. They also incorporate historical contrasts and contain an insistent facticity. The found material stubbornly confronts and resists the directed material. Kluge has emphasized the centrality of serendipity in his work: "We hold fast to our doctrine: To find is more important than to invent. Finding is the decision in favor of provocation, since I now have the possibility of fortuitous chance."[10] Such happy accidents, he claims, are based on "attentiveness" to experience rather than a blind imposition of authorial intentions upon reality.[11]

Most of the found material discussed above is not accompanied by its own sound. The still photos, illustrations, and silent films obviously have no sound, and Kluge often strips the sound out of the other motion picture and video footage, replacing it with his own.[12] However, found sound does play an important role in Kluge's films, especially in the area of nondiegetic music.

Unlike most Hollywood directors, and even many New German filmmakers, Kluge has never employed a composer to create a musical score for his films. Rather, his extensive knowledge of music and his penchant for citation incline him to use preexisting music. His selections range from the classical (Bach) through the romantic (Wagner) to the popular (tangos from the 1930s) and even to current avant-garde music (Luigi Nono). It should be noted, however, that the occurrence of any contemporary popular music is relatively rare in Kluge's films.[13] In this respect Kluge's adherence to high culture standards is quite consistent. The popular is clearly bracketed as a historical phenomenon, an artifact for examination and cataloging. The popular must always be denied its immediacy. It must be removed from its context so that it can be observed at a critical distance.[14]

The cinematic material that Kluge himself has directed, both documentary and fictional, might also be regarded as "found," in a sense. He uses actual locations rather than sets, often employs nonactors ("real people") rather than professional actors, and encourages his actors to improvise, to find their own dialogue and action. Some of his most felicitous images are accidents. Kluge cites as an example the shots of Gabi Teichert setting off to dig in the snow: the blue tone was the result of a camera operator forgetting to use a filter.[15] Adorno has suggested that such accidents and improvisations are useful antidotes to the total control that the film industry likes to impose on its products: "vis-a-vis the culture industry—whose standard excludes everything but the predigested and the already integrated, just as the cosmetic trade eliminates facial wrinkles—works which have not completely mastered their technique, conveying as a result something consolingly uncontrolled and accidental, have a liberating quality."[16] From such a perspective, Kluge's self-proclaimed status as a film amateur may aid rather than hinder his attempts to achieve modernist effects.

As noted in the last chapter, Kluge does not see documentary and fictional sequences as antithetical—he sees them as two interrelated modes, each critiquing and containing the other. With the exception of *Strongman Ferdinand*, all of his fictional films include documentary material: dramaturgically interruptive interviews and shots of landscapes, buildings, and public events such as political demonstrations, party conventions, or police exhibitions. The use of documentary footage serves to shift the tone and texture within the fictional film. The documentary sequences seem more immediate, more unpredictable, and more newsy than the dramatizations.

The fictional/documentary distinction is further blurred by the insertion of fictional characters into real public events. The appearance of a Roswitha Bronski, Inge Maier, or Gabi Teichert among politicians, public officials, or ordinary citizens often results in an awkward artificiality, which comments critically on both the fiction and the event. Such footage looks more documentary than fictional: the camera work is shakier and the shots are sometimes grainier, improperly lit, or incorrectly exposed. One prominent example of this is the extensive footage at the SPD convention in *The Patriot*.

Many of Kluge's purely fictional sequences also have a documentary look to them. They often lack the composed, controlled predictability that one encounters in mainstream cinema. A number of formal techniques in the production process contribute to the diversity and unpredictability of Kluge's narrative sequences. A consistent determination to create an anti-illusionistic cinema is carried out through a frequent but unsystematic breaking of cinematic conventions in both image and sound recording.

Characteristic of Kluge's films is a jumpy, awkward, and at times even amateurish camera style. This gives his films the loose, spontaneous liveliness that characterized many art films of the 1960s. The lighter sync-sound equipment that had recently become available encouraged more camera movement, more hand-held work, and more unusual camera positions. Although some of the oddness of Kluge's visual style is attributable to his use of more than one camera operator in the same film,[17] more significant is his intentional manipulation of camera angle and film speed. Both are related to a modernist emphasis on both the constructedness of the film (and the world it records) and on the materiality of the medium.

Kluge often seeks unusual camera angles to show people and processes from an unfamiliar and revealing position. In *Yesterday Girl*, the trial sequence contains a shot of the back of the judge's head, which appears particularly thick and immobile. In the collaborative film *Krieg und Frieden* (*War and Peace*, 1982–1983), a long take in a kitchen shows just the legs of a woman moving around the room. In the many operatic sequences in his films, Kluge almost always shoots from behind the stage (normally from the wings). Here is an instance of Kluge capitalizing on a limitation. Unable to shoot from the auditorium without disrupting the performance, he goes backstage to show the changing of costumes and sets, the prompter whispering lines and the performers watching themselves on a live television monitor. Most importantly, he reveals the performance as a construction, as a staged reality, breaking its illusion by showing the effort required to create it. By showing what is not normally shown, these unusual angles also prove more interesting or unsettling to a viewer who has been trained to expect more conventional shots.

In his later films, Kluge often displays a modernist tendency to distort the images, or render them abstract in certain ways. Sometimes
an image is fractured by reflections in windows or metal surfaces. In
other cases, the camera picks out abstract patterns—such as those
formed by the lighted windows in high-rise buildings at night—that
push the viewer away from the story and into consideration of formal
qualities of the image.

Although Kluge's films lack complex tracking or crane shots—
which would not be feasible given the low budgets he usually works
with—the camera is still relatively mobile. In addition to hand-held
shots, Kluge often films from automobiles. This footage, which often
depicts cities at night, is frequently shot at slow speeds so that when
it is projected the movement of light and color is accelerated and the
images become a sensory spectacle. The end of the collaborative film
Der Kandidat (*The Candidate*, 1979–80) has a particularly dazzling
sequence of hand-held, time-lapse shots with flashing, multicolored
lights forming abstract patterns.

Kluge, like Eisenstein and Vertov, has repeatedly experimented
with such alteration of the speed of on-screen action. Fast action is
used not only to increase the visual stimulation, but often to show a
process that would not be visible at normal speed. Time-lapse shots
show lights blinking on then off in high-rise buildings as night
changes to daylight. Clouds race through the sky; stage hands hur-
riedly complete set changes behind the opera curtain. The ubiquity of
this technique indicates its importance to Kluge. Time-lapse allows
him to compress time so that a relatively invisible movement is revealed or an entire process becomes visible. An example is the fast-
action sequence of police at a house demolition in *The Middle of the
Road Is a Very Dead End*. The police seem to move around like dolls;
according to Kluge, this technique reveals—in a way that regular
speed photography could not—their unconscious nervousness about
what they are doing. "I can only express this in the form of a temporal
totality, as it were a close-up of time." [18]

Less frequently, Kluge slows down the images, using either slow
motion or other techniques to stop the action entirely. Sometimes, as
in a shot of the soldier between two fronts in *Odds and Ends,* it is
difficult to tell whether the image is a freeze-frame or simply contains
no movement. The inclusion of many still photographs and stills from
old movies enhances the ambiguous status of his images. In *The Power
of Emotion* and other of his later films, Kluge sometimes slows down
old films to such a slow pace that the flicker between each frame of

the original is visible. Duration of visual experience becomes problematized for the viewer, making explicit Kluge's conception of cinema as a "time-machine" and forcing the spectator into different temporal rhythms.[19]

All of these practices are relatively rare in mainstream cinema. When they do occur, they function to reinforce the narrative, often by portraying the psychological state of a character. In Kluge's films, they tend to draw attention to the materiality of the images, force comparisons between one material and another, and emphasize the filmmaker's experimentation and manipulation of the material. The distinctive aspects of Kluge's camerawork are employed analytically in a modernist critique: reality is dissected to show that it is neither natural nor inevitable.

This disruptive style is also evident in Kluge's approach to sound recording. In his narrative as well as his nonnarrative shooting, Kluge minimizes the importance of synchronous sound. Many shots of characters alone—walking, driving, thinking—have no live sound.[20] Also, the dialogue that does occur in Kluge's films often has the quality of found material, consisting largely of distorted or exaggerated imitations of certain types of people. The language of the bureaucracy is frequently mocked by Kluge in dramatizations of educators, lawyers, judges, and other officials. In *Yesterday Girl,* for example, both the judge and the social worker cannot understand Anita or be understood by her because they speak entirely different languages. The judge rattles off incomprehensible legal jargon and the social worker prattles nonsensical pieties, which Anita mechanically repeats like a good catechist. Finally, the social gathering in the halfway house contains a stream of clichés intoned simultaneously by the social worker, the house mother, and a cleric as if in a musical round, the same phrases being repeated slightly out of sync.

In Kluge's later films, he introduces a variant of this mock monologue/dialogue: the mock interview, which turns on miscommunication, wordplay, and stubbornness. Often the process and techniques of the interview are foregrounded in these satires. For example, in *The Blind Director,* Dr. Gerlach keeps complaining about the poor job the interviewer is doing, not asking proper questions, and not knowing what he wants to find out.

These various techniques consistently question the status and function of dialogue. By foregrounding the process of communication and manipulating the constituent elements, Kluge undercuts the credibility of these characters. Their conversation seems forced and stylized rather than natural. Kluge's use of voice-over narration re-lieves the dialogue of its traditional narrative burden. The alternation between minimalist and ironically exaggerated dialogue constitutes a distinctive stylistic trait of Kluge's films.

Both modernism and postmodernism are very concerned with lan-guage. Kluge's more modernist use of dialogue stresses the difficulties involved in communication, the missed meanings and the resultant frustrations. The multiple simultaneous vocalizations suggest traces of the Dadaists' simultaneous poetry, where several poems in different languages were all read aloud at the same time.[21] Unlike postmodern-ism's multivocal expressions of diverse subcultures, Kluge's suppres-sion and channeling of dialogue is more a multifaceted expression of his voice than an embodiment of true diversity. Despite the improvi-sational quality of much of the dialogue, its direction and function seem controlled by Kluge. This is further heightened by Kluge's prac-tice of later adding voice-over narration.

These image and sound recording methods break with narrative conventions. The stylistic excesses and extremes interrupt the narra-tive flow to remind the spectator that the images, sounds, and silences are not revelations of reality but manipulations of it. The fact that they are employed sporadically or inconsistently gives Kluge's films a cer-tain spontaneous quality. Kluge seems to scorn a smooth and invisible construction in his films, preferring to flaunt their flaws and show their seams.

MONTAGE: MANIPULATION AND JUXTAPOSITION

> But the film is governed not only ideologically but also struc-turally by the principle of discontinuity, the juxtaposition of incongruent elements. Just like the whole of modern art that rejects the classical principles of unity, so the "filmic" form is based upon the juxtaposition and erratic juncture of antitheti-cal realistic and imaginary, rational and irrational, temporal and spatial motifs. The structure of the film which develops in this way is expressed most obviously in the principle of montage.
>
> —Arnold Hauser[22]

For most feature films, postproduction is a relatively straightforward process of assembling the footage that has been shot into a preplanned narrative sequence. For Kluge's films, however, the postfilming phase is the most important and most creative.[23] Given the large amount of found material and Kluge's desire for narrative subversion, an almost endless number of possibilities present themselves at this stage. Kluge's postproduction is not merely an editing process, but an opportunity to reshape the raw materials he has gathered. Two principles seem to predominate. First, Kluge attempts to frustrate and stimulate the viewer through surprise, shock, and interruption. Second, Kluge tries to promote new associations and connections. The first principle is essential to the second: only by the disruption of conventional relations and the fragmentation of apparent totalities is radical juxtaposition possible. This tension between chaos and reordering, between deconstruction and reconstruction, is worked out on the levels of both form and meaning. Kluge first manipulates the raw material to heighten difference and emphasize the materiality and artifice of construction, then he combines this altered material using several different modernist montage practices.

One important technique of image manipulation involves the use of the framing mask or iris. Although present even in Kluge's early films, it becomes a more prominent stylistic feature in his later work. Occasionally it is diegetically motivated: a shot of a character looking through binoculars is followed by a point-of-view shot of the object being looked at, framed by the twin circles of the binoculars. One example occurs at the end of *Occasional Work of a Female Slave* when the security chief spies on Roswitha.

In most instances, however, such narrative pretexts for the masks are lacking. In Kluge's earlier films, the masks were almost always black circles surrounding a central image. Miriam Hansen has pointed out that this is just one of many features of Kluge's films that is closely linked to primitive cinema. "Besides direct quotations from silent films, Kluge borrows techniques and conventions like fast-motion and time-lapse photography, which visualize the passage of time; tinting, iris masks, and dream balloons; long takes and traveling shots that are relatively independent of narrative motivation; written titles which assume an (often mock) expository function, offer commentary, or quote from diegetically unrelated sources."[24] In Kluge's films, however, the mask exceeds its silent film function of focusing spectator attention on a particular object or person. For Kluge, the mask is a striking alteration of the graphic composition and frequently serves to accentuate the antiquity of the footage. It also differentiates Kluge's films from contemporary cinema.

Kluge does not employ the mask in any predictable manner, however. For example, in the *Aida* sequence in *The Power of Emotion,* the first few shots are masked, then the mask disappears for a few shots only to return again in the succeeding few shots. Sometimes he will use different types of masks within the same sequence. This random and intermittent application of the stylistic element prevents the spectator from either ignoring it or decoding a pattern to its use. By refusing the viewer either solution, Kluge cultivates the problematic quality of the device.[25]

An effect similar to masking is sometimes achieved by using only small lights to illuminate part of a photograph or drawing. For example, in *The Candidate,* a blue light in the lower left corner shows one figure in a political cartoon, then in the opposite corner a red light comes on to illumine the candidate, Franz-Josef Strauss, as an acrobat. Not only does this type of illumination vary the size and shape of the cinematic image, but it is also an inexpensive way of introducing motion, drama, and a particular mood to still photographs and drawings.

Sometimes Kluge alters images to make them look like they are from a previous era. In *The Power of Emotion,* Kluge took footage of a contemporary performance of the opera *Die Sache Makropulos* and attempted to make it look like footage from the 1920s, the time at which the opera was first performed.[26] In other instances, he prints new color footage in black and white, perhaps to emphasize connections to the silent era, perhaps just to vary the texture of the images. In *Odds and Ends,* for example, different shots from the same narrative sequence alternate from black and white to color in no discernibly systematic way. Kluge has argued that his frequent juxtaposition of color footage and black and white is essential to stimulate the viewer.[27] "If one takes color film seriously, then I can't understand how one can make a 90 minute color film, because the eye adapts and after a while I can no longer accept colors. The eye abstracts to a certain extent from itself, and, if you will, has seen a mediocre black and white film. The eye can only notice colors when it is surprised."[28] The black and white is necessary to provide a pause during which the eye can readjust itself. "The movements of a constant re-adaptation to colors should contain something like a shock."[29]

Especially in his later films, Kluge likes to employ multiple exposures. Sometimes he juxtaposes very diverse images such as a battleship and a woman's face. In other instances, he duplicates the same image in a different part of the frame. At the end of the *Aida* sequence in *The Power of Emotion,* the frame is split into three layers of moving images, each of them from the *Aida* film. All of these different kinds of multiple exposures serve to create more dense and complex images. They are more interesting to look at and also more challenging to the viewer—both to identify the subjects and to understand their relations to one another.

One last element of Kluge's visual style is added in the postfilming stage: intertitles. These occur in all of Kluge's feature films, even *Strongman Ferdinand,* and constitute a stylistic signature.[30] As indicated earlier, these titles are anachronistic imitations of those used in silent films. Since these titles are often quotations, they are also within a modernist tradition of citation and allusion. Harvey Gross suggests that "in the decade of modernism before the First World War, composers, painters, and poets all experimented with outright parody and the subtler forms of critique: allusion, quotation and reminiscence."[31] The most direct influence on this aspect of Kluge's style was Brecht's epic theater—indeed a number of Kluge's quotations are taken from Brecht.[32] Already in the filming stage of *Yesterday Girl,* Kluge intended to use intertitles: "I would like to use few chapter headings, so as not to disturb the flow of the plot. But on the other hand I cannot totally renounce them, since I would like to give the film an epic structure. The headings have thus an organizing function."[33] In Kluge's early black-and-white films, these intertitles are always white letters on plain black backgrounds.[34] In his later, mostly color films, these white titles are almost always mounted on a light blue field.[35]

Although these titles have become an expected stylistic feature of Kluge's films, they remain disturbing as formal interruptions and because their meanings are often allusive or elusive. The sources for most intertitle quotations are not cited. *The Patriot,* for example, has at least three such unattributed quotations: "Brightly we read in the cloudy sky how thick the winter days are. A slow life is long";[36] "The more closely one looks at a word, the further it recedes";[37] "For a thousand years the dew fell. Tomorrow it won't. The stars enter a new house. Approximately."[38] Although each of the quotations is straightforward enough in itself, its relation to the preceding and subsequent images is not so simple to work out, particularly since one does not have the leisure to reread the quote and review the surrounding footage.

Another difficulty with the titles is that they occur unpredictably throughout the text. Sometimes they will appear regularly at the beginning of a sequence; for example, the series of titles about the opera in *The Power of Emotion* ("Plot," "Lighting," "Movement"). At other times they occur in the middle of a sequence, as in *The Blind Director* where the title "The Delivery of the Child" occurs only after the footage of the traffic accident. In *War and Peace,* sometimes as many as five intertitles are placed immediately after one another. These unpredictable interruptions keep the spectator a bit off balance and allow Kluge the maximum flexibility about when and whether to use intertitles. Like the voice-over commentary, the intertitle sometimes conveys information that is not delivered by the dialogue or action and frequently comments ironically or obliquely on the images to reduce spectator involvement in the story. The function that Brecht claimed for the theatrical device of the poster seems also to apply to its cinematic equivalent, the intertitle. Benjamin quotes Brecht:

> The poster is a constituent element of "literarized" theatre. "Literarizing involves punctuating 'representation' with 'formulation'; gives the theatre the possibility of making contact with other institutions for intellectual activities." [39]

Intertitles allow Kluge to connect his films to literature and critical thought.

Not only does this provide a way of introducing different kinds of material, it also serves as a way of interrupting the narrative and breaking the narrative illusion. Kluge also claims that the intertitle provides an important pause in the flow of cinematic images: "In silent films the titles always excited me. Since, from a literary point of view, the titles are mostly idiotic, hardly informative or well-placed, I asked myself why I like to look at them. I am glad to see them because at that moment my brain begins to work and has a moment to evolve independent fantasies. Then I am glad to see pictures again." [40]

Critics have not been the only ones to note the prominence of montage in Kluge's work; he often mentions it in his own writings and interviews about film. Obviously, his use of extremely diverse raw material makes the juxtaposition of these elements much more visible and problematic than in most commercial films, in which all the material has been produced specifically for a particular film. On the other hand, once the principle of discontinuity has been introduced to the audience, the filmmaker has freed himself from many of the constraints and conventions that make editing so painstaking. For Kluge, in a sense, anything goes. He generally employs two different approaches to editing, depending on the type of material at hand. When he is dealing with scripted dramatizations that he has originated, the editing constitutes a variation on the classical cinematic norm. When he is dealing with more diverse, less narrative material, then his technique is considerably more innovative.

Even in Kluge's later films, fictional narratives tend to predominate over other types of material. These narrative sequences are edited in a modified continuity style. For the most part, events are recounted in sequential order, with an intelligible, if attenuated, plot line. Kluge depends heavily on nondiegetic sources to provide narrative information that would be too difficult and costly to film himself. This results in a certain elliptical style, where temporal, spatial, and causal connections are clarified, if at all, through commentary or intertitles rather than through the images themselves.

Already in Kluge's first feature, *Yesterday Girl,* the editing is very abrupt. Scenes are juxtaposed without transitions and, within scenes, jump cuts and other temporal elisions abound. A love scene becomes a wrestling montage. Sometimes parts of different scenes are intercut. Nonnarrative materials such as drawings of a city, an interview, or a child's storybook are interjected between and in the middle of scenes without motivation or explanation. Scenes of a Jewish cemetery are inserted, like documentary B-roll, into a conversation about German history. This quirky editing results in the brisk pace of this film and similar sequences in other Kluge films. But Kluge also employs a variety of techniques to slow down the pace. Shots are often held longer or started earlier than in classical Hollywood cinema, leading frequently to uncomfortable silences and strange facial expressions. Often, reaction shots do not seem to work because the timing is wrong.

Variance from classical continuity style is attributable partly to an improvisatory style of shooting and partly to indifference or antipathy to smooth continuities. Sometimes cuts are accentuated acoustically because the room tone drops out on cutaways. Sometimes the same shot is used in two different scenes, presumably because no other was available to the editor. Jump cuts are apparent in most of his films and often seem intentionally disruptive.[41] In other cases, they seem merely convenient compromises. But the carelessness in continuity is symptomatic of a director who is less concerned about creating an illusion of reality than he is about recounting the gist of a story or critiquing society.

The pauses and sometimes slow pacing seem to be intentional interruptions, emphatically reflective but noncommittal. Head-on close-ups, for example, seem to challenge the viewer to stop and think: what is going on here, what is she thinking now? In *The Blind Director,* early in the Polish film factory sequence, all of the actors look toward the camera as if waiting for the director's command. After a few seconds, they turn to each other and begin to act. In this instance, Kluge's editing leaves in what most film editors would take out: evidence of the production process. The beginning of the shot could easily have been snipped off, but Kluge chose not to.[42]

Miriam Hansen, among others, has pointed out that Kluge rarely uses character point-of-view shots in his films. By minimizing this staple of continuity editing, he not only forgoes creating strong spatial and temporal links between shots (and between on-screen and off-screen space), he also abjures a primary device for developing the spectator's psychological identification with the filmic character.

Such departures from conventional continuity editing are not systematic in Kluge's work, but their relative frequency within the dramatized segments confirms the notion that for Kluge continuity is subordinate to other values. One of these values is certainly his commitment to producing films at relatively low cost. Indeed, what is more surprising than such continuity lapses is the degree to which Kluge adheres to continuity conventions, despite his commitment to montage disruption. Even in his later films he tends to keep the dramatized stories or scenes intact, with relatively few interruptions of extraneous material. There remains a strong tendency toward narrative economy within such scenes (even though Kluge's economy may be directed at different dramatic effects than Hollywood's). Kluge's narrative montage, like most aspects of his work, maintains a dynamic tension between coherence and fragmentation.

Instances of Kluge's more radical editing approach occur outside of—or rarely interrupt—the dramatized narrative sequences.[43] These sequences include the nondramatized shorter narratives, documentary sequences, and, most importantly, the montage sequences or mini-essays in which Kluge associates freely between different subjects and images. These montage sequences are the most provocative aspect of Kluge's work. This montage practice demands a close analysis if we are to understand how his films are constructed. But before doing so we must look at one key montage element used in both his narrative and nonnarrative sequences: sound.

Unlike most mainstream commercial filmmakers, Kluge does not take for granted that the sound track will be subservient to the picture track or that the relation of sound to picture will be direct or redundant. Although Kluge prides himself on never postdubbing dialogue, synchronous dialogue constitutes a relatively minor aspect of his use

of sound.[44] In all of his films, sound functions as a relatively independent element that can be used not only to reinforce the image, but to
contradict it, comment upon it, or even ignore it. Creating a sound
track is for him not merely a matter of syncing up the picture to the
audio voice track and then adding a music score. For Kluge, as for
many early practitioners of the sound film such as Eisenstein and Fritz
Lang, the relationship between sound and picture must be renegoti-
ated in each cut.

> The introduction of sound permits polyphonic reality, which previ-
> ously only could be indicated consecutively. . . . The modern devel-
> opment, which film has achieved internationally, is moving toward an
> emancipation of sound and especially of the language of film. One can
> here no more say that the word is superior to or is subordinated to the
> plot, or the picture to the word or the plot to the object of the plot.
> The realized work eliminates this kind of hierarchical notion.[45]

One important respect in which this is evident is the use of silence.
In a film like Lang's *M*, the lack of sound is frequently as forceful as
the dialogue or music. Similarly, in Kluge's films, the abrupt silences
during subtitles and montage sequences seem uncomfortably sparse
and unfinished to filmgoers conditioned to expect a continuous bed
of music and dialogue. Kluge often accentuates the silence by strip-
ping out apparently indispensable sound from found footage. In *The
Candidate,* he removes the entire voice-over from a civil defense film,
leaving a ludicrously macabre image: a group of people relaxing in a
living room wearing party clothes and gas masks.

Voice-over narration is not only Kluge's most distinctive narrational technique, it is a privileged stylistic device for unifying the heterogenous bits of material in his films. The voice-over provides a consistent tone and an omniscient organizing presence, even when the
words it intones are abstract or puzzling. It is used over dramatic,
documentary, and, most importantly, montage segments. Sometimes
these montage sequences have little or no narration, especially the
short interludes—the sequences of nondiegetic shots of trees or
clouds or water.

But in most Kluge films, narration is never absent for more than a
few minutes. The gentle irony of Kluge's voice continually reassures
the spectators and reestablishes their position as critical observers
of the pictures. Even if the spectators do not understand the interconnections between successive images or between sound and image,
they can be confident that the narrator does. Kluge's presence as the

narrator lends the voice-over both authority and a special, personal flavor. It raises specifically modernist questions of the presence of the author in the work and the constructedness of the aesthetic object.

As indicated above, almost all of the music in Kluge's films is found sound. This means that he does not have the luxury of fitting a score exactly to the rhythm and timing of the edited film. He must either cut the picture to fit the music or cut the music to fit the picture. The former practice is certainly not unknown in Hollywood, particularly in musicals and in opening sequences such the beginning of *Saturday Night Fever*. But this practice occurs much more frequently in Kluge's work and is particularly crucial to his nondramatized montage sequences, which constitute perhaps the most intriguing part of his work.

In those instances when he cuts music to fit the picture, the sound editing can be done either surreptitiously or obtrusively. In most instances, standard Hollywood practice calls for "sneaking" the music in and out, that is, gradually fading it in and out when the timing of music and picture do not match exactly. Although Kluge sometimes follows this practice, more often he accentuates the manipulation by bringing in the music at its full dynamics, sometimes in midphrase, and then cutting away equally abruptly. One notable instance of an abrupt halt in music occurs near the end of the *Aida* sequence in *The Power of Emotion*. After a moment of silence Kluge comments: "What the opera is silent about! The people will not stand by while a couple in love is buried alive." Here the music track pointedly calls attention to both the presence and the content of the narration.

In general, the music in Kluge's films is a more vital presence than it is in Hollywood films because his is stronger music. Typically, Hollywood music is composed to reinforce the visuals without calling attention to itself. Kluge's found music, however, was composed to stand on its own and already has an established reputation either as instrumental music or as song. The strength of the music and its familiarity from other contexts often overpowers the images. Its ostentatious interjection and termination also distracts from the visuals.[46]

Infrequently, Kluge mixes several different audio tracks for a simultaneous aural montage effect, similar to his use of multiple exposures on the image track. One striking example in *The Power of Emotion* accompanies shots of reflections from the facades of skyscrapers. A rather sad orchestral piece begins but is soon punctuated by the rattle of jackhammers. The tension of this audio juxtaposition comments on the images of hard, metallic urban beauty.

Sound functions as a very strident and obtrusive element in Kluge's work. It is interruptive in the same way that Brecht wanted his songs to interrupt the drama. Moreover, sound has become an integral part of Kluge's strategy for low-budget filmmaking. By using preexisting music he reduces soundtrack costs. Voice-overs free him from some of the demands of dialogue. The use of sound effects has also helped him enliven still footage and build montage sequences from heterogenous available materials.[47]

ANALYSIS

The opening sequence of Kluge's 1982 film, *The Power of Emotion,* is representative of the range of materials, styles, and editing techniques occurring in all of Kluge's films after 1977. This thirteen-and-a-half-minute sequence consists of eighty-one shots, which can be grouped into seventeen different segments. The analysis below is necessarily somewhat extensive because of the substantial variety of visual and aural information that Kluge presents to the spectator. The audience must process all of this within a relatively short time, and then keep it in mind as the film proceeds—and this constitutes only a small portion of the film as a whole.

This opening sequence can be segmented in the following manner:

1. Opening credits
2. 5 shots of skyline and airplanes (2 min. 25 sec.)
3. Main title (9 sec.)
4. 1 shot of WWI tank (23 sec.)
5. 5 shots of burned baby (20 sec.)
6. 28 shots from *Kriemhilds Rache* (*Kriemhild's Revenge,* Lang, 1924) (1 min. 17 sec.)
7. 11 shots of funeral (2 min. 42 sec.)
8. 5 shots from old film: departing train (34 sec.)
9. 3 shots from old film: officer quotes Hölderlin (36 sec.)
10. 5 shots from old film: uniformed man and woman (18 sec.)
11. 2 shots from opera (49 sec.)
12. 5 shots of mock interview with singer (1 min. 20 sec.)
13. 2 shots of skyline and river (47 sec.)
14. 2 shots of fortune teller (30 sec.)
15. 4 shots of lovers (34 sec.)

16. 1 shot of woman (15 sec.)
17. 1 shot of sinking battleship (22 sec. total—7 sec. superimposed over previous shot) [48]

The opening credits are white on light blue, unaccompanied by any sound. The first image is of Frankfurt at night; the overture from Wagner's *Parsifal* begins softly on the sound track. In time-lapse photography, the lights twinkle on and off in the night skyline and then the picture begins to lighten as dawn breaks quickly. Straight cuts connect another shot of skyscrapers in the morning light and two shots of airplanes flying past high-rises. The last shot in this first segment is of the sun behind a cloud with trees and smokestacks visible in the lower portion of the frame.

This first segment is fairly unified. The shots all depict aspects of modern metropolitan life in juxtaposition to nature and the passage of time. The dawning of the day seems an apt image for the beginning of the film and is echoed in the increasing volume and movement in the musical score. For viewers familiar with opera, the source of the music may suggest certain possible associations: opera (as an institution of a particular historical era and class), Wagner (his personality and significance for the Third Reich), the themes of this opera (spiritual redemption, search for the grail), and finally the meanings of this particular passage (the morning prayer, faith). For those less familiar with opera, the music does not have these rich associative possibilities. However, it does carry strongly emotive connotations. Beginning with a feeling of calm, emotion mounts steadily as the volume and tempo increase.

The images differ from those of most classical films in two respects. First, there are more images and they are held for a longer time than would be necessary to establish the location of the film. Second, the time-lapse shot is not at first very noticeable, but, once the technique is perceived, it raises the question as to why it was employed. The spectator may now anticipate that other images may also be manipulated as the film continues.

The first series of shots ends as the musical passage concludes. The segment is bracketed at the end by an intertitle announcing the name of the film, again in white letters on a light blue background. Like the opening credits, this title is also unaccompanied by any sound. The title itself is abstract and somewhat troublesome: *The Power of Emotion*. "Power" connotes action and will, almost anthropomorphizing "emotion," as if feelings were autonomous of the human beings who actually experience them. Moreover, rather than specifying one emotion (The Power of Love, The Power of Anger) in the title, Kluge generalizes to include all feelings. The title is more provocative than illuminating.

The complete silence on the soundtrack continues disturbingly into the next segment, which begins with old footage of a World War I tank moving toward the spectator. The blue-tinted shot is masked as if seen through binoculars, leading the viewer to guess that this might be a point-of-view shot of an enemy soldier watching the advance. The next shot, however, does not reveal a soldier with binoculars, but is instead the beginning of a totally different segment. What promised to be a continuity link, becomes a disorienting shift in time, space, texture: A full-color close-up shot shows a burned child's face wrapped in bandages. At first it is difficult to identify what the subject is, because of the bandages and the extreme close-up position. The succeeding four shots of the burned child are almost as hard for the spectator to process. They are also close-ups or extreme close-ups, were shot from very unusual angles, and average only about four seconds in duration.

Rather than explain this sequence or even provide a delayed establishing shot, Kluge uses a straight cut abruptly to change the locale, time frame, and visual texture of the image. Shots from an old movie portray half-naked men handing out weapons. Like the tank shot, this footage is also framed as if by binoculars. Then a circular mask encloses a Teutonic warrior and a blonde child. Kluge's first voice-over provides minimal information about the action: "This child doesn't have long to live." Then other shots follow from the climax of Lang's 1924 film *Kriemhild's Revenge*. Although Kluge does not identify the film, his voice-over commentary does identify Kriemhild and Hagen and explains much of the on-screen action. To many educated Germans, both the tale and the Lang film are already well-known. Hagen kills Kriemhild's child and she in turn slays Hagen. Twelve of the twenty-nine shots have no framing mask. Fifteen are masked by a double circle, but sometimes this includes a vertical dividing line and sometimes not. Kluge alternates groups of three or four shots with similar masking or nonmasking but in no clearly discernable pattern. Many of the shots are tinted blue or yellow, and again no consistent pattern seems to emerge. These random variations prohibit prediction and create material contrast between shots from an identical source.

Twice during this *Kriemhild's Revenge* footage, Kluge slows the images almost to stop-action. The first instance marks the central event of the segment. Hagen draws his sword in slow motion and then, while Kluge's voice explains ("So Hagen slays the child"), the picture cuts to a slow motion shot of the unsuspecting child at play as the blow is about to descend upon him. Both of these shots are masked with double circles. Then Kluge replays the two shots at regular speed, without masks and starting the first shot at an earlier point than in the previous instance. The alteration of the length, speed, and masking of the shots makes it difficult to identify them as repetitions. The other instance of slowed motion in this segment occurs near its conclusion. The Huns' camp begins to burn, and Kluge slows the images almost to a stop so that they flicker on the screen.

If the first segment of the film after the credits seemed to be a series of urban establishing shots, that assumption is confounded by segments 4 through 6. Only segment 5 (the burned child) is set in contemporary times and could perhaps be occurring in a modern metropolis. The clips from old movies are not contextualized as the viewing experience of one or more characters within the diegesis (in fact, we have not yet seen any such characters). Nor is any one of these three segments very substantially related to the other two. They share a certain grotesqueness of subject matter: war, severe injury, and murder/revenge. But the emotions, the situations, and the styles are very different. Causality and unity of place and time are obviously not organizing principles among these three units. Each of these segments is bracketed by straight cuts, which give the viewer no clue as to passage of time or change of subject. Although each of the segments is largely comprehensible, even if its original context is unknown to the viewer, the relationship between segments is difficult to fathom. The viewer does not have the leisure to go back and reexamine the components for possible relationships. More images crowd onto the screen, which must be scrutinized, identified, and connected.

The first synchronous sound sequence follows: several shots of people in dark suits seated in a large room, who rise together as others proceed soberly into the hall. The German viewer would recognize Bundestag President Jellinger, escorting a frail woman dressed in black, followed by Helmut Schmidt. As the picture cuts to a shot of a skylight, the off-screen sound of an apparent eulogy begins abruptly in midsentence: " . . . it soon became clear what he achieved on these trips in terms of guaranteeing jobs. . . ." As the oration continues, the audience members are visible, but not the orator, who is the focus of their attention. Then a shot shows an orchestra beginning to play

 Die Macht der Gefühle (*The Power of Emotion*): The chancellor at a state funeral

Bach's "Air for the G String" in a very stately tempo as a woman in the first row dabs her eyes with a handkerchief. Kluge intercuts an apparently exterior shot of a wreath with Chinese characters on it. By this time the viewer has almost certainly concluded that this is a memorial service. More shots of the audience include Helmut Kohl sitting beside the SPD leader Herbert Wehner, and Chancellor Helmut Schmidt dozing off.

The orchestral music continues, but the picture cuts abruptly to an old film. A conductor blows his whistle and then in reverse shot salutes a train as it begins to leave the station. As an older woman waves a handkerchief at the departing train, an off-screen male voice intones: "Accept me, accept me into your ranks that I do not die a common death." A young woman runs past the crowd following the train as the voice continues: "Yet gladly will I sacrifice myself for the fatherland."

The train leaves the station and the picture cuts to a blue-tinted medium shot of a German officer seated and continuing to recite the poem. The shot tracks in to a close-up, then jump cuts to an extreme close-up of his face, now tinted purple, as he finishes his recitation. Kluge fades the picture to black as the sound track continues: footsteps echo across a wooden floor and a different voice says "Hölderlin, beautiful."[49] The picture cuts to another, older film (the sound track is more crude) in which a naval officer tells a woman: "Yes, but a person notices just a minute before the departure of the train that he has forgotten the most important thing."[50]

These four segments are tied together both by sound bridges and by certain thematic connections. The funeral music overlaps into the train departure. After this music fades out, then the officer's voice and the original movie score from the subsequent segment begins, about twenty seconds before the train segment is finished, and carries

I *Die Macht der Gefühle* (*The Power of Emotion*): "Live on O Fatherland and don't count the dead."

▌*Die Macht der Gefühle* (*The Power of Emotion*): "So then how do you play [in the first act] 'with a spark of hope in your face?'"

through its own segment. On the thematic level, the funeral, the train departure, and the naval officer's comment are united by the notion of saying goodbye, while the funeral and the Hölderlin quotation are tied together by the conjunction of death and the nation. The last three segments also share a similar origin: all were excerpts from German feature films of the Nazi era. None of these segments after *Kriemhild's Revenge* has had any intertitles or voice-over commentary. No information is provided about whose funeral is being shown or what odd films are being excerpted: indeed, it is almost impossible to tell whether these old clips are from the same film or from two or three different films.[51]

The end of the previous segment is marked by an abrupt sound and picture cut, at which point we see an opera performance, shot from the wings. The shot begins in midsong and continues until the end of the scene when the man drags the woman off stage. A very short backstage shot is then followed by a mock interview of an opera star.

This begins with an over-the-shoulder shot and continues in a shot/ reverse-shot documentary style. The only unusual aspect of the interview is the insistence of the singer that in each performance of the first act he is still optimistic because he does not know how the opera will turn out—it could have a happy ending. This belief in a happy ending is also central to Kluge's own project: "For years I have been attempting through literary and filmic means to change the opera stories: to disarm the 5th act. . . . I feel a deep disbelief in the tragic; against the melancholy with which our culture seems to be infatuated."[52] He hides a central theme within a comic interview. Again, in this sequence there is no commentary and no identification of the opera being performed.

The next sequence returns to the Frankfurt skyline, this time viewed from across the river. As an oil barge slowly slides by in the foreground, Kluge plays a melancholy hit from 1939: "Sometimes one must say Adieu. . . ." Aurally, this ties back to the previous farewells while the visuals relate to the opening shots of the film. Just when the juxtaposition of images is beginning to draw some connections, Kluge cuts to a dark screen. A light comes on illuminating part of the screen to show a still photo of a gypsy fortune-teller's face. Another light

▌ *Die Macht der Gefühle* (*The Power of Emotion*): Frankfurt skyline

 Die Macht der Gefühle (*The Power of Emotion*): Woman with jewelry on her hands

comes on to illuminate the many rings on her hand. The picture fades to black. Then we see a light illuminating her hand above some tarot cards. The music continues as the image fades to black again. It fades up on a still of two lovers in a circular frame mask. The fades and the masked stills continue: another pair of lovers almost kissing, a woman sitting, a man watching a woman finish disrobing, and finally a double exposure of a blonde woman. This latter image remains on the screen while another image comes up: a smoking, sinking battleship.

As the song comes to an end, Kluge's voice-over commentary finally returns. "People who can no longer stand something endure it even longer; then they suddenly break out brutally and without warning." The commentary ends at the same time as the picture does. One wonders what this has to do with a sinking battleship: is he describing a mutiny? Rather than a summary of the previous sequence, this comment constitutes a kind of sound bridge or introduction to the next long narrative sequence, the trial of the woman who shot her husband. However, the commentary ends before the first shot of the next sequence begins, so it is not really a bridge. The abrupt change of visuals does not immediately provide a retroactive clarification of this voice-over transition. If Kluge had faded to black before the commentary, or even if he had left out the comment altogether, the shift into the fictional sequence would have been smoother. Instead he tricks the viewer into trying to apply the voice-over narration to the wrong images. This results in some confusion and frustration.

The most salient stylistic characteristic of this thirteen-and-a-half minute sequence is its extraordinary diversity of sources, subjects, textures, colors, and tones. There is a great range in types of images: still photos, old movies, a dramatized interview, documentary footage of a funeral, urban landscapes, and a clip from an opera. In other parts of the film, Kluge inserts old book illustrations, newsreel footage, and interviews. Most of the filmic material is contemporary, but a substantial portion bears the marks of an older origin.

Although Kluge's montage style will be discussed below, it must be mentioned that his methods of juxtaposition tend to heighten rather than reduce the contrast between different types of material. Moreover, it is evident that Kluge manipulates the raw material to make the visual and aural diversity and discontinuities more striking. The superimposition of two images (e.g., woman and battleship) increases their density and complexity. In the clip with the Hölderlin quotation, he breaks the visuals into three parts by tinting the second shot purple and by blacking out the last part of the clip. His masking and tinting techniques in the *Kriemhild's Revenge* clip alter these images so that they too seem less continuous. In addition to manipulation through repetition and slow motion, Kluge also speeds up the pace of the original footage by shortening many shots and eliminating many others altogether. Kluge's one minute and twenty second clip is a condensation of the last thirty-three minutes of the original film. All of these techniques constitute visible alterations that heighten the disjunctiveness of the film images.

Similarly, Kluge manipulates the relationship between the sound and the picture in unpredictable ways. In some instances, such as the funeral music, the sound is used to bridge two very unrelated shots. In other cases, the abrupt shifts in sound underscore the abrupt shifts in the visuals and viscerally shake the viewer into a new mood and subject. Kluge sometimes takes away sound from the image, making the viewer somewhat uncomfortable and forcing her/him to deal more immediately with the images. In the most extreme case, Kluge uses the sound to mislead the viewer, as when the narration does not quite fit the images presently on the screen, but is appropriate for those about to appear next. This motley variety of fragments flaunts its collage construction and challenges most cinematic notions of coherence and unity. Yet an underlying intelligence cannot be ignored, and the viewer is forced to look for alternative kinds of coherence and to discover nontraditional sorts of patterns.

The key to Kluge's obviously constructed but enigmatically organized style is his montage. How does his montage function? Several patterns and techniques emerge from a close examination of Kluge's editing practice. First, he seems to gather clusters of images that have a certain similarity of subject. These clusters or segments are the basic building blocks for his films. Within each of these clusters of shots, relationships are fairly clear. In most instances, there is a temporal and spatial relationship as well as a continuity of subject matter.[53] Often, the cohesion of the shots within a particular cluster is apparent to the viewer by the similar material qualities of the shots, and the different qualities of the surrounding segments. For example, the burned baby footage is in color, slightly reddish, and recorded on a grainy film stock. It is preceded by a masked and blue-tinted, black-and-white shot of a World War I tank and followed by a masked, yellow-and-blue-tinted black-and-white shot from *Kriemhild's Revenge*. The funeral footage is also distinct from the surrounding footage—it's in color and was shot in wide angle from a few limited positions, with uniform, slightly bluish lighting.

Nevertheless, it is not always easy to tell where one such cluster or segment leaves off and the next begins. The sound bridges often connect very different-looking material, while cuts in sound will occur in the middle of a shot or between similar kinds of shots. The most visible common feature of the cluster of shots is often a similar origin (for example, old movie footage), but this commonality may be more incidental than substantive. The viewer must figure out what similarities these shots have that are important for this film. It is not enough merely to recognize, for example, that these are all shots from old movies.

Excluding the titles, the length of these segments or clusters of shots ranges from fifteen seconds to two minutes and forty-two seconds. The individual shots range from one second to forty-five seconds in length. In most cases, this duration allows the spectator sufficient time to identify the subject of the shot and its historical period, to consider what the most significant aspect of each shot is, and to try to connect this shot with previous shots in this segment and with earlier segments. It is this last process that is most difficult. One has few clues as to how long the present segment will continue and no way of anticipating what the next segment might be. Unlike films such as *Berlin, Symphony of a Great City* or *Man with a Movie Camera*—which are organized temporally around the progression of a day, with clusters of shots grouped into units such as eating or sports or going to work—no such overarching framework is here discernable. A certain associative flow is often suggested: war—maiming—death—funeral—farewell, for example. But one often senses that the order is rather arbitrary, the pieces somewhat interchangeable. Not only is anticipation impossible, the lack of an overarching structure makes it much more difficult to remember, let alone understand or integrate, the previous material. Details are most easily grasped and retained when they are seen as a part of a larger pattern. By inserting seventeen distinct and relatively independent clusters of shots into a space of thirteen minutes, Kluge has created a difficult organizational task for the viewer. Although some of these clusters do seem to fall into larger groups or sequences—such as the four clusters involving the funeral and farewells or the shots of boats and lovers during the song "Adieu"—these larger sequences are less coherent than the segments or clusters that comprise them, and they do not, in turn, easily comprise larger units.

Sound is an important montage tool that can be used either disjunctively to emphasize difference or cohesively to unify diverse visual material. The five shots of the first segment are unified by the musical score and cut off from the surrounding material (the titles) by silence. The length of the five shots was timed to coincide with the length of the musical excerpt. Indeed, it appears that the first shot was backtimed so that the breaking of dawn would correspond with a crescendo and resolution in the music. Similarly, the various shots of boats and lovers are timed to correspond to the length of the song. The most disjunctive and powerful use of sound is the abrupt sound and visual cut from *Kriemhild's Revenge* to the crescendo of an opera duet.

The observations and connections made above are the result of multiple viewings utilizing stop action to observe individual frames. The average viewer of a Kluge film has no such opportunity. The film continues to wind through the projector or scan across viewers' television sets with no opportunity to slow it down or take a second look. Unlike a story or novel, where one can page back to verify one's memory or read difficult passages several times, film presentations normally offer no such possibilities. Furthermore, Kluge films are not easily obtained at a neighborhood video store either in Germany or abroad. The serious devotee must look to Kluge's interviews and writings for clarification of confusing or obscure aspects of the film.[54]

Kluge's extratextual commentaries reveal how rich in associations and meanings the filmic images are for Kluge. The actual image on the screen is merely a shorthand sign for a vast web of information and ideas. Kluge himself clearly loves to trace objects to their origins, to explore their historical context and interrelationship with other ideas and events. Most of this is either absent or barely suggested in the film. Rather, the images are uprooted from their original context and placed in juxtaposition with other uprooted images. This radical uprooting presents the spectator with two viewing alternatives: either try to guess Kluge's structure and associations or create new ones.

Kluge's eclecticism is not limited to the actual materials of which his films are composed; it is also evident in the sources and development of his own unique modernist style. In particular, although Kluge's montage style shows the influence of Eisenstein, Vertov, and Brecht, it differs in significant ways from all three.

Several commentators have remarked that at least two major modes of montage are discernable in Eisenstein's films. His earlier work exhibits a dialectical model of montage as a juxtaposition of opposites. His later films employ a more synthetic, associational montage practice.[55] Kluge's work manifests a tension between these two modes. On the one hand, within the small clusters of shots there is often an associational coherence, both of material and of theme or subject. Sometimes, such associations serve as links between the clusters; more often, though, there is an abrupt interruption. In most cases, two subsequent clusters are composed of very different types of material, contrasting in color, in age, in degree of movement, or in their status as documentary or fiction. Less evident in Kluge than in Eisenstein is either rhythmic editing or graphic contrasts or matches between consecutive images.[56] The major theoretical difference between the two, however, is Eisenstein's unabashed willingness to control the emotional, intellectual, and ideological responses of his audience. Whether working dialectically or synthetically, he was fully aware of his own ideological program and eager to communicate this to his spectators. Such audience manipulation is extremely problematic for Kluge, who claims not to want to force any particular interpretation on the audience. As will be further explicated in the next chapter,

Kluge claims his films are merely provocations for "the film in the viewer's head." Eisenstein, in contrast, wanted to deliver the character's "inner monologue" to the audience.[57]

Like Vertov, Kluge distrusts fictional cinema, particularly the traditional American model,[58] and both filmmakers regard documentary production as an experimental process to reveal a reality that lies hidden beneath external appearances.[59] This calls for a variety of innovative camera and editing techniques, which not only explore reality but self-reflexively reveal the constructedness of the film itself and the materiality of the medium. In addition, it demands a deconstruction or defamiliarization of the objects being shown. This leads to an emphasis on process and production rather than a reification of the finished product.

Although the two filmmakers' shooting experiments are very similar—odd angles, altering films speeds—more important are their montage similarities: heterogenous materials, radical juxtapositions, and superimpositions. For Vertov, what is most significant about montage is the interval between the shots: "The school of the Kino-Eye requires that the cine-thing be built upon 'intervals,' that is, upon a movement between the pieces, the frames; upon the proportions of these pieces between themselves, upon the transitions from one visual impulse to the one following it."[60] Kluge also talks about the gap between the shots, but sometimes he seems to take this more literally, not only as the various differences between the shots but as the temporal space between them.[61]

Kluge's later films are much more diverse and fragmented than either Eisenstein's or Vertov's, not the least because Kluge insists on combining both documentary and fictional styles. Although Eisenstein's films were often fictional reenactments of historical events or conditions, and Vertov's films were documentary manipulations of reality, Kluge embraces both filmic modes, regarding them as dialectic polarities that imply and critique one another. As a late modernist, however, Kluge's films lack the didactic/political program that unifies and propels the Russian montage. However, he has not yet reached a postmodernist position where he would abandon his fundamental impulse of social criticism.[62]

Kluge's fractured and variegated style leans heavily upon a filmic dimension unavailable to either of the Russians until late in their careers: sound. In any case, Kluge seems much less visually oriented than his predecessors. The music and, even more important, the narration are essential to providing both coherence and disruption in his films. Kluge's notions of montage seem most strongly influenced by Brecht. Not only does he employ a variety of Brechtian devices (intertitles, quotations, use of still photos and film clips, nonrelated episodes, songs) but his overall aesthetic purpose seems much closer to Brecht: interruption, maximum diversity of material,[63] destruction of illusion—all with the purpose of removing the spectator from an emotional involvement with the characters and the plot.[64] Although Brecht's ideal spectator may be more purely analytical and Kluge's may be more imaginative (employing fantasy), both seek an active spectator who does not simply absorb the material presented.

In summary, the analysis of this film has revealed several distinctive aspects of Kluge's modernist style. First, he utilizes a great variety of materials, which are intentionally and disruptively manipulated to emphasize their diversity and the process of construction. In addition, certain signature stylistic devices appear throughout this film and throughout Kluge's ouevre as a whole: the recurrent use of stills and old movie clips, often masked or colorized; the use of intertitles and his voice-over narration; the emphatic and contrapuntal use of sound; and the associative/interruptive quality of his montage, based often on thematic or subject connections and material differences. The associative patterns and relationships are often difficult to discern and are impossible to predict. At work is the modernist principle of confounding expectations and precluding anticipation on the part of the spectator.

The discussion of Kluge's overall style, and particularly of his montage practice, cannot easily be separated from questions of meaning. Apart from the material texture of the images, Kluge's montage practice derives less from visual principles than from conceptual connections. Seldom is his cutting based on graphic matches or oppositions or on composition or motion in the frame. Images are the concrete expressions, illustrations, or symbols of ideas and feelings. For Kluge, montage is a method of showing relationships and contrasts, most often between unlikely pairs or groups of objects.

Kluge's modernist style is of prime importance for the functioning of his films because fragmentation and collage are necessary methods for disrupting old verities and conventional viewing habits. Ripping objects out of context and mounting them together in a new one is essential for revealing the reality that is hidden and suppressed by society.[65] Yet the power of the juxtaposition of elements is dependent on how much of their old context they carry with them into the new one. If Kluge were an abstract filmmaker concerned only with visual surfaces, with shapes and movement, then the spectator would only need to learn how to look at the images. But for Kluge, the images themselves carry a great deal of meaning and he believes that this meaning, this original context, always accompanies these images even when they are transplanted into a new context. Viewers may not always agree: what is self-evident to Kluge may not be so to the spectator. To understand the interconnections and contexts, the viewer must understand the images as completely as possible. On the most elementary level, the viewer must be able to identify the referent: is that a shot of a burned baby or of something else? If the viewer can identify the person, place, time, and situation of the image, then the levels of possible interconnections are increased, and the relations become more complex.

Although the resonance of any art work depends on the experience that the viewer brings to it, an artwork is more or less esoteric depending on the degree of specialized experience it demands, and on the extent to which such experience is available to the viewer. Kluge notes approvingly that film is accessible to much broader audiences than is high culture, but he insists on construction principles that make the films difficult for these wide audiences.[66] Kluge's later work in particular presupposes a level of cultural literacy available to few outside Germany's borders, and to a limited public stratum within those confines. The next chapter will investigate the questions of how audiences attempt to make sense of Kluge's films. It will examine the themes and subjects that recur in these films and analyze the devices that Kluge has employed to help audiences understand them. What kinds of patterns are discernable in the ragpicker's patchwork quilt?

This analysis will focus on Kluge's 1985 film *The Blind Director*, which can be regarded as the culmination of many elements and tendencies found in earlier Kluge films. However, the social and aesthetic context of this work was undergoing significant alteration. The transition from a modernist to a postmodernist discourse requires a brief excursus into this new theoretical terrain.

2
A Modernist
in a
Postmodern Era

Excursus into an Altered Landscape

What then is the postmodern? What place does it or does it not occupy in the vertiginous work of the questions hurled at the rules of image and narration? It is undoubtedly a part of the modern. All that has been received, if only yesterday (modo, modo, Petronius used to say), must be suspected. . . . In an amazing acceleration, the generations [of artists] precipitate themselves. A work can become modern only if it is first postmodern. Postmodernism thus understood is not modernism at its end, but in the nascent state and this state is constant.

—Jean-François Lyotard [1]

The mid-1980s marked a significant change in the work of Alexander Kluge. His film aesthetic had gradually evolved into extremely fragmented films whose theatrical distribution had significantly shrunk. A new interest in the aesthetic and political possibilities of television induced him to abandon, at least temporarily, the big screen for the small one. Although Kluge's social theory remained grounded in a critical approach to capitalism's bureaucratic rationalism, the society in which he was working was changing. The internationalization of capital became more evident as the media followed other enterprises (oil, electronics, automotive) in overstepping national linguistic and legal barriers. Consumerism was proving itself triumphant over communism; advertising and commodification were penetrating public spheres in the German Democratic Republic and the rest of Eastern Europe, as well as invading private spheres such as the home and leisure activities, more thoroughly than ever before.

New resistances were also emerging: new nationalisms, racisms, and fundamentalisms. More diverse voices—of women, gays, and ethnic and other cultural minorities—were struggling to be heard. Scholars and social critics began to talk increasingly of a postmodern era and of postmodern art. The neat dichotomies and clear contradictions of the preceding one hundred years seemed less clear, more complex as the Soviet Empire began to crumble and the American Empire, itself exhausted by the Cold War, no longer knew who its enemy was and had neither the energy nor the resources to exploit its victory.

If modernism is an amorphous concept, then postmodernism is doubly so, not the least because of its dependence on the notion of modernism. Like modernism, postmodernism is used to describe a diversity of aesthetic practices, ideas, and styles, but in this case without the benefit of even the limited historical perspective available in discussions of modernism. Writers like Fredric Jameson have traced the origins of postmodernism to fundamental shifts in post–World War II society, which initiated corresponding shifts in aesthetic practices. The new social formation has been labeled variously "post-industrial society," "late capitalism," the "information age," or "consumer society." In postwar aesthetics, the contradictions and limitations of modernism became more acute and apparent on philosophical, institutional, and stylistic levels. Philosophically, the high/low culture split, the notion of the rational subject, and confidence in progress all became increasingly problematic. Institutionally, high modernism had lost much of its negative force as it became the dominant discourse in architecture, literature, theater, the academy, museums, and workplaces. Stylistically, the late modernist tendency away from representation and toward abstraction, the abandonment of ornament and figuration, and the emphasis on simplicity, functionality, and constant innovation left artists with fewer and fewer aesthetic possibilities.[2]

Especially since the late 1970s, artists have been trying to broaden their options in a variety of ways—many of which have been labeled postmodern. From one perspective, postmodern art can be seen as abandoning purity and exclusivity for diversity and inclusion by appropriating materials and styles from many different cultures: traditional Western culture, mass culture, subcultures, Third World cultures. This postmodern inclusivity and polyphony is regarded by some cultural critics as an abrupt break with and repudiation of modernism. Others, such as Lyotard, see a much more complex interrelationship.

More than most contemporary artists, Kluge's work stands as a bridge between modernism and postmodernism. Although critical of rationality, he has not abandoned it; rather, he has attempted to adapt the Enlightenment project to current conditions. His aesthetic practice employs aspects of the modernist tradition: varied artistic materials and styles are incorporated in a modernist social framework to create new aesthetic approaches. Some of these solutions, however, seem very similar not only to modernism but also to approaches and perspectives that have been labeled postmodernist. Todd Gitlin's description of postmodernism is largely apposite as an explication of Kluge's cinematic method: "It is completely indifferent to questions of consistency and continuity. It self-consciously splices genres, attitudes, styles. It relishes the blurring or juxtaposition of forms (fiction-nonfiction), stances (straight-ironic), moods (violent-comic), cultural levels (high-low). It disdains originality and fancies copies, repetition, the recombination of hand-me-down scraps."[3] Ihab Hassan has produced a binary list that contrasts qualities of modernist and postmodernist art, which include the following:

Modernism	Postmodernism
form (conjunctive, closed)	antiform (disjunctive, open)
purpose	play
design	chance
hierarchy	anarchy
mastery/logos	exhaustion/silence
distance	participation
genital/phallic	polymorphous/androgynous
root/depth	rhyzome/surface.[4]

Although one might argue about elements of this list, undoubtedly Kluge's work has many affinities with the categories on the right. However, the categories on the left are significantly consonant with several bedrock features of his productions. Especially relevant are two sets of Hassan's dichotomies: purpose/play and depth/surface, which relate to the flow of images in postmodernism: "It takes pleasure in the play of surfaces, and derides the search for depth as mere nostalgia."[5] Although Kluge's films and writings seem to endorse the notions of play and pleasure, of openness to and celebration of a variety of cultural stimuli, his images always point to more serious purposes and meanings below this surface.

Andreas Huyssen has suggested that the key characteristic of postmodernism is the disappearance of the chasm between high culture and low culture: "The great divide that separated high modernism from mass culture and that was codified in various classical accounts of modernism no longer seems relevant to postmodern artistic or critical sensibilities."[6] In this respect, too, Kluge's position is ambivalent: he never doubts the chasm, but feels compelled to bridge it.

Two kinds of responses have been made to postmodernist critiques of modernism. The first claims that there has been no decisive rupture with modernism, simply a shift in emphasis from one aspect of modernism to another. Most of the descriptions of postmodernism could equally well apply to at least some exemplars of an older modernist (or avant-garde) tradition. Open forms, chance, anarchy, silence, combination, fragmentation, discontinuity, and irony are almost ubiquitous in modernist work. Postmodernism has tended to expand backward in time, claiming what were considered modernist artists as its own, redefining modernism more narrowly.[7] Defenders of the modernist position have argued that, while important aesthetic changes have occurred over the past two or three decades, these do not constitute a break with modernist sensibility and style, but mark a new phase in its development.

Other critics, however, while recognizing the reality of postmodernism as a phenomenon, believe it is a regressive and possibly momentary reaction to modernism. They have pointed out that, at its worst, postmodernism abandons the critical negativity and skeptical resistance of modernism for an easy and ahistorical affirmation, one that delights in all the excesses and contradictions of late capitalism. The new confidence that there is space for art within the culture industry leads to an underestimation of the powers of the latter for cooptation. Postmodernism is charged with complacency and complicity in commodification.

Defenders of postmodernism praise its anti-elitist attitude, its inclusive rather than exclusive strategies.[8] No longer is art the reserve of a privileged class of white males. Art is no longer afraid to sully its hands by interacting with popular and mass culture. However, many proponents of postmodernism have sought to distinguish two antithetical strains. The first is more affirmative and often commercial. E. Ann Kaplan refers to this as "coopted postmodernism," as distinguished from "utopian postmodernism."[9] The latter, more critical and politically informed (if not politically aimed) postmodernism that she and others embrace has many affinities with a critical or political modernism—the establishment of definite standards, a mistrust of commercialism, cooptation, "facile eclecticism,"[10] and an appeal to particular kinds of audiences in particular settings (the academy, art institutions, political gatherings). This kind of postmodernist art would interact with mass culture (Kaplan cites Joan Braverman's deconstructive video, *Joan Does Dynasty,* as an example), but it is not to be confused with it. The high art/low art distinction may not have died so easily after all, particularly if one sees mass culture as an important component of low art.

The critical postmodernists do, however, differ from the modernists in some very important ways. Most evident is their endorsement of the liberating potential of popular cultures—in the sense of art produced by the people, particularly by "the Other": women, gays, blacks, and Third-World peoples. And they wouldn't limit this aesthetic activity to the traditional artistic forms of high culture: other media and genres must be explored and taken seriously.

Although one should not ignore the significant differences between the modernist and postmodernist sensibilities, neither should the similarities and continuities connecting them be overlooked. Modernism is seen as traditional and even old-fashioned by its successor, a movement that nevertheless embraces many of the assumptions that were key to modernism: the fetishization of the new, a fascination with contemporary society and its technologies, and, on a formal level, the valorization of collage and combination. Like modernism, postmodernism opposes closure and is concerned with materials, self-referentiality, and intertextuality. These connections and shared values account for much of the difficulty that scholars have had in separating the postmodern from the modern. It is perhaps most useful to see postmodernism not as the opposite of modernism, but as a sensibility or attitude emerging out of modernism; one that, while chafing at some of its prejudices and limitations, incorporates and transforms much of the basic impulse of modernism to keep it moving forward critically.

Postmodernism gave itself a host of new media, new styles and contents, and even new audiences, because the aesthetic sensibilities of modernism had by the 1970s and 1980s filtered down into everyday life and mass culture. Postmodernism takes the modernist notions of collage much further by drastically mixing media, genres, styles, and contents. It is less esoteric and serious than modernism. And postmodernism is less concerned with pure form, less concerned with any form of purity, less convinced that artistic radicalism has anything to do with political radicalism, and is more willing than modernism to tarnish its artistic integrity by direct contact with popular culture and the marketplace.

Despite legitimate complaints that much of postmodernism is too affirmative of society, one can agree with Kaplan that many manifestations of postmodernism maintain some critical, polemic quality. In some instances, this is directed at the targets of modernist critiques: capitalism, consumerism, bureaucracy, and technology. In other instances, the polemic is addressed primarily to the esoteric and self-important quality of modernist high art. This critique is tied to similar polemics within modernism that were championed by the historical avant-garde. As Huyssen suggests, postmodernism could be regarded simply as a new collection of efforts to solve, paper over, reformulate, or eliminate the impasse of modernism: high art versus mass culture. To the extent that Kluge maintains the extant framework of this high art/mass culture split, reemploys devices of the historical avant-garde, or helps widen the chasm, he remains a modernist filmmaker. To the extent that he produces new solutions to this dilemma, we may, perhaps, be able to speak of him as a postmodernist.

Most of Kluge's media work after 1985 has utilized postmodern technology, and much of it addressed postmodern social conditions. His television programs were created through digital video technologies, which offered him wonderful new opportunities for image manipulation. They were distributed through terrestrial, cable, and DBS technologies to homes in Germany, Austria, and Switzerland. Images were recycled from every possible source: his own films, those of his contemporary New German directors, from old films, books, and still photos.

The next two chapters will examine how Kluge's aesthetic and theoretical approach, however, remained remarkably consistent with his earlier work. Kluge continued to utilize montage in a purposeful, not merely playful, way, creating polarities between which the viewer's attention could move: polarities of aesthetic material, polarities of visual texture, historical polarities, contrasts of theme and style, juxtapositions of interviewer and interviewee. Kluge's social critique remained anchored in a Frankfurt School rejection of mass-produced consciousness and an affirmation of autonomy and individual experience.

Chapter 5 analyzes thematic and content elements in Kluge's cinema by focusing on his 1985 film *The Blind Director*. Although the subject of this film is the emerging social forces of what has been called postmodernity, both the themes and methods are related to his previous films. Irony abounds in this film, particularly in the many parodied interviews. But this imitation is the opposite of a postmodern pastiche: it is always sardonically critical of the character types and the activities that are being lampooned. This film's ironic stance toward the new media and the new era is particularly striking because Kluge himself was investing his energies in this new *Schrott,* this new scrap, and was in the process of becoming a "man in a hurry," shuttling from city to city and from meeting to meeting.

Chapter 6 discusses the institutional context of Kluge's television work and consequent developments in his modernist aesthetic. Working in a mass medium, he was more interested in the insights of high-culture and academe than in an analysis, critique, or celebration of mass, folk, or third-world cultural production. The content of his programs brings the historical perspective of opera and the silent cinema to bear on contemporary life. While processing variegated visual material and interviewing hundreds of people, Kluge maintained control over his programming and always left his distinctive personal stamp on it. The interviews were curious, probing, ironic, and quasi-anonymous. The electronically manipulated visual montage was rich, dense, and challenging. His television work also raises the postmodern problem of the imbrication of resistance and recuperation: Who is using whom? The voracious appetite of the media seeks out even its enemies as fodder, which it can disgorge as bland pulp. Yet the continual attacks on Kluge and his programming by the German media moguls attest to the fact that his work is not completely digestible within the new media's alimentary system.

In the 1980s, Kluge's work comes closest to becoming postmodern, and most clearly demonstrates the continuity between elements of postmodernism and modernism. One Kluge scholar, Manas Ray, situates Kluge's work between Brecht's political modernism and postmodernism, but places him closer to the latter. Of particular interest to Ray is "the way that Kluge conducts the debate between the guiding insights of postmodern practices and the claims of history. Taking inspiration from the theories of history of Benjamin and Bloch, Kluge embarks on a project of 'redemption.' His is a historicized postmodernism which excavates the innumerable histories of his nation to speak against the very repressions of History itself."[11] Ray emphasizes the centrality in Kluge's work of a "dialogic exchange of past and present," in which a suppressed past continually returns. The grand narrative of history has ended in polyphonic discontinuity.

However, Kluge also insists on more than relativism or the end of history. The title of his penultimate film, "The Attack of the Present on the Rest of Time," is clear evidence that any dehistoricization that takes place in postmodernity must be resisted. Ray acknowledges that "central to Kluge's production is a fundamental desire to understand and grasp history, coupled with a profound awareness of all that keeps that desire from being realized."[12] Although Ray labels Kluge's work postmodern, he does not conceive of postmodernism as the antithesis of modernism. The relation between the two is temporal, and postmodernism only partly negates its predecessor: "the thesis of postmodernism can claim the end of modern times without necessarily abandoning the *project of modernism*."[13] It is this project and critical spirit that continues to inform the later media work of Alexander Kluge.

5
The Film in the Autor's Head

MAKING MEANING

> I would like in this film to show a photograph of the classical cinema "from the perspective of today." What is that: today? Events such as mass unemployment, the closing of the ship-yards, the call for a thirty-five hour work week, structural changes of the industrial sector, consciousness industries, and so forth are, as far as feature films are concerned, unfilmed. Each of those themes contains a provocation towards film and, to be sure, not only in the direction of a reproduction, but in the direction of a cinematic translation.
>
> —Alexander Kluge[1]

Kluge's statement of purpose for his 1985 film, *The Blind Director,* is a good indication of his ongoing preoccupation with contemporary social reality. From as early as the Oberhausen Mani-festo, Kluge's critique of the film industry included an attack on the content of mainstream films. In his view, most commercial films, and especially those manufactured by the old German film industry, were irrelevant to the concerns and needs of contemporary audiences.[2] Vast areas of human experience went unrepresented and unexplored on the screen. The cinema of entertainment relied on old genres and for-mulas, turning toward an idealized past or an unrealistic present for its subjects.

Throughout his career, Kluge has attempted to deal with subjects that were often considered unsuitable for filming because they were too controversial, political, intellectual, or just too ordinary to be of interest to most filmmakers—or filmgoers. Kluge's penchant for the ironic rather than the dramatic has made him less interested in tradi-tional narrative than in unnoticed contradictions and unlikely associations. His political instincts and acute sense of the contemporary mood and situation have inclined him to deal with current themes and issues. Like many modernists, Kluge expends much of his energy grappling with what he finds to be the often unpleasant reality of modern life.

With the exception of his few science fictional flights into the future—which are essentially distorted reflections of contemporary problems—all of Kluge's films are set in the present. While, in his later films, a number of the fictional and montage sequences deal with historical subjects, they do so only to counterpoint the contemporary materials that constitute the bulk of these films. This emphasis on the present was particularly noticeable during the highly politicized 1970s, when many German filmmakers retreated into the adaptation of canonized literature—such as *Effi Briest, Woyzeck,* or even *The Tin Drum*—to render their social criticism in more oblique forms. Kluge was not interested in producing large-scale costume dramas or adapting other people's writings.[3] Instead, his films have taken on such topical subjects as abortion (*Occasional Work of a Female Slave*), student/police confrontations over house occupations (*The Middle of the Road Is a Very Dead End*), the national mania for security (*Strongman Ferdinand*), revolution and reaction (*Germany in Autumn*), nationalism (*The Patriot*), resurgent conservative politics (*The Candidate*), and nuclear armaments (*War and Peace*).

Perhaps even more important than his attention to the large political topics of the day is Kluge's engagement with the conditions of everyday life in the modern era: "I believe strongly that the real script editor is always close observation of daily life. I am saying that the script editor is not the filmmaker, but rather his attentiveness and his capacity to understand what 'daily life' means."[4] Indisputably, Kluge is an extremely perceptive observer of contemporary social reality. Throughout his work, a number of modern issues and themes recur in varied guises: the alienated individual in an impersonal and institutionalized society; the isolation of the individual from others and the difficulty of relationships; sexuality in contemporary life; the past as pretext and context for the present.

Many of these themes represent concerns voiced earlier by Adorno, Horkheimer, Benjamin, and others associated with the Frankfurt School. They understand modern society as a warped and instrumentalized version of rationalism. This instrumental reason seeks to turn all aspects of human life, both public and private, into predictable, controlled behavior. All human action and intercourse becomes quantifiable and commodified. The primary instrument for standardization and homogenization in the private sphere is the culture industry, which mass produces and commodifies art.

In his efforts to escape the paralyzing aesthetic dilemmas posed by this critique—especially for someone determined to work in the mass media—Kluge has adopted several different strategies. The first has been his ongoing attempt to wrest media from the exclusive control of the culture industry, insisting that artists be allowed to revert to a preindustrial, artisanal form of organization in order to create genuinely autonomous art using these media. Secondly, he has argued for films that do not just entertain, but speak to real concerns of the audience by addressing contemporary problems. Finally, he has continued to insist on a spectator-based cinema: the production of meaning is not simply the concern of the artist, but of the spectator as well.[5]

Inherent in this last concept, however, are tensions that Kluge himself has never definitively resolved. His modernist social critique requires a communication of meaning from the artist to the spectator. The artist is controlling the arrangement of images to create an intended effect in the audience. At the same time, Kluge's rejection of the top-down control administered by the "consciousness industries" calls for a democratic process, whereby meaning is created by the active involvement of the spectator. The audience must be free to organize the filmic experience for itself, but how is this possible when it has been preorganized by the filmmaker? How open or closed are these films? How much control does the author exert?

Similarly, his democratic impulses incline him to seek the largest possible audiences. But the more democratically open the work is to multiple meanings, the less appealing it is to mass audiences, which have been trained to rely on generic conventions and to accept more closed texts that emphasize preferred meanings. The aesthetic properties that mark films as autonomous works of art and not mass products, and those qualities that incorporate critical values, also serve to distance audiences from such works, literally as well as figuratively. Spectators stay away from these films in droves, and the portion of the mass medium represented by Kluge's films becomes an esoteric one.

The Blind Director, Kluge's penultimate feature film, is a useful work for exploring these subjects, themes, and meaning-making processes. Like most of Kluge's films, it is informed by many of the critical assumptions of the Frankfurt School, and it explicitly addresses several fundamental modernist issues: the role of the mass media in mod-

❙ *Der Angriff der Gegenwart auf die übrige Zeit* (*The Blind Director*): A head full of images

ern society; the relation of the film to both producer and audience; and the distinctive features of contemporary reality and their relationships with the past and the future.

However, many of the subjects and themes in *The Blind Director* can be regarded as postmodern. Particularly prominent are socioeconomic relations in the era of the new media—which in Germany include not merely cable, direct broadcast satellite (DBS), and fiber optic transmission of television, but computerization, videotext, and other technologies of the information age. Kluge's attitude toward contemporary society—whether postmodern, modern, or both—retains many features of the modernist social critique. In 1975, Kluge wrote that "the motive for realism is never the confirmation of reality, but protest."[6] Almost ten years later, this critical attitude still prevails in *The Blind Director*. The film stands in opposition to any postmodern celebration of contemporary society. Even the more critical side of postmodernism is less pessimistic in tone and is more engaged with the vitality of different forms of resistance and the creative possibilities of popular culture than is Kluge's work. Although Kluge portrays certain aspects of contemporary society that are often thought of as postmodern and utilizes some of the latest techniques for the propagation and manipulation of images, this is carried out from Kluge's distinctively modernist perspective: the artist laments the latest manifestation of modernity even as he appropriates its images. For Kluge, the new media constitute a further "industrialization of consciousness": a mode of "repression through consumption, through entertainment."[7]

THEMES AND SUBJECTS

> Kluge's film aesthetics reveal with exceptional clarity a certain compulsion to repeat; there is hardly a motif that does not crop up again in some other situation, that is not tried out, rehearsed once more, rearranged, and illuminated anew by different contexts.
>
> —Gertrude Koch[8]

The title of a film often announces the genre, themes, or subject of the film. To a certain extent, Kluge's film titles, as unwieldy and unusual as they are, achieve similar purposes. The original German title of *The Blind Director* is *Die Angriff der Gegenwart auf die übrige Zeit,* or "The Attack of the Present on the Rest of Time." This title indicates that the film probably does not belong to any ordinary genre and that its themes will be prominent and abstract. It announces a serious social critique and warns the spectator that interpretation will be a necessary part of the viewing process. The title is an interpretive clue to the film as a whole, but one which itself must be interpreted: the title explains the film as the film explains the title.[9]

"The Attack of the Present on the Rest of Time" designates temporality as an important theme, and this recurring motif does play a primary role in unifying the otherwise heterogenous material of this film.[10] The title's implicit criticism of the present (as aggressor) suggests the modernist's critique of modernity: present society is indicted for obliterating (or at least leveling) all tradition and historical consciousness and for destroying any optimism about the future. These indictments are also remarkably similar to critiques leveled at the ahistorical (or antihistorical) nature of postmodern society and certain strains in postmodern art. The film illustrates instances of contemporary society's two-pronged attack, against both the past and the future, and it attempts to locate more concretely those forces in the present that are playing this destructive role. Among the most prominent contemporary themes in *The Blind Director* are: the metropolis, the pace of contemporary life, displacement from the social work-place, assaults on human relationships by an impersonal society, the commodification and perversion of sexuality, scrap as a new industry, the decline of cinema, and the ruthless ubiquity of the new media.

For Kluge, as for many modernists, the metropolis is the key site and a major protagonist in contemporary society.[11] In his previous feature film, *The Power of Emotion,* the city also was a prominent sub-ject. In that film, Kluge compared modern cities to the ancient me-tropolis of Babylon: "Babylon was destroyed for building high rises." In the "screenplay" for *The Blind Director,* Kluge states that the "illu-sion of the city" is one of the film's three main themes. According to Kluge, most people believe that cities will get better, that they will remain full of activity, and that they can be shaped to meet human needs and desires. "The real relations show no ambition in this direc-tion. The reconstruction of the city will soon be finalized. We will enter the 21st century with cities which are very similar to those which we now have before our eyes. The idol of the city, for example Florence during the Renaissance, belongs to the continued existence of the illusion."[12] Characteristic of the city is this reconstruction, the destruction of the old to make way for the new—skyscrapers, pedes-trian zones, underground shops, and new city centers.[13] Ironically, it is the "urban renewal" of high modernism that he is here attacking, the inhumane and monolithic urban planning that sets out to stan-dardize what was diverse. The film itself is less explicit in the devel-opment of this theme than the screenplay predicts. The promised ex-tensive filmic essay on urban reconstruction shrinks on celluloid to just a series of transitional shots, without commentary. The high-rises glitter with lights and reflections, each window an identical box with slightly different contents. The buildings are often shot in fast action, but function basically as cold, aesthetic objects—the background against which the film's mininarratives unfold.

But the film's narratives do describe the lifestyles of typical contem-porary urbanites. Indeed, the major characters are explicitly types, not individuals, and are introduced as such through intertitles or narra-tion: "the men in a hurry," "the superfluous woman," "the calculating woman," "the home worker." Kluge is less interested in rich character-ization than with the way people adapt to and are shaped by their social roles. His audience does not identify with these people, only observes them. Both the important and the worthless pass before us: the scrap merchant, the busy executive, the chauffeur, and the or-phan; the movers and shakers as well as the moved and shaken.

All of them either move to the tempo of the post-industrial metropolis or are cast aside. Their lives are disrupted and reshaped by the reconstruction of the city, where labor is no longer concentrated in factories and offices. An increasingly large workforce sits isolated at home, hunched over computers, connected only by wires to the outside world. The whole Broch family clusters around their new hearth, the computer. As in the nineteenth century, this new cottage industry also exploits child labor to tend the machine, but this time the apparatus is electronic rather than mechanical.

What is important about these lives is not the dramatic incident, high emotion, or fantastic events typical of Hollywood films, but ordinary activities, the daily routine. Broch sits in front of the computer or on the toilet. Gertrud Meinecke cooks; the chauffeur drives. The executive paces, waits, walks out of buildings, and climbs into his car. Gertrud manufactures long lists to explain the rhythms of the little girl's life.

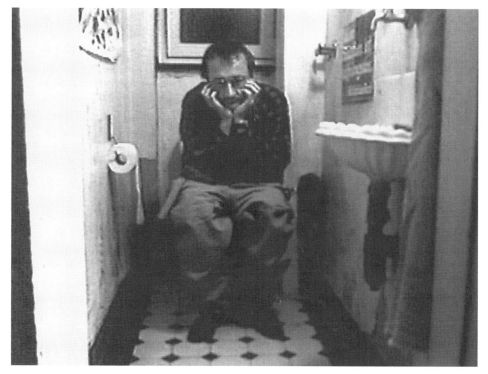

❚ *Der Angriff der Gegenwart auf die übrige Zeit* (*The Blind Director*): The home office

Even the daily rituals of domestic life are invaded and dislocated by impersonal social forces beyond the individual's control. The computer brings work and its strict schedule (two fifteen-minute exercise breaks per day) into the home. Broch's family must constantly monitor the computer, and he is summoned by whistle from the bathroom when the machine needs him. The implacable demands of business shuttle the hurrying man from city to city, keeping him from his family, and disrupting the plans of his wife. The individual can struggle to assert or maintain routine, but such struggle seems ineffectual. The child cannot undo the car wreck that tore her from her parents, nor can Gertrud resist the court order that takes the child away. The economic factors that displace the doctor from her office are as irresistible as they are unforeseen. Thus, Kluge applies the Frankfurt School critique of the implacable forces of administration—appropriately so, now that not just the workplace but leisure time and domestic life have been completely colonized.

In *The Blind Director,* relationships are rare and tenuous. The rhythms of contemporary life seem to exclude friendship and intimacy. The dismissed doctor has no one to turn to but a stranger, the cinema ticket seller. The blind director comments that in these times it is impossible to love. The two executives discuss a marriage that is based on neither friendship nor love, but on discord and weakness. The man cannot tell the woman that he does not love her, because it would upset her too much. Alienation continues to be the modern condition.

Sexuality is organized rationally as a commodity: singles rely on dating services to find partners; a woman, apparently a prostitute, masturbates a male client. In other Kluge films, prostitutes not only commodify sex, but themselves become commodities, bought and sold by pimps. Sexuality does not seem to lead to any lasting harmony or intimacy. Perverse sexuality can, however, have salutary consequences, as in the revival of a young woman through necrophilia.[14]

The expression of sexuality in Kluge's work is singularly nonerotic. In part, this relates to the distanced position of the spectator and the ironic tone of the films. The viewer is not invited to identify with the sexual fantasies of the characters. Nakedness occurs rarely and is treated in a matter-of-fact manner. The body is simply a part of ordinary experience, and sexuality is simply another bodily function. When sexual acts are recorded in Kluge's films, they are stripped of the romantic trappings of fantasy: a hand job is manual labor.

Several critics have commented on this absence of eroticism. Miriam Hansen has noted that the unflattering portrayals of male bodies are "linked to a critique of institutional authority." She goes on to point out, however, that "to the extent that these bodies are deliberately devoid of erotic imagination and attraction, they throw a shadow on the very possibility of relations between the sexes." [15] Heide Schlüpmann, writing about *Artistes at the Top of the Big Top: Disoriented,* agrees that "although the phallus has apparently lost its menace, the eroticism between the sexes has not thereby been salvaged—it too has been lost." [16]

The subject of scrap occurs several times in *The Blind Director.* Baudelaire's ragpicker has now been transformed into a businessman, profiting from the planned obsolescence and disposability of modern society. The interview with a scrap entrepreneur reveals that these are scrap-intensive times. Shots of crushed cars being grasped in giant, mangling pincers alternate with images of conveyor belts dumping twisted and torn bits of metal. But not just outmoded consumer goods are junked: human beings who have outlived their utility are treated like scrap.

Kluge suggests equivalencies between scrap and both cinema and the new media. On a purely visual level, shots from *Die Wunderbare Lüge der Nina Petrowna* (The Wonderful Lie of Nina Petrowna, 1929) are optically processed so that they are flattened and stacked on top of one another, four images in the frame at once. A graphic match edit juxtaposes this stack to piles of flattened cars, suggesting a similar fate for both products. While cinema may be, as Kluge says, "superfluous" today, there is also a suggestion that the new media are simply tomorrow's scrap: two businessmen cannot decide whether to invest in waste or in the new media. Similarly, the reporter who normally covers the new media is assigned to interview the scrap dealer.

The decline of cinema is one of the major themes of this film. While most of Kluge's films are also littered with cinematic scraps from the past, nowhere else in his work is Kluge so explicitly concerned with the problems of the film medium. Not until this period, when private television experiments were further reducing cinematic audiences, did Kluge fully realize the moribund condition of cinema. *The Blind Director* becomes the filmic occasion for exploring the nature and history of film itself. The cinematic scraps in this film are sometimes narratively motivated, but more often not. One interesting example occurs when the doctor quits her job, goes to a movie theater, and buys a ticket. Then, footage is shown from an old film: tinted shots of trees and fast moving clouds; colored drawings depict attractive men and women in thirties-style clothes. Rather than recording the doctor's cinematic experience, these shots seem to suggest the clichés of the classical film tradition. The footage is neither an excerpt from (or an imitation of) a contemporary film, which is what one expects to be playing in the theater, nor is it an excerpt from or imitation of an old film. However, the next shot shows the doctor back at the ticket booth and the narrator informs us that she never even bothered to go inside the theater at all. This information retroactively reinforces an interpretation of these shots as Kluge's commentary on film and removes them further from any diegetic status. Unlike the cinema of the early 1970s, which was an important experience and source of inspiration for the likes of Roswitha Bronski (from *Occasional Work of a Female Slave*), the cinema of the early 1980s goes unwatched. It cannot even amuse or distract, let alone inspire, this depressed, superfluous woman.

Old footage of clouds and a 1930s film clip of a man emerging from a limousine are other small fragments from unidentified sources that seem to float randomly on the surface of the film. As mentioned before, the footage from *Nina Petrowna* is radically smashed, spatially and temporally. The duration of four different sequences from the film is reduced by running them simultaneously. The scraps have been dislocated from their original source and fail to function narratively. These scattered cinematic remnants hover on the edge of oblivion, rescued momentarily by Kluge in a film that few viewers will actually see. Such a precarious position for the cinematic tradition is not just a contemporary phenomenon, however. A mininarrative tells the story of a caretaker of a Polish film studio during the Nazi occupation. In order to protect the facilities and the films, the caretaker and his wife encourage a romance between their daughter and a German soldier.

Toward the end of the film, Kluge includes shots of Auguste Lumière and some selections from his films, followed by a documentary clip about the design and operation of a motion picture camera. This sequence constitutes a cinematic restatement of comparisons Kluge has often drawn between his filmic innovations and the silent cinema. In the mid-1970s he wrote: "Thus it is not a contradiction if one expresses a callous modernity, that is, the formal principles of the present in the most primitive forms of the silent film. I link my films to the silent cinema not for stylistic reasons, but because it is vital to remain radically open to the elementary roots of film, so long as the total construction of the cinema remains only a program."[17]

This material on the history and apparatus of the medium leads directly into the final lengthy segment of the film, entitled "The Blind

Director." This sequence is both an examination of the film production process and a personal rumination on the role of the filmmaker and the future of cinema. The director, his head full of images, claims to hate images. Blind, he can no longer see what he is doing and depends on his assistants, who are afraid to tell him the truth. Despite a long film career, he has reached a creative crisis: unable to explain what he is doing, unable to complete the film, uncertain of his future. The journalist from earlier in the film conducts two key fictional interviews during this narrative: one with the director and one with the producer. Both of these fictional interviews are filmed in black and white, an ironic comment on the factuality and realism normally connoted by this absence of color.

One important factor in the demise of cinema is the arrival of the new media. The two businessmen who contemplate investing in the new media see the process as involving the closing of movie theaters and the distributing of images through telephone wires. Kluge points out in his narration that it is a mistake to think of the new media as being solely a matter of entertainment: they constitute a new industry, one that creates the new *Heimarbeiter* (home worker). The displacement brought about by this new form of work isolates workers and breaks down the social bonds of work relationships. The home is no longer a defense against the outside world. It has been penetrated by the rationalization and regimentation of the workplace.[18]

The problems in the contemporary situation Kluge portrays are not new. They are chronic, if increasingly acute, issues. His analysis of the city is not so different from Georg Simmel's at the turn of the century:

> The deepest problems of modern life derive from the claim of the individual to preserve the autonomy and individuality of his existence in the face of overwhelming social forces. . . . An inquiry into the inner meaning of specifically modern life and its products, into the soul of the cultural body, so to speak, must seek to solve the equation which structures like the metropolis set up between the individual and the super-individual contents of life.[19]

Adorno and Horkheimer developed the same themes in their *Dialectic of Enlightenment*:

> Yet the city housing projects designed to perpetuate the individual as a supposedly independent unit in a small hygienic dwelling make him all the more subservient to his adversary—the absolute power of capi-

talism. Because the inhabitants, as producers and as consumers, are drawn into the center in search of work and pleasure, all the living units crystallize into well-organized complexes. The striking unity of microcosm and macrocosm presents men with a model of their culture: the false identity of the general and the particular.[20]

The difference between these critiques and Kluge's is that now the conditions are worse, as new spaces are invaded and more subtle forms of oppression and manipulation are introduced. The result is exploitation, alienation, and meaninglessness: a thoroughly modern condition.

All of the various themes and subjects discussed above have important temporal dimensions. Most often this is the conflict between the new and the old. Contemporary society is represented by the metropolis, by the scrapping of the past, by the disruption of traditional social patterns of work and home, and above all by the new media, which are rapidly bringing to a close the ninety-year history of the cinema. Past traditions, relationships, and modes of living are rendered obsolete or superfluous.

Each of the narrative segments in *The Blind Director* is dominated by the implacability of time. The "men in a hurry" never have enough time as they rush from meeting to meeting. The superfluous doctor has nothing but time, now that time has passed her by. The wife of the "man in a hurry" has no time with her husband, and her time as a wife may soon expire—the omniscient narrator tells us that she is ten years older than he, and he will leave her in four years. The blind director's time is also up—stranded between the studio and his room he must wait two hours before an assistant comes along to help him. The Polish sequence occurs at New Year's eve, a privileged time for Kluge and for most people because it symbolizes the passing of time, the fleeting moment between the past and the future. Similarly, Kluge emphasizes the temporal aspect of many of the nondramatized film fragments. Many shots have a clock with whirling hands superimposed over part of the main image. Thus Kluge provides the viewer with at least one thematic tool for making associations among such heterogenous material.

On two occasions in the film, the concept of time becomes not just a motivating factor but the main subject. Both are short fictional sequences. In the first, an interviewer questions Dr. Gerlach about his almost mystical theory of temporal cycles. Gerlach has observed that the twentieth century could be broken into groupings of sixteen years, each consisting of four four-year periods. He begins by pointing out that 1984 is sixteen years after the height of the student protests in 1968, but also sixteen years from the beginning of the next century. As in most of these mock interviews, little information is transmitted, but a critique of both the language and the inane obsessions of the interviewees is clearly communicated.

In the second sequence, a professor expounds the differences between *chronos* and *kairos* to a colleague. The speaker is oblivious to the fact that the auditor has no time for such interminable discursions, because in an hour and a quarter he must deliver a lecture himself. The professor explains that the Greeks used the word *kairos* to convey the notion of a particular opportune moment in time. Nevertheless, he continues, its radically interruptive quality has a certain malignant aspect to it. *Chronos,* on the other hand, stood for duration, for the unfolding of time, and was symbolized by an old man. The distracted colleague is unable to seize the moment, either by listening to the monologue or by interrupting the speaker to attend to his own preparations. Thus, Kluge's irony here operates on multiple levels, as the professor must step back into the classical past to find categories to deal with a contemporary phenomenon. Yet this very investigation of the past obliterates his awareness of what is happening in the present. On the other hand, his colleague represents the modern situation of the person in a hurry, with no time to understand why he is in this condition.

In writing about the film, Kluge pursues the distinction between *chronos* and *kairos* further. Surprisingly, for a man whose sense of timing (*kairos*) has always been so superb, and who has celebrated this trait in the name of his own production company, Kluge conveys some serious criticisms of *kairos:* "All these stories are about the present, which is about to expand itself. Kairos fights against chronos";[21] "the principle of the present rages against the principle of hope and the collective illusions of the past. We live in a present, which for the first time would be in a position to raise itself up as ruler over all other times."[22] Many early modernists took exactly this position about modernity: the present is attacking the past. This was either lamentable or laudable; it was also apparently inevitable. More than one hundred years later, the intensity and the completeness of this attack seem to have increased significantly. As a former history student, Kluge finds this absolute subordination of the past threatening, but not necessarily inevitable. Resistance to such usurpation can begin by writing a book or making a film.

Many descriptions of postmodernity seem to posit a social condition very much like that which Kluge describes: the iconoclasm of modernism has been taken one step further. No longer is there merely an antagonism between the past and the present, but the past is subsumed into a permanent present. The instantaneous nature of contemporary electronic technologies makes obsolescence obsolete. A fad is gone before it has fully emerged. But its exile is only partial and momentary, because it can return again at any time. This infinite series of instantaneous global communications that characterizes contemporary life is paralleled in the arts.

While the term "postmodernism" suggests that chronological temporality is still operative, postmodernism's retroactive digestion of modernism and all other artistic phenomena—regardless of their moment of origin—suggests an infinite expansion of the present in both directions. The mass media generate a circulating flow of reproduced images that have become completely cut off from their sources, their contexts, and their meanings. Their kaleidoscopic interchangeability forces attention on the "play of surfaces" rather than on any anchoring referents. While it can be argued that this is precisely the result that Kluge moves toward in his montage practice, this does not seem to be his primary intention. If such depth has disappeared, it is more an occasion for regret than rejoicing. For Kluge, there still seems to be some insistence on the signified as well as the signifier, some notion that there is a *Zusammenhang,* a context and a coherence between images, a conviction that meaning can be made.[23]

MAKING MEANING

These modern/postmodern subjects and themes are organized by Kluge and the viewers in distinctive ways. While the tension noted above between the filmmaker and the spectator as rival or complementary sources of meaning may not be unresolvable, it cannot be dodged. In writings and interviews, Kluge often downplays the role of the filmmaker in order to exalt the role of the viewer. Moreover, Kluge attempts to expand the notion of cinematic experience to include less cognitive and more emotional modes of reception. Nevertheless, the privileged mode of reception is interpretive rather than sensual, and the privileged source of meaning remains the filmmaker. Indeed, the author is more important in these types of films than in more formulaic productions in which meaning-making is easier for the spectator. This question of cinematic authority is explicitly raised in *The Blind Director* and in Kluge's writings about the film.

In its exploration of the historical demise of the cinematic medium, *The Blind Director* can be regarded as Kluge's eulogy for a dying institution.[24] Despite Kluge's long-time devotion to cinema, however, his view of the medium is by no means that of an infatuated lover, blind to the faults of his mistress. In fact, Kluge's attitude toward classical cinema is quite ambivalent—both fond and critical of it. On the one hand, he portrayed himself in the 1960s as an ardent cinema goer who preferred action movies.[25] "In my opinion it is impossible to transform the cinema into an institution of moral education. People go to the cinema in order to be entertained there in 'attentiveness without strain' (Walter Benjamin), that is, with a certain casualness."[26] Nevertheless, Kluge has repeatedly launched attacks on mainstream cinema as a repressive institution, a perversion of the real interests of the spectators through "bad taste," "clichés," and "conformity."[27]

Classical cinema has functioned almost exclusively through fictional narrative. While the viewers expect such films, they are also, according to Kluge, bored by them. Their "attentiveness towards enacted scenarios [is] worn down by the friction" of repetition.[28] Kluge suggests that this is a function of both form and subject matter. As he claims in the quote at the head of this chapter, cinema has been unable or unwilling to turn its camera on many of the most important aspects of modern life.

This surplus of unfilmed real-life experience has created a "congestion," Kluge suggests, that can only be unblocked by employing a nonclassical film approach.[29] "In such cases where there is a congestion of experience or translation, the form of the essay film is necessary. I know no other possibility for quickly conveying such an abundance of material."[30] Images must be organized in nontraditional ways. Thus, *The Blind Director* functions as both a critique of classical cinema and as a prototype for a nontraditional approach: the essay film.

Kluge does not, however, actually explain why an essay film is necessary to show real-life experience nor does he define the precise nature of this new cinematic model. He has suggested elsewhere, however, that reality cannot be read directly off of surfaces, but is relational. Kluge remarks: "On the subject of realism, Brecht says: of what use is an exterior view of the AEG if I can not see what is going on inside the building in terms of relationships, wage labor, capital, international investments—a photograph says nothing about the AEG itself."[31] If *The Blind Director* is in fact an example of the new model, then the essay film seems to be a method for conveying ideas by using nonnarrative material and associative/interruptive montage. But by rejecting traditional narrative and formal conventions, Kluge creates difficulties for his audiences in understanding his films. One critic who has been very sensitive to the process of watching a Kluge film is herself a filmmaker, Helke Sander. She observes that Kluge's montage style "jumps from point to point" and overwhelms the audience: "We require time to take up unfamiliar trains of thought and to assimilate them. However, we find that Kluge is already on the next train of thought when we have hardly managed to reach the last one. This is of course, stimulating, intellectually refreshing, and of genuine entertainment value, but it quickly becomes tiring."[32] Inundated with images and associations, the viewer often gives up.

As early as 1968, Kluge began efforts to remedy this problem. One early attempt involved an arrangement with a movie theater to allow patrons to view the same film a second time by presenting their used ticket stubs. Kluge felt that repeated viewings would permit the spectator to reflect further on the meanings of *Artistes at the Top of the Big Top: Disoriented.*[33] Most of Kluge's other strategies for furthering spectator comprehension have involved his direct and personal intervention. Each strategy is caught up in a fundamental dilemma, however. On the one hand, Kluge is aesthetically and politically committed to maximum ambiguity of meaning and audience freedom of interpretation. On the other hand, Kluge's political modernism promotes a program of social change, a process that requires a certain clarity and precision of filmic expression and interpretation. Included in this program is the *training* of spectators to think *independently*—an objective that most starkly embodies this contradiction.

Kluge's intervention in controlling the meaning-making process can usefully be divided into those activities that occur within the film itself and those that take place outside it. In the former category are the film's dialogue and narrative events, which are planned by Kluge, but to which other members of the crew, especially the actors, contribute substantially. The choice of images and the sequence of juxtaposition also control what kinds of associations the viewer will make between these images. The title of the film and the intertitles give important clues—although often enigmatic ones—about how the film should be subdivided and how the parts fit together. Perhaps most important is the voice-over narration, delivered by Kluge himself, which has a privileged status in explaining what is happening and providing a perspective about those events. The more open and ambiguous the images, the more important the narration—even if it, too, is at times enigmatic, terse, or ironic.

Outside the borders of the film itself, Kluge has been unusually active in organizing meaning. Like any pragmatic filmmaker, Kluge has submitted to countless interviews by the popular and more elite press. In these interviews, Kluge provides many clues and connections that help journalists and readers understand the film. Usually these comments are somewhat oblique and scattered. In earlier interviews, Kluge makes connections between his work and that of other contemporary or past filmmakers. In later interviews, he either introduces very abstract notions or employs metaphors and more concrete analogies, often drawing upon his unique status as both a social philosopher and literary figure. Indeed, Kluge's normal mode of argument is exemplified by his films: he moves by association from subject to subject and idea to idea, utilizing many specific anecdotes as illustrations, and often speaking in a personal verbal shorthand. The following remark by Kluge actually describes one of his most frequent expository strategies: "This is hard to explain, but easy to understand through an example."[34] In dealing with reporters, Kluge's charm and intelligence enable him to deflect criticism and explain away difficulties. The result has been surprisingly favorable press coverage. One first-time critic, in fact, remarked that Kluge had so charmed her colleagues at a press screening that they asked him no difficult questions and resented it when she asked one.[35] Another critic has commented: "If I always heeded my own opinions, then I would be of the opinion that Kluge was not such a good filmmaker. But then Kluge would come along and prove to me precisely what good films he really makes. In reality I should have been convinced that he is a brilliant theoretician. But now instead I would be of the opinion that he is a brilliant filmmaker."[36]

More than most filmmakers, Kluge has used public screenings as opportunities to initiate discussions with the audience, which can help shape the immediate reception of the film and the subsequent circulation of meanings about the film. Kluge has sometimes recut films based on these discussions (e.g., *Strongman Ferdinand* and *The Patriot*). Such discussions are conducted in a question/answer format rather than as formal presentations. Kluge is adept at turning questions back to the audience or questioner when he does not care to answer them himself.

One of the most important means for Kluge to control the reception of his films has been through publication of the screenplays for his films. Kluge's early film books were simply printed versions of the filmed screenplay.[37] These were a useful way for viewers to review the films in order to make sense of them.[38] The book for *Occasional Work of a Female Slave* in 1975 marked a change. It included not only the script, but other materials that were not part of the finished film. Of particular interest was a response to feminist criticism of the film, which will be discussed later.

Subsequent film books have included short stories, production notes, interviews, photos, drawings, and other related materials. These are presented in the form of mixed media collages, with varied typefaces and layout to create a stimulating visual experience, which corresponds to the montage style of the later films. All of these books provide the Klugephile with additional information, such as notes on sources, authorial intention, processes of construction, and alternative versions. Although these materials are neither comprehensive nor fully explanatory, they are very helpful in identifying both the original context and the most important aspects of the film images, verbal quotations, and music—often precisely what is missing in the films themselves.

Such supplementary information can be extremely useful to a confused spectator. Many spectators feel that they understand most of the parts of the film, especially the narrative sections, but they are not sure how they all fit together and seek extratextual help. However, both within and outside of the film, Kluge maintains a tension between providing viewers with interpretive information about the film and withholding information so that spectators can make of it what they will. Kluge controls the interpretation both by what he explains and by what he declines to explain. The problems of what such films mean and how that meaning is produced is raised in *The Blind Director*; the journalist interviewing the director says: "I've seen all thirty-two of your films, and I'm very interested in them, but I can't seem to comprehend what is going on in this last film." The filmmaker seems both truculent and baffled himself. He is tired of answering such questions, whether posed by the press or by his own mind. Is there a red thread of meaning or not? Is there a preferred reading? Or can the film be understood on several different levels by different kinds of viewers?

The screenplay of *The Blind Director*, published as *The Attack of the Present on the Rest of Time*, provides answers to some but not all of these questions. It emphasizes the key roles that the city, the cinema, and, above all, time play in the film. The most important exegetical problem is the interrelationships between the myriad individual narrative and nonnarrative fragments in this film. In the book, Kluge suggests that the viewer consider time not only as a thematic link between fragments but as a formal one as well: "The stylistic connecting link, at the same time the occasion for a certain comic effect, which responds to the seriousness of the situation, is the *Category of Time.* Film time, 'condensed dramatic time of the city,' life time—it is understood that there are time battles, which take up whole lifetimes." [39] Thus, Kluge does provide interpretive clues: the shots do have meanings and intended effects. He draws our attention to such devices as fast action/time lapse photography (moving clouds, traffic, and high rises at night) or the abrupt insertion or curtailing of images and sound as ostentatious manipulations of cinematic duration. Similarly his reference to the "condensed dramatic time" emphasizes how his shortened narratives frustrate normal feature film time expectations, where a film must last ninety minutes even if it only contains ten minutes' worth of ideas. The film book is a key method for Kluge to provide information about both the individual details of the film—such as the sources and referents of shots, quotations, and musical excerpts—and about the multifaceted connections and associations that he makes between these various details.

Kluge's theoretical writings and other extratextual interpretive activities distinguish him from most other filmmakers. His articulate explanations allow him to continue to refine or change the meaning of the film after the shooting and editing is finished. For many spectators and critics, it becomes virtually impossible to see the film in isolation from the bulk of extratextual information that is available. Kluge provides ready-made handles, catch-phrases, and interpretive clues to explain what is often abstract or inchoate material. It is much easier for commentators to simply impose his schema on the film and find examples, than to see a Kluge film as it is.

Kluge himself has called into question the relevance of theory to filmmaking: "Theory, which is what you learn at the university, is very important, but it doesn't have much to do with production." [40] While it may not be very important in the production phase, theory may be quite useful in the distribution/exhibition phases. It often seems that Kluge's theory is invented after the fact, to explain what has happened rather than providing a priori principles for organizing experience onto film. [41] Norbert Jochum describes a critic's screening of *The Pa-*

triot in which the reels were inadvertently screened out of order. At
the end of the screening, Kluge explained the problem to the befud-
dled critics and went on to assert, as paraphrased by Jochum, "it really
makes no difference and the film is just as good even with the trans-
posed reels and one could have constructed it so at the outset. Actually it was so good this way, that [I] might decide to have it shown this
way in the future."[42] Jochum reports that Kluge "developed a theory
for this on the spot and all of us wrote it down, it was totally conclu-
sive even for the young critics."[43] Kluge's theoretical and interpretive
material does not explain everything, and may sometimes be too
dense or abstract to follow, but it does provide the critic and spectator
with some insight into the film in the filmmaker's head.

THE FILM IN THE VIEWER'S HEAD

> For tens of thousands of years, there have been films in hu-
> man heads—streams of associations, daydreams, experiences,
> sensory perceptions, consciousness. The technical invention
> of cinema has simply added reproducible counter-images to
> these.
>
> —Alexander Kluge[44]

Despite the clues and peripheral information Kluge pro-
vides to interpret *The Blind Director* and his other films, he explicitly
resists definitive interpretation of his cinematic work. He has often
said that the film in the spectator's head is more important than the
one on the screen. The space between the shots belongs to the viewer,
to make associations not only with other parts of the film, but with
his or her own life experience. Reality is not just relational and contextual, but is shaped by human perceptions. These are controlled by
desires, wishes, memories, and dreams: the fantasy, which protests the
oppression of reality and which fights against fatalism. Kluge argues
that the spectator brings this fantasy to the cinema, and the director
should allow space for it to operate during the course of the film.[45]
"The spectator must simply rely on his sensibilities, allow his phantasy free reign. Rather quickly the spectator will interject his own
memories, his own experiences and above all his own phantasy into
the film."[46] In another interview, Kluge explains further: "The [film]
language is a kind of crystal lattice, which provides the viewer with a
conceptual structure. That is, he develops thoughts himself out of his

personal problems, I only put the tools in his hand. Illusion shouldn't be promoted, but rather the spectator should be led through the specific stimulations, which the films provide him, slowly to a filmic language."[47]

In *The Blind Director,* the film in the spectator's head is embodied in the figure of the blind director, who can no longer see the film on the screen at all, but whose head is full of images. The narrator also emphasizes that the secret of the cinema is that for every image of light there is an equal moment of darkness. Kluge asserts here that it is not just the space, the associations, between shots, but the space between individual frames that allows the spectator to create her or his own film. This claim seems rather unlikely. The alternation between the extreme brightness and darkness, as well as the two- or three-bladed projector shutter results in the spectator seeing the light, not the darkness. The eyes and brain are involved in the processing of information from the light even during the instantaneous periods of darkness. Like Kluge's experiments with double projection of out-of-phase strips of film, this seems another largely ineffectual use of this piece of mildly interesting information.

Nevertheless, Kluge has an additional and more compelling argument against the tyranny of the author in the meaning-making process. He asserts that not every image should be understood completely. "We must make films which thoroughly oppose such imperialism of consciousness. I encounter something in a film which still surprises me and which I can perceive without devouring it. I cannot understand a puddle on which rain is falling—I can only see it; to say that I understand the puddle is meaningless. Relaxation means that I myself become alive for a moment, allowing my senses to run wild: for once not to be on guard with the police-like intention of letting nothing escape me."[48] This seems to be an argument for viewing films on a purely perceptual rather than rational level. This approach reveals a certain kinship with some of the abstract avant-garde films of the 1960s—and perhaps with some videos of the 1980s—where the flow of visual and aural sensations is totally absorbing and without any apparent referential meaning. While few of Kluge's images can be said to be empty of all referential content, Kluge does suggest here one possible model for experiencing his films. The spectator could merely watch the images flow by without trying to comprehend them at all. This would be easier under certain conditions than others: the elimination of dialogue and narration would certainly help—a situation that Kluge often sets up in his interludes between mininarratives. A lack of knowledge about the events and people portrayed would also help. An altered state of consciousness that encouraged sensory rather than cerebral activity would further facilitate such viewing modes.

However, few viewers rely primarily on such strategies for watching Kluge's films. As many film reviews of *The Blind Director* indicate, most viewers see his films as puzzles that must be solved. Nevertheless, it is not necessary to dismiss Kluge's comments as merely a technique for discouraging questions of authorial intent. Kluge may simply be arguing against *always* trying to understand everything: sometimes the less cerebral approach is more appropriate. Certain parts of Kluge's later films seem less meaning-laden and more sensory. The interludes are moments of less narrative or intellectual information. Most often these sequences have no dialogue or voice-over narration to create verbal meanings. These sequences seem to function as breaks in the film rhythm. In some instances, the pace slows down: pleasing and calm visual images are complemented by soothing music. In other cases, the pace speeds up through fast-action photography and fast cutting. An increase in visual stimulation is accompanied by more up-tempo music. The former instances encourage the viewer to relax or may provide an opportunity to reflect about what has preceded this moment, much the same way that Kluge regarded silent film intertitles as a welcome occasion to start thinking. The quicker-paced sequences, in contrast, would seem to encourage the spectator to shift into a different, more sensory mode of viewing. In both types of pacing, however, the viewer is still engaged in some meaning-making, some interpretation, even if at a reduced level. For Kluge, the puddle is an apt metaphor for a different way of perceiving. For the viewer, it is very difficult not to try to understand what the metaphoric function or meaning of the puddle is, particularly when Kluge spends so much of the film commenting on such images.

As mentioned in the previous chapter, Eisenstein's theory of intellectual montage tried to simplify each shot into an unequivocal statement, which could be combined with other shots to achieve a precise effect in the viewer. Whatever overtones or connotations were present in each image should reinforce this effect.[49] For Kluge, images seem to have multiple, often autonomous levels of meaning and varied connotations. This polysemy hinders any linear progression of ideas. As Stuart Liebman has noted: "A range of possible implications ranges over the weave of images and sounds, but the point remains elusive, more felt than comprehended. Meanings proliferate and radiate outward toward other sequences, producing . . . as much perplexity as illumination."[50] Each image suggests a variety of other associations as well as ruptures. Each shot opens onto many alternative pathways that could be followed. The subsequent image is almost never necessary, it is simply one of many alternatives. Sometimes the link between images is purely graphic or stylistic, other times it is expressive of a mood or illustrative of an idea.

The common German literary metaphor of the "red thread" of meaning is mentioned by the journalist in *The Blind Director*. This metaphor seems applicable to Kluge's mode of film construction, because it suggests a meandering, sometimes obscure path. A thread of meaning winds through Kluge's films in various directions, sometimes moving laterally, sometimes doubling back on itself. But the metaphor does not fully account for the complexity of this and other Kluge films. Perhaps it would be better to think of the film as containing many different threads of meaning, winding in various directions, sometimes splitting, becoming tangled, occasionally disappearing and sometimes reemerging later.

Kluge's notion of "letting the senses run wild" does give both the filmmaker and the viewer a new freedom. The director is free to include bits that neither abet the narrative nor constitute the logical building blocks of an essay. Indeed, almost any bit fits. In *The Blind Director,* this is demonstrated by the substantial discrepancy between the screenplay and the actual film. Several planned narratives were apparently never shot. Two screenplay sketches turn up in Kluge's next film. Several important sequences that were not mentioned in the screenplay are included in the film, most importantly the blind director narrative. The finished film contains a clip of the African prostitute, most of whose story is told in *Odds and Ends*. There is an interchangeability of segments between films as well as within each film. This directorial license is very useful for Kluge: both for its pragmatic cost-saving and for its liberating quality. It encourages spontaneity, experiment, serendipity, and the exploration of the unconscious.

This combination of the pragmatic and the spontaneous is particularly attractive to a planner like Kluge who appreciates the role of whimsy and accident: "Meanwhile I abandon myself to the flow of chance. The director can strike precisely at that moment, when he has discovered an accident which is better than any picture I could think up."[51] This spontaneity characterizes both the filmmaker's role in the production of filmic material and the spectator's role in producing meaning: "To bring the thoughts of others into the world spontaneously, that is Socrates' method. This is what I like, too."[52] The viewer is also given permission by the director to find meanings that Kluge himself did not know were hidden there. Part of the creative task is thrust onto the viewer. What Kluge seems to be working toward is presenting on the screen a semiorganized experience, which can then be reorganized by the spectator. But despite the important role of chance and found material, these films are not random or unorganized. The material is deliberately selected, reworked, and mounted together by Kluge. One can contrast this montage style to the random clicking of a TV remote channel changer. Much more thematic and stylistic systematization is present in Kluge's films than one gets from channel surfing.

The problem is that the cinematic experience of Kluge's films is both too organized and too chaotic. Kluge's many interpretive clues, the recurrence of thematic motifs, and the prior training of the spectators all encourage them to seek intentionality. The more educated the audience—and Kluge's is undoubtedly quite well-educated—the more highly developed this tendency and the more adept the viewers are at identifying the multiple connotations—identity, source, and context—of the images and sounds. Kluge himself says: "The threads in my films are not apparent to everybody. These films are made for certain situations. Everybody in these situations knows the context."[53] But who understands the entire context? Some observers have suggested that Kluge makes films only for a select group of his peers, Germans of his age and educational background. For almost everybody else, the films may be too chaotic to organize. Helke Sander has commented: "We don't simply want to be overwhelmed by an unfamiliar chaos, but want instead to organize our own. We must protect ourselves from being overwhelmed by a chaos constructed by another, even as we are pleased by its presence in the work."[54]

A successful encounter with a Kluge film does not necessarily demand a full understanding of the meanings that these images have for the author. As with any text, even classical Hollywood films, consumers with different levels of viewing skills may still derive enjoyment from the parts they do understand and gloss over the less obvious meanings that could be found. This multifaceted approach to film meaning is consonant with Kluge's overall principles of operation, which are inclusive rather than exclusive, eclectic rather than purist. Such an approach is rich in contradictions and allows the filmmaker maximum latitude in the creation as well as the interpretation of his work.

Politics

> For it is a special kind of confusion whenever I measure reality according to the rigid schema of a party position; and it is also partisanship whenever I produce an abundance of images without political differentiation. This partisanship consists then in my not taking a position—one of the most aggressive partisan postures.
>
> —Alexander Kluge[55]

While Kluge's political modernism raises many contemporary issues, he has found ways to do so that do not directly and fundamentally threaten the social order. His associative montage technique and resistance to linear argument have been key factors in enabling—but also limiting—the political impact of his work. His films rarely exhort or take direct political positions. He is the intellectual analyst, not the political organizer. Although often critical of institutions or personalities, Kluge rarely draws explicit conclusions. His style is satirical and ironic, his tools are the curious fact, the searing insight, the behind-the-scenes point of view, and the interesting allegory. Seldom, however, are these utilized in a cumulative fashion to present a strong and clear point of view.

Kluge's most political films are the three collaborative projects of the late 1970s and early 1980s, *Germany in Autumn, The Candidate,* and *War and Peace.* The first seems an indictment of repressive state security measures. It does not, however, directly take up the underlying issue of revolutionary politics/terrorism; rather, it captures a mood of paranoia and repression. One sentence occurs at the beginning and very end of the film: "After a certain point it doesn't matter who started it, it simply has to stop." While Kluge's sympathies seem to be with the young mourners at the Baader, Ensslin, and Raspe burial, the film is far from an affirmation of the revolutionaries' cause. It seems rather a call to all forces in the constitutional democracy to act constitutionally. Miriam Hansen connects this political stance to a modernist aesthetic:

> The films' refusal to adopt an unequivocal stance towards the events, however, is closely related to its politics of perception and concept of montage. Though certainly more accessible than a traditional avant-

garde or experimental film, *Germany in Autumn* to some extent shares
the modernist impulse of Kluge's aesthetics. To project a *Gegenöffentlichkeit* [oppositional public sphere] for and through new modes of
discourse betrays a utopian element, not unrelated to the enterprises
of historical modernism in painting and poetry.[56]

In *The Candidate,* Kluge and his associates become actively involved in the campaign against Franz-Josef Strauss, candidate for
Chancellor of West Germany. Created almost completely from archival documentary material about Strauss, the film nevertheless has a
clearly partisan perspective. Though voice-over narration is added
(much of it not spoken by Kluge), most of it consists of factual background material rather than critical or ironic commentary. This objective approach in general relied on the words and actions of the politi-
cian himself to create a negative self-portrait.

In *War and Peace,* the subject is nuclear war. This is an indictment
of the whole tendency toward nuclear proliferation, particularly in
central Europe and on German soil. The juxtaposition of propaganda
films, nuclear holocaust dramatizations, military celebrations, and
protest constitutes a sharp critique and a poignant plea for change; no
alternatives are suggested, however, and no program for action is
spelled out. In all three films, Kluge is adept at social criticism, particularly of governments and politicians. But the basis of this criticism and its programmatic consequences are unstated in the films
themselves. Too often, Kluge seems to blunt the political impact of his
work with his penchant for irony or obfuscation.[57] Rather than making a point clearly, he prefers to obscure it in an aphorism.

Similarly in *The Blind Director,* the new media, urban life, and time
become interesting intellectual conundrums or occasions for satire
rather than objects of analysis. In a devastating review of *The Blind
Director* in *Der Spiegel,* Maxim Biller calls Kluge to task on this point:

> A divine offscreen voice asserts: "Time cannot make any of that which
> has happened unhappen." Or: "The power of the fate of yesterday lies
> in the fact that none of the participants has the time to reflect upon it."
> Or: "For hundreds of years people have behaved in a makeshift way.
> The present expands itself." Where is this going? Sparkling bon mots
> from the feuilliton, l'art pour l'art, hot air; mystifying circumscription
> of concepts—instead of impaling them with reason, Kluge gives them
> a dark tinder. So they degenerate into intellectual ornaments, without
> sense and content, without any enlightening thrust. The movement (of
> the sixties) has lost its last priest.[58]

This avoidance principle in Kluge has several functions. First, it prevents too much retaliatory pressure on his work.[59] This is a lesson well learned from the Frankfurt School, which was able to keep its social critique in the intellectual rather than the political arena, and hence remain unthreatening and unthreatened in a liberal democracy. Second, the use of irony and abstract aphorisms supports his claim to intellectual and artistic legitimacy and prevents his commentary from seeming simple or shallow. Third, it obviates the necessity of inventing or embracing any specific political program, which would inevitably entail making some mistakes.

Kluge would no doubt argue, with some justification, that such criticism misunderstands his objectives and is not truly democratic in its assumptions. He does not want to be a leader, a model, or an agenda-maker. One major problem for both society at large and for various radical movements has been an overreliance on leaders. The point is rather to organize from below, or, in Benjamin's words, to encourage "consumers" to become "producers" of art works.[60]

While there is indeed reason for Kluge to reject a leadership position, this excuses him neither from making his criticism as sharp and focused as possible nor from suggesting some modes of activity that may be more positive and useful (rather than merely comic and incompetent). It is disingenuous for Kluge to imply that he does not also participate in the making of meaning in his films. The spectator's activity may be important, but it is secondary, both chronologically and conceptually to the activity of the filmmaker.

Irony and Humor as Modes of Meaning

> Parody, reminiscence, and critique can all be subsumed under a generalized concept of irony. I am not referring exclusively to irony as a particularized gesture of language, as a rhetorical device, but irony as Nietzsche understood it: as the period style of the modern world and of its spiritually deprived inhabitants, the epigones.
>
> —Harvey Gross [61]

Despite the seriousness of the themes that Kluge takes up in his films, humor is an essential ingredient in these concoctions. Although the genre of the films seems a cross between documentary and narrative melodrama, they almost always include comic characters and scenes. Much of the humor is satirical and directed toward bureaucrats (teachers, lawyers, judges, administrators) or other self-

▌*Die Macht der Gefühle* (*The Power of Emotion*):The accused

important figures (businessmen, celebrities, policemen). The humor mostly derives from linguistic confrontations and distortions. Already in *Yesterday Girl,* there were several satirical sequences involving the social worker and the other pious religious figures. In *The Power of Emotion,* the examination of the woman who shot her husband brings forth illogical and contradictory testimony that confuses both the judge and the accused herself.

In Kluge's later films, the humorous scenes are most often mock interviews: the opera singer in *The Power of Emotion;* the scrap dealer, Dr. Gerlach, the film director, and the producer in *The Blind Director.* In these interviews, a tenacious but somewhat naive interviewer attempts to extract useful information from a stubborn and opinionated interviewee. This format is one which Kluge knows intimately as a participant. After twenty years as a subject of interviews, Kluge switched to the other side of the microphone in the 1980s. By the time of *The Blind Director,* Kluge was conducting frequent interviews for his private television programs. The interview is perhaps the key genre in this era of personality cults and is ripe for caricature by Kluge, a skilled practitioner of both evasion (as interviewee) and wily pursuit (as interviewer).

Humor is not confined to the interview situation, however. It is often present in dialogues, for example the couple in *The Power of Emotion* discussing love as if it were a financial transaction ("If I love more than you, you owe me change") or the dialogue about marital *Zank* ("squabble") and *Zwist* ("strife") in *The Blind Director.* Sometimes the humor is situational (Ferdinand's antics or the blind director), but in most cases it is linguistic. This play with language is one aspect of Kluge's work that has strong affinities with trends in both modernism and postmodernism. Kluge is an acute observer of the power of language to shape and distort reality, to control situations and people. His parody and wordplay, the shifts in discourse, and the multivocality of his films link his work back to Joyce, Kafka, and Brecht, and forward to younger contemporary writers.

The parody and satire in Kluge's films is an important source of pleasure for audiences. Even the less sophisticated viewers can take pleasure in the mimicry of pietists and bureaucrats. While occasionally the comedy in Kluge's films can result in real belly laughs, more often it simply elicits a smile. Farce is less common than irony, and the irony is typically communicated verbally through the voice-over narration. The distanced, reflective nature of irony makes it an effective tool in Kluge's effort to distance the spectator from the film's action. Whether this leads to any critical thinking by the viewer independent of the narrator is arguable. Spectators are positioned by Kluge outside the narrative and above the characters. The spectators' superiority of knowledge and insight encourages a condescending attitude toward the characters.

The ubiquity of this ironic narration has important implications for the themes and subjects of the film. If the tone is often ironic, it becomes difficult to take anything seriously. The great themes are deflated, and all meaning becomes reduced to the wry smile of a somewhat cynical sophisticate.[62] Every seriously engaged individual seems to become a comic type for Kluge. The ironic commentary on their unsuccessful utopian quests undercuts Kluge's basic assertion that fate is not fatal, that alternative realities are possible, and that tragedy is not inevitable.

Representation of Women

> In the construction of their own new forms, women may well
> react against some elements in modernism and will almost
> certainly challenge some current definitions of what an artist
> does and what her relationship to her audience can be.
>
> —Ann Barr Snitow[63]

One critique of modernist art has been that it was predominantly masculine and excluded feminine voices. For a male filmmaker, however, Kluge has been extremely interested in depicting women and their experiences: most of his protagonists are women. In *The Blind Director,* though only two of the narratives feature a woman protagonist, the mode in which they are presented is typical of the techniques that Kluge has employed throughout his career. This mode of portrayal provides an interesting case to test the degree of control that Kluge exerts in the construction of meaning in his films and exemplifies the ironic distantiation of his work in general.

First of all, the actions of female protagonists are often portrayed as ill-advised, pointless, or merely metaphoric. In *The Blind Director,* both the social worker and the superfluous doctor seem to be emotionally isolated and ineffectual. When confronted by unexpected problems of contemporary life, they seem incompetent to resolve them. Like Anita G., their solution is to flee. Such incompetent/irrational behavior characterizes the female protagonists in almost all of Kluge's films. Despite their utopian goals, they offer neither utopian nor premodern modes of more humane social organization. Nor do they demonstrate any contemporary positive models for emulation or adaptation by women viewers.

Moreover, the characters are singularly inarticulate, further indication of their nonrationality. In the social worker sequence in *The Blind Director,* which runs a total of twenty-one-and-a-half minutes, the main character speaks only thirty-three lines, which constitute only one hundred seconds of the fifteen minutes she is on screen. Her dialogue comes in two bursts: a few sentences rejecting the advances of a blind date, and her persistent attempts to communicate the needs of the child to its new guardian. In the eight-and-a-half minute superfluous doctor segment, the female protagonist speaks less than a minute. Other than reading aloud a medical report (thirty-five seconds), her only other dialogue involves one question about the new doctor and later the purchase of a movie ticket. Nothing in their dialogue directly expresses the characters' motivations, feelings, or thought processes; indirectly, we get only the most general information (anger or frustration) from their words.

What is most problematic in Kluge's representation of women is not just that this minimal use of dialogue deprives them of their own voices. More important, Kluge substitutes for their voices the ironic, detached narrator, who often provides the only clues as to what is going on in the character's mind. In talking about *The Patriot,* Helke Sander argues:

> The protagonist Gabi Teichert, however, is pieced together through commentaries and only rarely gets to speak for herself. When she does open her mouth, she either reads texts to others or attempts to reconstruct the writings of others, such as the *Ode to Joy.* . . . Gabi Teichert, in search of another German history, may roam about the woods with a shovel and dig in the earth, bore a hole into books and saw them up, but she is never allowed to formulate her own questions. She bores, digs, and saws blindly, as it were. The commentary explains to the audience what she is doing and what she means by her actions.[64]

The same could be said for other Kluge (anti-)heroines: Anita G., Leni Peickert, Roswitha Bronski, Inge Maier, Rita Müller-Eisert, Frau Bärlamm, Gertrud Meinecke, and others. The characters seem like voiceless puppets, scurrying around, while the male narrator explains and criticizes their thoughts and actions from a position of omniscience. This, critics charge, is another, and perhaps more sophisticated, patriarchal ploy for depriving women of their own voices.

Miriam Hansen has pointed out some of the problems posed by Kluge's narration in *Germany in Autumn:*

> While Kluge's voice is important to breaking the spell of the image track and disrupting unmediated identification with characters, its own status remains unquestioned. Separated from the body, a voice is more likely to resume functions of authority and closure proper to traditional documentary and narrative genres. In particular, this appears problematic in the context of a sexual division of labor: a disembodied male voice "explaining" a female character who is physically present on the screen only underlines the general dilemma of transsexual identification and projection.[65]

Despite this criticism, Hansen has raised several arguments in Kluge's defense. First, looking back to some of Kluge's earlier films, she has pointed out that he uses a variety of narrators other than

himself. Different voices of different sexes comment on the story in
Artistes at the Top of the Big Top: Disoriented, and, in *The Middle of the
Road Is a Very Dead End,* the protagonists themselves narrate over the
visuals. This polyphony eliminates the identity between author and
narrator, making the commentary less "consistent" and "authoritative."[66] Second, she has argued that even when Kluge himself narrates,
he undercuts his own position of authority through irony, shifting
positions, ambiguity, and the posing of alternative rather than definitive interpretations: "Voice-over comment in Kluge's films often explains less than its reassuring tone suggests; it tends to complicate
the discursive situation rather than to add continuity and closure."[67]
Hansen argues that, by undermining its own authority, the narration
yields up its "control over character intention; the figure takes on a
life of its/her own, as she is engaged in a project that neither narrator
nor spectator as yet understands. Taken as a separate strand of discourse, Kluge's voice-over consistently shifts its stance and mode of
articulation, deconstructing itself as it goes along."[68] She also points
out that much of the dialogue in these films is improvised. The ac-
tresses themselves have a voice in what they will be saying: "In a film
like *The Patriot,* which neither has a script nor gives direction credit,
the dialogues were invented by the actors who speak them."[69] Kluge
has himself often acknowledged the importance of the actors in developing not only their dialogue but even the direction of the film as
a whole. One of his chief recourses against feminist criticism of *Occasional Work of a Female Slave* was to point to the insistent demands
of his sister Alexandra that he change the script.[70] These arguments
by Hansen and Kluge suggest a dispersal of authorial control, which
would create certain contradictions or polysemy in the text. These in
turn would allow or even force the viewer to participate actively in
making sense of these conflicts and multiple meanings.

While Hansen rightly points to the cryptic and elusive qualities
sometimes present in Kluge's narration, and to the improvisatory
quality of the dialogue, one ought not take this argument too far.
First, despite some exceptions, almost all of the narration in Kluge's
films is by Kluge himself. Second, much of his narration is straightforward, providing exposition or direct access to the characters' minds.[71]
Moreover, when character dialogue does occur, Kluge sets its parameters, proposes tentative lines for the actors, directs them, and ultimately selects those lines that he wishes to be included in the film. In
addition, the total amount of dialogue is so small that it constitutes at
best a minor part of the characterization. Lastly, because of the paucity

of dialogue and the elliptical quality of the visuals, the viewer is very dependent on the narrator—whether he is always reliable or not.

B. Ruby Rich, in an article entitled "She Says, He Says: The Power of the Narrator in Modernist Film Politics," argues that the Kluge audience is "thoroughly under the sway of the narrator" largely because of the intentional destruction of illusion and character identification:

> While Roswitha is not a properly constituted character in the realist sense of character unity and psychological motivation, she is nevertheless a compelling presence on screen and the nominal focus of the film. Her persona as well as her distillation of the film's narrative and political concerns do lead to an audience engagement with this "Roswitha." In the best modernist style, such an engagement is then distantiated and fractured by Kluge's devices of narration, extrapolated references, etc. Thus cut off from the characters (who in fact remain a mystery to the viewer, devoid of any visible subjectivity and relieved of all psychology) and from the possibility of identification with these characters the viewer must turn elsewhere.[72]

Modernist theory would suggest that identification is replaced by cognitive, critical activity on the part of the spectator, but Rich argues that this does not happen in Kluge's films. The omniscience of the narrator, who is privy to information unknown to both the character and the viewer, makes him the new object of the viewer's identification. Rich continues: "The narrator, in his display of wit and wisdom, wins the respect of the viewer over the course of the film. The viewer, in turn, repays this narrative generosity with a downright chumminess, uniting in a spirit of smug superiority with the narrator over and against the character(s)."[73] This becomes especially problematic when the narrator is male and the characters female. The male author/narrator "consistently undermines the film's female protagonist."[74] Rich cites several instances in which Roswitha's apparently successful actions are made to look irrational only through the intrusions of a superior narrator's comments.[75]

It is interesting that despite such criticism throughout the years, Kluge has continued to utilize primarily female protagonists and the male voice-over narrator. To some extent, these devices do work to create a critical, active audience—at least among some feminists. However, they do not seem to be encouraging the film in the viewers' heads through indeterminacy. Rather, their contradictions seem to focus the attention of the viewer on the interrelationship between the film on the screen and the film in the head of the author—who is personally present on the soundtrack. Anger and frustration, not fantasy, are stimulated here. Nevertheless, these too are responses that—like visual pleasure, contemplation, curiosity, and surprise—fall within the broad range of Kluge's aesthetic program. And ultimately they may lead to constructive work by the viewer. Stuart Liebman has observed: "A space is thus opened up for the film's spectators, whose efforts to decipher its meanings, fueled as much by resistance as by assent to what Kluge has constructed, will result in their own revisionary constructions, the 'films in their heads.'"[76]

While the themes and subjects of *The Blind Director* constitute only a portion of those occurring in Kluge's numerous films, they illustrate the important role such themes play in holding his montage fragments together. This function is particularly crucial in his later films, where no overall narrative operates to unify the diverse parts. The essay film is more dependent on ideas than are the picaresque narratives of the earlier era. However, the thematic and subject diversity is also important in assuring the complexity and difficulty of these films. If the treatment of the themes were more logical and developed, and if there were fewer themes, then the meaning would be clearer. This would result in a more communicative model of cinema, which Kluge seeks to avoid. Whether the spectator creates his own film from the semiraw material that Kluge presents, or attempts to solve the puzzle of what was in the mind of the filmmaker, or simply gives up because the film is too difficult, the effect is to challenge traditional notions of how cinema should function and what cinema is.

It is important to note again at this point that the cinema that Kluge is rebelling against is not a modernist one. Because of its relatively young tradition and its early application as a mass medium, cinema's artistic status was always ambiguous and less a site of aesthetic struggle than the more traditional artistic media. Because of the strong industrial commitment to a realistic, novelistic mode of film product, modernist experiments were limited, and modernism never became the dominant style and sensibility that it was in other fields. Thus, the prime target of his attacks is the Hollywood feature film, which, he claims, falsifies reality and limits fantasy.

His solution is an active spectator, who is distanced and critical, but also extremely sensuous. It is in his notions of the spectator and spectatorial activity that Kluge seems to be closest to a postmodern sensibility. The spectator is the producer of the film: he or she must be allowed to perceive and enjoy the art work. The filmmaker must carefully refrain from asserting too much control in this process.

Thus, chance is valued as a limitation on the artist's control. The result should be a polysemic art work with an open ending.

To some extent, Kluge does create an open polysemic text, but this is always in tension with a preferred reading, a first reading that corresponds to the author's original stream of associations and connotations. While it is possible to appreciate the film without understanding the mastercode, the presence of a mastercode is felt in the intertitles, the narration, the supplemental books and interviews, and especially in the commentaries and interpretations of popular and scholarly critics. The films are not self-sufficient experiences equally accessible to all, they are not the juxtapositions of readily understandable cultural images. They are difficult and challenging puzzles: boxes inside boxes, for which one must find the proper keys. Although Kluge's films may point the way to a more populist practice that might still be critical, they do not embody it.

The next chapter will examine Kluge's move from the former dominant mass medium, film, into the most important contemporary one, television. In the process, he begins extensive use of the postmodern art form par excellence, video, with all its possibilities of electronic image manipulation. In some ways, this transition into television may narrow the gap in Kluge's work between an elite and a more popular aesthetic. In other ways, this gap seems even more accentuated in the new medium.

6

Kluge on Television

HIGH CULTURE MEETS THE SMALL SCREEN

One cannot simply criticize such a complex system as television through writing, but rather by actually making products oneself.

Don't complain, create!

—Alexander Kluge [1]

On Pentecost Monday, May 23, 1988, following a game in the football championships, RTL-plus broadcast a videotaped performance by a black gospel group, The Golden Gate Quartet. The singers came on stage, a Las Vegas-style nightclub set, and sang such songs as "Michael Rowed the Boat Ashore" to an appreciative crowd of tuxedo-clad Germans, who clapped along in time to the music. As the curtain fell on the quartet, the programming returned to a live female announcer in the studio. Wearing a red jogging suit and running shoes, she was reclining upon a large couch later revealed to be shaped like a giant foot. In German, she welcomed "friends of culture to *Ten to Eleven*, [2] our cultural broadcast under the direction of Alexander Kluge." She informed the audience that this material had never been shown before: "They are documents of their time, and several, via 'trick' of course, have been put in original theaters. Now, unfortunately, some of these no longer exist. *Ten to Eleven*. Good entertainment."

Squeezed between an American gospel group and a deodorant commercial featuring a close-up of a bare-breasted woman running across a beach is Kluge's "cultural window" in German private television. What seems an odd, even absurd, juxtaposition is, on closer inspection, an absolutely logical, if not inevitable, development in Kluge's work, both from an economic and a formal perspective. Kluge's television enterprise is a utopian expedition into the forbidden terrain of private television, the dominant mass medium, the temple of low culture. His self-imposed mission is to upgrade it, redeem it, and in the process keep film art alive until it can flourish again in the twenty-first century.[3] This modernist missionary zeal is both stubborn and adaptable. The same individual who attempted—with considerable success—to remake German film as high art now wields the same modernist forms in the attempt to transform television into an art. This involves reinventing both television and modernism. Comparing himself to the cinematic pioneers Lumière and Méliès, Kluge has undertaken a search to discover the specificity and materiality of television, its limitations and potential. Also like film's forefathers, he must determine which formal techniques, critical practices, and available resources can be adapted to this new situation. All of these questions must be worked out under temporal and financial constraints—not unlike the economic difficulties that have left their mark on his cinematic style.

INSTITUTIONAL CONDITIONS OF PRODUCTION

Alexander Kluge's decision to begin producing television programs in 1984 for the new private television network SAT 1 surprised not a few observers of the West German media scene. For decades he had attacked the commercialism of the entertainment industries and struggled against conservative political and social forces. Now he was joining a consortium of generally conservative newspaper publishers, led by the right-wing tycoon Axel Springer. SAT 1 constituted a direct challenge to the public television networks in Germany, which were accused of being too high brow, too unpopular, and not sufficiently entertainment-oriented. Opponents of private television—including Kluge and many of his friends and associates—had long feared that commercial broadcasting would inundate distinctively German productions in a flood of American and American-style programming: game shows, old Hollywood movies, and reruns of U.S. sitcoms and action shows. In the mid-1980s, Kluge himself rearticulated the media critique of his mentor Theodor W. Adorno to denounce the "new media" as the "industrialization of consciousness."[4] But since 1985, sandwiched between commercials, heavy metal concerts, and soft-core porn movies, Kluge's "cultural window" has reached millions of German homes each week via the private television channels SAT 1 and RTL.

Kluge has always been aware that rifts, rivalries, and contradictory interests within and between private industry and governmental spheres can provide opportunities for creating counterinstitutions and an "oppositional public sphere." His collaborative engagement in the cultural politics of the 1960s and 1970s resulted in broader distribution, legitimacy, and financing for German filmmakers through governmental and public broadcasting entities. In the early 1980s, a whole new set of private television institutions became available for Kluge and his cohorts to march through.

This opportunity presented itself at a critical moment in the development of German cinema. Not only had Kluge's own recent films struggled at the box office, but cinema attendance as a whole was down in Germany. The dynamic force of the New German directors was dispersed. Fassbinder's death, global peregrinations of Wenders and Herzog, and international coproductions by other directors diminished whatever cohesion of vision and values had once been present. The cinema appeared under siege and a strategic retreat by directors into television seemed to Kluge the best prospect for film's survival into the next century.

> If I had a wish, like one gets in fairy tales, I would wish the whole New Media to disappear. Since I can't make them disappear, then instead we must use these New Media to protect the film medium. Since we can only do this through aggressive action, we must take the New Media seriously. We want to develop an island or a show-window of high-quality, exciting programs. Thereby we can simultaneously obtain the financial means to be able to invest again in film.[5]

Thus, Kluge's antipathy toward the television medium and the promoters of private television was not necessarily a barrier to his participation in it, particularly if the political/economic situation was such that he could guarantee control over his program content. This situation came into being in 1984. Forces that had been building for almost thirty years had become irresistible.

Since the 1950s, the courts and the Social Democrats (SPD) had successfully blocked efforts by the Christian Democrat/Christian Socialist (CDU/CSU) coalition to establish private television in West Germany. The arguments for increased diversity and more entertainment had not proven effective. The Social Democrats were strong supporters of a British-style public broadcasting system and feared that the arrival of private systems funded by conservative publishing interests could threaten the character and very existence of the public stations. Market pressures might alter television's commitment to educational and cultural programming, cultivation of German producers, and programming with a distinctive national identity.[6]

In the late 1970s, however, the establishment of private television began to be justified based on economic/technological grounds rather than political and programming diversity. The development of "new media" (cable television, videotext, fiber optics, direct broadcast satellite television) was seen both as inevitable and as essential to the growth of West Germany's high-tech industries. Moreover, direct broadcast satellite technology threatened complete disregard for national boundaries, which had already been encroached by conventional broadcasting in neighboring countries.[7] In this mood, cable television experiments involving private companies were established in several locales in the early 1980s.[8] Despite the very limited success of these experiments, it was clear, at least to Kluge, that there was no turning back, and that an opportune moment for action, *kairos,* had arrived. While the situation was still in flux, there was room to maneuver and create new positions. As a legitimate representative of high culture because of his critically acclaimed cinematic and literary work, Kluge could provide a certain respectability to the new commercial broadcasters as well as insure a certain political and cultural diversity to assuage critics.

Because of his close relationship with the public channels, serving on television funding boards and broadcasting almost all of his films on these stations, Kluge's decision might seem like an abandonment of natural allies.[9] However, Kluge was convinced that the bureaucratic public television institutions were not sacrosanct entities. In comparing public and private television, Kluge suggested that they are like "two different poisons":

That means that I would reject the hypocritical difference between the public system which buys American wares and the private commercial system which buys American wares. . . . I am only saying that the monster of the public system, which is creating a monopoly, will not be healed by the entry of the monster of the publishers' consortium, which strives equally to create a monopoly. There are in fact two monsters which seek to dominate people. I say rather: the public sphere consists of multiplicity and multiplicity consists by no means of monopolies, but of many autonomous, decentralized groupings.[10]

Kluge's solution to the modernist problem of monopolistic media concerns is both modernist and postmodernist: autonomous art produced by decentralized groups.

Kluge's first maneuver into private television on SAT 1 was through a long time acquaintance, Eberhard Ebner, publisher of the *Südwestpresse* newspaper in Ulm.[11] Together they formed Neue Medien Ulm, which acquired a 1 percent interest in the new channel. This ownership position obligated Neue Medien Ulm to provide 1 percent of the programming for the service. Since the independent-minded members of the SAT 1 coalition refused to yield editorial control to a central authority, Kluge, like other program providers, had complete artistic autonomy for his television series, *Stunde der Filmemacher* (Hour of the Filmmakers),[12] which began airing in 1985.

In 1987, Kluge was able to insure an even larger scope to his television operations. In return for terrestrial broadcast licenses in the densely populated (and SPD-controlled) state of Nord-Rhein Westphalia, RTL-plus and SAT 1 agreed to broadcast the programs of another Kluge group, DCTP (Development Company for Television Programs). DCTP was given its own license to insure that cultural and informational programming would be broadcast on the two major private channels. Partners in DCTP included 144 theaters, operas, symphonies, book publishers, and film directors, Spiegel publishing, and Dentsu, one of the world's largest advertising agencies.[13] Kluge himself maintains controlling interest.[14]

Kluge's decision to become involved in television, however, constituted neither the abandonment of his aesthetic standards nor the eschewal of cultural critique for a new postmodern enthusiasm regarding television's rich diversity. He has no illusions that the bulk of programming on private television will be anything other than American-style entertainment fare, which he has long opposed. Of their own volition, these broadcasters will offer virtually no opportunities for German filmmakers. But he is determined to create a space in this new media structure for alternative programming. His allies are the traditional high arts: literature, theater, and opera companies. He

I *Stunde der Filmemacher* (Hour of the Filmmakers): Connection to silent cinema

refers to his programming as a "cultural window" in private broad-casting.[15] Unlike postmodernists, who see culture as a large concept embracing high and low art forms of all kinds, including television programs, Kluge sees culture and television as contradictory terms. His reference to a "cultural window" is a reaffirmation of his commit-ment to the modernist battle against the "industrialization of con-sciousness," a battle which he is waging from within the most power-ful mass medium.

KLUGE MAKES TELEVISION

Once Kluge completed the complex political and legal negotiations to guarantee his "cultural window" in television, he was faced with an even more prodigious task. As a film director, he had produced a total of thirteen feature films between 1964 and 1984, an average of about one hour of film per year. Now, he was committed to producing more programming than this each week. Instead of a film budget of several hundred thousand marks, he had less than DM

5,000 per hour for his first television programs, *Stunde der Filme-macher.* His initial solution to these temporal and financial pressures was to involve other New German Cinema directors in this project. By enlisting such figures as Edgar Reitz, Volker Schlöndorff, Helke Sander, and Ula Stöckl, Kluge not only shifted a large production burden from his shoulders, but also gave the program a broader legitimacy. A rapid opening montage of still photos of New German Cinema directors at work, accompanied by the musical theme from Fassbinder's *Berlin Alexanderplatz,* further emphasized a sense of collective authority.

He soon had to abandon this anthology approach, however. The directors' unfamiliarity with the new medium, the low budgets, and the short deadlines yielded very uneven results and caused Kluge gradually to assume tighter control. Rather than commissioning works, he began to produce shows himself, relying mostly on interviews.[16] Typically, Kluge conducted the interviews himself—often discussing films with other directors or actors and interspersing lengthy film clips throughout the program. For example, he interviewed Bernhard Sinkel about his film biography of Hemingway that features Stacy Keach, and he interviewed Volker Schlöndorff about his production of *Death of a Salesman* that stars Dustin Hoffman and John Malkovich. He also interviewed other cultural figures, especially writers and musicians. The East German playwright Heiner Müller discussed Tacitus in one program, while Karl-Heinz Bohrer, the editor of the prestigious periodical *Merkur,* expounded on the French Revolution and the use of the guillotine in another. Other programs were simply excerpts from films by Kluge or his associates. In general, the choice of subjects for these programs bore witness to Kluge's admiration for high culture: literature, classical music, theater, opera, and the newest "traditional art," cinema.

With the advent of his new license in 1987 and a shift to shorter program formats (twenty-four or fourteen minutes), Kluge's television aesthetic also began to shift. Increasingly, programs began to incorporate material from traditional high culture sources, in large part due to his alliance with theaters, operas, and book publishers.[17] Access to sophisticated digital postproduction equipment at the Arnold and Richter (Arri) studios in Munich allowed Kluge to produce more sophisticated and faster-paced programming. A close examination of one particular program will allow us to understand the complexity, new techniques, and organizational principles that Kluge was able to develop.

PROGRAM ANALYSIS: THE MOUSE AND OTHER STORIES OR 16 FILMS IN 24 MINUTES

The May 1988 "cultural" broadcast introduced by the RTL announcer wearing the red jogging suit was a far cry from the primitive interviews of Kluge's first television programs. Instead of relying simply on the reputations of famous personalities to provide audience interest, Kluge now was engaging the viewer more directly with spectacle: a fast-paced whirl of motion, color, and music.

A tango starts up as four vertically squeezed shots of city traffic at night slide horizontally onto a blue screen: first the top and the third slide on from the left, then the second and fourth slide on from the right, turning the screen into a kaleidoscope of light and color. Then a tinted clip from the famous early film of workers leaving the Lumière factory is followed by footage of Auguste Lumière himself inspecting a strip of film. The image fades to black and then a page-turn wipe brings the white *10 vor 11* logo onto the screen. The tango fades abruptly. A white-on-green title, "16 Filme in 24 Min.," pops on inside a white and black rectangle. Ominous music by Luigi Nono begins and carries through the program's apparent title: *Die Maus und andere Geschichten* (The Mouse and Other Stories).

❚ *10 vor 11* (10 to 11): Auguste Lumiére inspects a film shot

The program itself is composed mostly of clips and still photos from old films manipulated in a variety of ways. In addition, computer animation, television announcers, time-lapse shots of a city at night, and shots of several symphony conductors in action are incorporated. Like Kluge's 1985 film, *The Blind Director,* this program's theme is film history, but with an emphasis on action: trains, car wrecks, airplanes, speed, travel, and finally romance, which is often frustrated or tragic. However, this cinematic theme is here developed not within a feature film, but in the medium that has replaced cinema—television. Hence a nostalgic rather than suspenseful mood unifies much of what is to follow. Formally, the program is integrated by repetition and variation, rapid pacing, and musical selections that unite diverse images.

The cinematic citations in this program span much of film history:

1. The Lumière footage.
2. A clip from a thirties sound film in which medieval soldiers besiege a fortress.
3. A sequence from an early film in which a couple in a car is too preoccupied with each other to see the train that smashes into them.
4. Silent film footage of stunt plane tricks.
5. A scene from a thirties or forties German film about two elegant lovers.
6. A clip from a German newsreel about the closing of a movie theater.
7. Three sequences from Kluge's film *The Middle of the Road Is a Very Dead End* about a romance between two Eastern bloc spies.
8. Shots of German aviators and planes from World War II.
9. Shot from a 1960s black and white film (woman drinking coffee).
10. A clip from the 1910s film showing a race car halt a train by straddling the tracks.
11. The final car crash sequence from Godard's film *Le Mépris (Contempt,* 1963).
12. Documentary footage of an orchestra performing at Bayreuth.

In organizing and presenting this material, Kluge constantly plays with viewers' expectations and mocks the conventions of the medium in which he is working. German television programs are often preceded by an announcer who provides an introduction to the material that follows. In addition to the RTL jogger, Kluge provides another announcer within the program, Sabine Trooger. Not only does she arrive late (five minutes into the program), she proves herself a most unreliable guide. Only after the train crash does she first appear in close-up to say, smilingly, "Nummer drei" (Number three). She returns a few moments later to announce "Nummer vier" (Number four) and then later "Nummer fünf" (Number five). After the next film clip, she comes on again and says "Nummer neun" (Number nine), pauses a moment and says "Nummer zehn" (Number ten), pauses again and says "Nummer elf" (Number eleven). A little later in the program, her function is taken over by intertitles: "Nr. 14," "Nr. 15," and "Nr. 16." At the very end, Trooger reappears in a medium close-up, now with a different hairstyle and dress, to announce (in German): "That was our window program, good night."

Thus, Kluge simultaneously mimics the television style, flouts its conventions, and reveals its constructedness. He does not set up the pattern until number three, skips six, seven, and eight, and then does not edit nine, ten, and eleven into their appropriate positions, thereby showing their original mode of production as one long take. He then skips to fourteen, which is presented not by Trooger but by an intertitle. Her final appearance also stresses the artifice of the program because she now appears in a totally different guise. All of this undercuts her authority and reliability as the announcer and organizer of the material. Although we are promised sixteen films, we are given only twelve distinctive sections of these minifilms. Indeed, upon closer inspection, one can see that the insertion of announcer and titles is arbitrary, sometimes corresponding to a major break between segments, other times not. Some segments contain excerpts from several films, others contain none. Rather than clarifying things, her presence interrupts, subverts, and deconstructs.

The old film clips themselves are manipulated in a variety of ways. The most significant involves the use of a tinted drawing or still photo of an old movie theater as a framing device. In the position of the movie screen, Kluge inserts a moving image—usually a clip from an old film. He uses the stunt airplane footage in this way. First it is shown in a cinema where the screen is fairly large. The film image, about one-third of the television screen, is relatively easy to discern. The clip is shown twice more in different theaters, each time with a progressively smaller screen until the clip is almost too tiny to discern.

This squeezing of the films (in both size and duration) is very self-conscious on Kluge's part. Unlike cable movie services, he apparently wants to emphasize that television does not and cannot duplicate the theatrical film experience. Cinema in Kluge's television programs is always a sample, a taste test, but also a transformation into something

▌*10 vor 11* (10 to 11): Movie still: Two Lovers

▌*10 vor 11* (10 to 11): Movie theater miniature: *Contempt*

new, a fundamentally different kind of experience. And he wishes the viewer to be aware of both aspects of this process.

The car crash from *Contempt* is also first shown squeezed into a minitheater. The second time, it is shown full-screen, but with the image now enlarged so much that the whole sequence seems shot in medium close-up. The shots of Camille's farewell note, which Godard had spliced into the crash sequence, are now removed but the sound-track has been left intact. Since the image track is now shorter, the soundtrack lags behind, out of sync. As the camera tracks past the wrecked car and dead bodies, the honk, screeching tires, and explosion are heard. This second sequence again bears the marks of its construction—it is very blurry and grainy, and the sound is obviously out of phase. By moving back and forth between the theatrical and other forms of presentation, Kluge again underscores the video medium and the process of manipulation.

The sequence in which the race car chases the train reveals another type of repetition and manipulation. Here, the film image is altered so that its mirror image is seen simultaneously—a double exposure. The train rushes toward itself, the car passes through itself, and the two sets of railroad tracks seem to converge. Each image becomes a spectacle as important as the chase being depicted—only more complex and with an internal tension that augments the emotional tension of the plot, even as it destroys the verisimilitude. On the Luftwaffe footage, Kluge performs different manipulations—squeezing and stacking the images and adding animation layers—but achieves similarly spectacular and distancing results. Interspersed with these complex fabrications are other unaltered film clips, intertitles, and animations accompanied by contrasting bits of music often cut off abruptly.

MAKING SENSE—THE VIDEO IN THE VIEWER'S HEAD

How does this distinctive montage style function for the viewer? Unlike most television shows, Kluge's programs do not fit into any familiar genre or preexisting schema. The program guides and on-air announcers refer to them as "cultural programming," but they are not complete performances. Kluge has argued, "One can only bring the arts into television as fragments, as trace elements. A drastic cure is necessary in order to let them revive in this medium."[18] His programs are also much more complex and unpredictable than "cultural magazines." Although appealing to the German respect for high culture, Kluge's productions carry out a modernist aesthetic of radical experimentation, critique, and interaction with popular culture and everyday life. Formally, Kluge's programs are more akin to two genres that have been developed specifically for the television medium: commercial advertisements and music videos. Both genres are normally fast paced, highly edited, and visually rich; but both are easier to understand than Kluge's constructions.

Commercials typically tell a very simple story about a product's qualities or effects and contain a behavioral imperative, either explicit or implicit: buy me! Whatever radical formal elements may be present in the shooting and editing styles of the commercial, the disruptive effects are blunted and recuperated by that clear and unambiguous purpose. Similarly, the fragmented style, radical cutting, and diverse images of music videos are organized by the songs and the personalities of the performers.

Kluge's fragments are somewhat more difficult to interpret. Although in some ways mimicking MTV—or perhaps simply looking to it as the most highly developed instance of a specifically television-oriented style—Kluge does not use the visuals to explain or illustrate the music. Rather, the music is secondary to and largely independent of the visuals, often starting or stopping abruptly. Second, Kluge's individual fragments are not a predictable three minutes in length. Some units are much shorter, others longer; indeed, it is often difficult to distinguish where one unit stops and the next starts. Each unit is not discrete and separate from the previous one but is felt to be related to the others stylistically and thematically (although these themes may seem obscure). Although Kluge's units lack closure and coherence, they interrelate on a fundamental level by being the expression of a single artist, an organizing intelligence.

Nevertheless, in Kluge's television programs as in his films, it is not always easy to interpret the relationship between one picture or series of pictures and the next. In this particular program, the use of the cinema theater as a framing device rather strongly urges at least the one preferred reading mentioned earlier: television diminishes cinema, both aesthetically and as an institution. Nevertheless, it is difficult to understand how, if at all, the subjects of the individual clips support this larger meaning. Are the crashes, for example, to be interpreted metaphorically as a cataclysmic encounter between the two media? Or is Kluge developing a totally separate second theme? Is the viewer's job to keep searching for more plausible explanations or does one ultimately conclude that the content is incidental or was chosen only as characteristic of the film medium? Or does one simply appreciate the rapid-fire sensory stimulation and not try to make sense of it?

Kluge's response to such questions would probably be noncommittal: do with it what you will. Kluge has often spoken of the pleasures to be gotten from the media, which include intellectual stimulation: "The cinema is an institution of pleasures. Above all for the pleasures of ideas."[19] But he also suggests that imagination and sensory pleasures are equally important: "The spectator must simply rely on his sensibilities, allow his fantasy free reign." He opposes the "imperialism of consciousness" that must understand everything.[20] Rather, media should "satisfy the pleasure interests of the viewer. The model is not the dramaturgy of the school class, but rather of the school recess; not the moral instruction by adults, but the phantasy of children among one another, even when the children have become adults, etc."[21] Perhaps Kluge's real purpose is to allow, or even force, the viewer to use a variety of viewing strategies, moving back and forth among them as seems appropriate.

These difficulties of interpretation are both intriguing and discouraging for audience members. Kluge refuses completely to organize the viewer's experience, but this reluctance can easily be mistaken for a lack of organization. Many of his programs utilize the technique of combining fragments of heterogenous but loosely associated material. Often he refers to these as "magazines" in the program titles ("Kurzmagazin," "Minuten Film Magazin," "Musikfilm-Magazin"), which underscore the diversity of components. Many shots recur in different programs, each time edited into a slightly different context. This associative montage finds a place for everything. Even the older, hour-long television shows get reduced into shorter versions of themselves. One critic explains:

> On TV, says Kluge, one can repeat everything, fetch back whatever was developed in the pictorial form of expression, the technique of painting and of the silent film, the film of the earlier and the later years. On TV, he says, one could even create a new cinema, a cinema for the middle-aged group. . . . Television as a reagent tube, in which the accumulated experiences of millennia mix together. Repeat everything.[22]

Yet this repetition is a variation, a transformation of the component images and sounds into new units and a new aesthetic.

Transition from a Film Aesthetic to a Television Aesthetic

Kluge's television work does not embody an abrupt stylistic rupture from his previous film aesthetics. The principles of associative montage, open construction, and reliance on an active spectator are still the dominant elements. The use of interruption, irony, visual and aural citation, and intertitles are all familiar to viewers of Kluge's films. Nevertheless, certain aesthetic adaptations and new emphases are notable in Kluge's television.

First of all, the digital video technologies provide Kluge with a whole new array of aesthetic possibilities, which allow new pleasures and pains for the viewer. Kluge's films frequently utilized montage sequences of still photos, drawings, and brief film clips. Now Kluge is able to create not only sequential montage (between frames) but montage *within the frame:* collages of multiple exposures, superimposed words, and figures. Although Kluge's films had featured irised images—the image within a black circle or double circle (as if through binoculars)—now he can squeeze, tilt, invert, mirror, or wrap images. Instead of expensive and uncertain optical effects, Kluge can play with a series of options until he finds the appropriate effect for a particular context.

> All these possibilities are fractures of pre-existing genres, each of which obeys different laws. When I put this all together, a bit of information results, an invention, made not by me, but by the computer editor, to his own amazement. The mistakes that we or the electronics make in this juxtaposition are in any case rich in invention: seven pieces are rubbish, but one is absolutely thrilling. I would say that more than half of the miniatures that we make we have not invented, but they have just turned up.[23]

The results of these experiments on the small screen frequently run counter to traditional television aesthetics of visual clarity. Kluge's cluttered and fast-paced images often are virtually illegible. At this point, the distantiation device functions so powerfully that it may discourage rather than encourage an active viewer. Some effects are so irritating that they become almost painful. One such trick favored by Kluge is a hard wipe, where a live action shot is pushed off frame by a continuation of the same image, which comes to rest for just a beat before being pushed off by its continuation. When repeated for thirty to sixty seconds, with occasional changes in wipe direction and alternations between black-and-white and color images, the cumulative effect can be extremely disturbing.

A second important factor in Kluge's television aesthetics is the extreme minimalization of narrative. Kluge was never very comfortable with traditional scripted film narratives involving actors. For his television shows he is producing no new fictional dramatizations. Narrative is now described rather than enacted, stripped to its bare bones of plot and character motivation. Often, stories are discussed in interview situations, sometimes presented in titles, or occasionally described in voice-over narration. Clips from narrative films, plays, or operas are still shown, but they are fragments rather than full presentations and are often visually distorted or altered. Rather than providing a video replay of a full, illusionistic drama, Kluge gives us a critical commentary, which may or may not be verbal.

A third difference between Kluge's television and film work is his own presence. In his films, he was often aurally present as the omniscient, ironic author whose sotto voce narration explained and critiqued the on-screen action. In his television programs, he has almost completely relinquished any voice-over narration. Kluge interprets the shift as follows: "The contact with the viewer in television cannot be as private as it still remains in the cinema. . . . The pace of television is too rapid to allow a whispering voice to generate intimacy." [24] Rather than narrating, Kluge has taken up another off-screen role: the unseen interviewer. Rarely is he actually pictured and nowhere in the programs is he identified, not even in the credits. Although this apparent minimalization of his own personality is in keeping with Kluge's modest mien, it may in fact enhance rather than reduce his authority. Interviewees continually look for approval to this off-screen presence, who repeatedly interrupts, finishes thoughts, demands precision of expression, and catches them off guard with personal questions designed to get behind the newsy, public-relations façade that all talk show habitués exhibit.

Instead of the informative commentary of the voice-over narration, Kluge's programs now frequently employ both intertitles and a running band of words at the bottom of the screen. The intertitles are no longer his cinematic white-on-blue words in simple and uniform typeface; increasingly they employ multiple fonts in various sizes arranged at skewed angles on the screen. A 1995 interview with author Heiner Müller presented a number of screens filled with written excerpts from one of Müller's poems; the screens and their contents were arranged in such a way that particular words and phrases were emphasized. The running strip of words is an even more common Kluge device, especially at the beginning of programs, to contextualize or raise questions that will be dealt with in the program. They normally run beneath a series of complex visual images at a rapid speed that makes it very difficult to read them while still deciphering the pictures.

The last and perhaps determining aspect of Kluge's television aesthetic is time. As mentioned above, Kluge must produce a great deal of television very quickly: three programs each week. *10 vor 11* and *Prime Time Spät Ausgabe* (Prime Time Late Edition) run on RTL and *News & Stories* on SAT 1.[25] Since Kluge produces virtually all of them himself, and has significant administrative tasks as well, he must work very rapidly. A normal work week for Kluge involves two days in the office and four days shooting and editing. This means less than two days per program. These production conditions have a significant impact on his aesthetic options. Most of the reserve material in his own archives—old Kluge films and outtakes—has been used up long ago. Programs are altered, recut, and recycled into "new" programs. New footage is commissioned (such as shots of the Eiffel tower for his series of programs on Walter Benjamin and the new "iron age" of the nineteenth century) and book illustrations, photographs, postcards, and other images are collected. Many programs include clips from theatrical and musical performances, honoring his commitment to provide a "cultural window" dealing with the traditional arts and utilizing the resources of his consortium (AKS).

Nevertheless, interviews have remained the staple of his programming, and have in fact become more predominant in the last several years. The complex visual products such as "16 Filme in 24 Min." are now the exception rather than the rule. Interviews can be shot fairly quickly, in a couple of hours, and combined with performance footage or a few illustrations and intertitles to make a program. The editing is relatively straightforward. Even these programs, however, bear the unmistakable stamp of Kluge: jump cuts, intrusive "amateur" visual elements (microphones poking into the frame, a bare light bulb right beside the interviewee's head, shadows across the face, poor sound quality), interruptions, and Kluge's unique, intimate, and intelligent interviewing style. As interviewer, Kluge is both the expert and the canny innocent who can ask the obvious question: "Why did you hesitate when I asked how old you are?" The low production values and ad hoc nature of the interview locales contrast sharply with the more elaborately designed sets and lighting of standard television studio interviews. Even within Kluge's own programs, the unpolished quality of these interviews (most conducted in the kitchen of his offices amidst shelves full of film canisters) proves a stark juxtaposition to the more sophisticated visual sequences he creates through digital video manipulations.

Although the overall objectives of Kluge's aesthetic seem to have carried over from his film work, the new possibilities and limitations of the electronic medium seem to result in new emphases. Viewers are still asked to create new relationships among fragmentary parts, to recontextualize uprooted materials, and to insert their own experiences into the process of meaning-making. But the provocations for this active viewership have altered: a miniaturization of narrative and image, the inclusion of more nonfictional material, a greater preoccupation with high cultural concerns, an increased visual complexity.

As with Kluge's film work, the response to his television work has been mixed. Although he has increased his viewership immensely by moving to television, his programs still attract a rather small audience when measured alongside more conventional programming. Executives of the private channels on which his shows air refer to him as a "Quotenkiller"—a ratings killer. They assert that ratings drop dramatically when Kluge's programs come on.[26] Helmut Thoma, head of RTL, refers to Kluge as a "parasite" whose programs suggest that he "bought out the black-and-white stock of the People's Republic of China: Stone-age television."[27] His objections are a response to Kluge's intentionally jagged constructions and rough textures.[28] Thoma finds it ridiculous that RTL has to broadcast these programs: "as if in the middle of a circus performance suddenly one presented twelve-tone music."[29]

In defense of his programming, Kluge has pointed out that he regularly gets around a million viewers and for some programs of topical interest about twice that many.[30] These figures, he claims, compare favorably to many other shows on private television and constitute a sizable portion of the population, whose viewing preferences deserve accomodation. According to Kluge, the demographics for his programming indicate an audience composed not primarily of media experts or academics, but of adults interested in self-improvement and continuing education programs. Despite the intellectually demanding nature of these programs, such viewers might well be attracted to Kluge's blend of personal life experience, social critique, and diverse cultural forms of expression.

The reception among the critics is also far from unanimous. Some find his programs pretentious, overly difficult, and, ultimately—despite Kluge's rhetoric about the active viewer—didactic.[31] In addition, some critics have scrutinized the financial aspects of these programs, suggesting that his compensation is excessive, and that some of these revenues could be used to support the work of younger visual artists.[32] Other critics, however, have been very impressed by his work. Kluge's cultural programs, according to one critic, "stand out from their surroundings of gameshows and erotic films like a literary bookshop in a redlight district. . . . With their bold contents as well as formal risk-taking, these television feuilletons are the pepper and salt in the program stew of the private broadcasters."[33] Another critic compares Kluge's work to that of Walter Benjamin: "'Ten to Eleven' is not Kluge's audiovisual *Arcades,* but it is proof of the potential endlessness and the depths of a fantastic production situation. One is able to use the whole pictorial universe of film and television, as Benjamin utilized the Paris National Library: to pull together material for a work that would describe and conceptualize an entire century."[34]

Recognition of the programs from other quarters has been equally mixed. His program on Anselm Kiefer's *Das goldene Vlies* (The Golden Fleece) received a great deal of notoriety when it became the subject of a legal case. A fifteen-second depiction of a castration caused church and state authorities to accuse Kluge of airing pornography and of glorifying violence. The courts ultimately found that the program was not censurable and, moreover, it was awarded the prestigious Adolf Grimme gold prize as one of the outstanding television programs of 1991.[35]

Kluge's entry into television marks a major shift in his career. Since his first television broadcasts in 1985, Kluge has produced only one feature film, *Odds and Ends,* itself a hodgepodge of outtakes and miscellany from previous productions, more fragmented and less successful than any previous Kluge film. Although he speaks of television as providing resources for a return to film, he has shown no serious inclination to return to the larger format.

His work in video has, however, become increasingly sophisticated and visually impressive. As someone who did not enjoy working with large-scale production crews or constructing traditional narratives, he is now able to work in a much more artisanal fashion—in a small video-editing suite with one or two technical assistants. He has used this complete artistic control to create complex, often beautiful, hand-crafted objects that incorporate contemporary and historical images and sounds. His imaginative innovations have resulted in programs far different from standard television fare: mini-essays full of sensual pleasures, wit, and the interplay of ideas and historical perspectives. Although the pace of production is relentless, television provides Kluge with ample financial rewards and artistic satisfaction.

The "cultural window" has not, however, subverted private television, won broad audiences, or achieved great critical acclaim. Kluge's television perhaps makes a small contribution to an oppositional public sphere, but its engagement with contemporary and historical social issues is distanced, abstract, and peripheral. It rarely provides a forum for new film and videomakers, the 1990s' equivalent of the Oberhausener outsiders for whom Kluge spoke in the 1960s. Although the other DCTP magazine shows, particularly Spiegel-TV, have generated considerable public attention and excitement, Kluge's have not had this kind of impact.

Nevertheless, Kluge does provide yet another model for guerrilla action against powerful institutions. The contemporary artist cannot wait for a patron, but must make space for his or her own work. Like capitalism, the mass media must expand or die, and this imperative will create opportunities for financing and exhibiting innovative work that has its own integrity. Ironically, he has found an ally in the most thoroughly commodified aspect of the media, advertising: "According to Kluge, the AKS (Arbeitsgemeinschaft Kabel-Satellit) proceeds now as before to produce a public sphere that is as independent of cartels and big business as it is of the public television stations. The great advertising budgets of the world are the only capital that have the financial scope and an interest in attractive, cultural productions."[36]

Kluge's programs serve as both models and encouragement to experimental video producers. If Kluge is actually able to realize his dream of a Europe-wide cultural channel, with a multiplicity of offerings, he may indeed provide a significant public forum for a broader group of producers—including less established artists—and engage a far larger audience than he is now reaching.[37]

FILM AESTHETICS/TELEVISION AESTHETICS

Aesthetically, Kluge suggests that all experience can be organized into art and that film and video have much greater potential than has thus far been tapped. Although his own works have not fully realized this potential, and he admits they may be a bit too "academic," they are nevertheless noteworthy attempts to bridge the distance between high and popular culture without denigrating either.[38] As indicated, Kluge's film and television works differ in several ways from one another. The television programs are shorter, utilize advanced digital-image manipulation, and are produced under more strict time deadlines. More than even his later feature films, they are freed from narrative expectations and can develop autonomous modes of organization and investigation (within financial and temporal constraints, of course). However, the montage principles that Kluge has developed in his feature films are still employed here—often through direct quotation. Because the programs are much shorter, the mnemonic demands on the viewer are much fewer. The pace seems to have quickened, with more elements squeezed into a shorter time frame. Montage within the frame allows for more information and visual stimulation to occur in a shorter time. Kluge still depends on associations and disjunction, tenuous connections, uncertainty, and surprise.

Perhaps the most salient difference lies in the dissimilar modes of reception of the two media. Television's mobile audience—browsing through numerous channels—must be attracted and entertained as well as challenged. Kluge himself speaks of these videos as "amusing" and "attractive programs." [39] The emphasis increasingly shifts to complex visual formation and manipulation. Identification *with* characters is further reduced, but identification *of* images is also more difficult with the spatial fragmentation and recombination of images. Compared to his cinematic work, these television programs present even more visual information for the brain to process, and the temptation for the spectator to lapse into a more passive reception of the flow of images becomes more seductive, especially when they are so colorful, animated, and varied. The anchoring presence of the authorial voice-over has vanished, replaced by an unreliable narrator or a speeding stream of written commentary that competes with the images for the spectator's visual attention. With more complex images and less helpful narration, the possibility of understanding all or even most of the images seems increasingly unlikely. As the images race by, the eye lingers on this or that object, the mind leaps from one aspect to another, ignoring those parts that do not seem to fit or seem less interesting. The modernist artist and art form have been transplanted into the postmodernist medium, and in the process have been accelerated, jazzed up, made more flashy. Increasingly, in his most sophisticated productions, Kluge is providing visual pleasure—something that he has talked of for years, but seldom achieved for most viewers. Now the flow of sensory stimulation is sufficient to carry people past some of the rockier spots of incomprehensibility. At this point, Kluge most closely approaches not only a postmodernist style, but a postmodernist sensibility: a play of visual surfaces.

Perhaps the most important difference from his film work, however, is that Kluge's flow of images has been inserted into the surrounding flow of images, which threaten to—but do not quite—engulf it. Kluge's program with its time-lapse cloud shots may be succeeded by a weather show with similar time-lapse cloud shots, but the context is not quite the same. Kluge still wants to maintain a critical difference, to be more than entertaining: to communicate, or at least evoke an active participation of the spectator. Whether or not he achieves this purpose, the viewer does sense that something different and difficult is going on here. While swimming in the midst of the postmodern stream, Kluge continues to drag his feet on the bottom. He still laments the modern/postmodern condition and attempts to call it to account. Dredging up history—be it Tacitus or Robespierre, Brecht or Hitler, Lang or Godard—he maintains his "attack *on* the present *via* the remnants of time."

7

Recollecting the Fragments

CONCLUSIONS

If we have to lead something, we lead it both as the avant-garde and the *arrière-garde*. The avant-garde is a concept valid for the early bourgeois period, but not for the end of the bourgeoisie. At this time, it may be necessary to be behind and bring everything forward.

—Alexander Kluge [1]

The primary argument of this book has been that Alexander Kluge's film and television work constitutes a pragmatic appropriation of a modernist aesthetic. Its second major proposition is that Kluge, as a late modernist, anticipates many aspects of a postmodern aesthetic, while retaining a fundamentally modernist perspective. This final chapter will summarize the factors supporting these conclusions and then suggest ways that these insights may be helpful for further work on Kluge, New German Cinema, and the modernism/postmodernism debate.

MODERNIST SENSIBILITY, MODERNIST STYLE

Kluge's world view derives from one strain of modernist sensibility that, in this book, is designated "political modernism." This sensibility is inclined to innovation and a break with past tradition, and undertakes a political critique of capitalist social reality. As discussed in chapter 2, this political modernism helped shape Kluge's critique of the German film industry in the early 1960s. He argued that existing film production was too profit driven, completely uninventive, and cut off from contemporary issues and everyday life. The formative experience for him, to which he has referred on several occasions, was witnessing the subordination of Fritz Lang's aesthetic integrity to the economic imperatives of an institutional hierarchy. As a result, the cornerstone of Kluge's cinematic practice and cultural politics became the notion of creative and financial independence: the director as both author and producer. This financial independence meant not only freedom from the constraints of a hierarchical industry, but insulation from the demands of the market. Kluge's practical strategies for moving toward Adorno's goal of more autonomous, less instrumentalized art involved the establishment of public and private institutions, and in effect turning himself into a political/cultural counterinstitution.

As argued in chapter 5, this political modernist sensibility also shaped the subjects and themes that have appeared in his films. From Anita G. on, his characters have moved through a contemporary urban landscape like refugees. With suitcase in hand, the homeless Anita walks nervously past policemen assigned to a building demolition. Ten years later, a similarly burdened and homeless Inge Maier skirts police and students fighting over evictions and house demolitions. Both Anita and Inge are isolated individuals, fugitives from both the law and the intimacy of personal relationships. Kluge's heroines are alienated from the oppressive institutions of contemporary life: big business, big government, and even the family. Most are unemployed. Even Gabi Teichert with her teaching sinecure faces a career crisis. But the silhouetted long shot of Anita or Inge carrying a suitcase across a bridge symbolizes not only flight from the grim alienation of an administered society, but also a quest for utopia, a totally different future. As Leni Peickert remarks, "The longer you wait for Utopia, the better it gets."

Not only is Kluge's work motivated by a modernist sensibility, it is executed in a modernist style, which manifests itself both in the narrational strategies discussed in chapter 3 and the innovative techniques of production and editing analyzed in chapter 4. Kluge's productions reject the fundamental structural device of classical cinema narratives: closure. None of Kluge's films ends happily and none even achieves a sense of culmination (be it positive or negative) that would provide a retroactive coherence to the film as a whole. All end on a tentative note: nothing is gained except experience, but nothing is final, either. Ferdinand in the paddy wagon, Roswitha in the wurst stand, Gabi Teichert staring out the snowy window and thinking about a better history to be made—these are not simply the ends of stories, they are also the beginnings of new stories, sequels that Kluge leaves to viewers' imaginations.

Kluge's elliptical narratives also abandon basic principles of realistic narration: causality, linear temporality, and coherent spatiality. Accident and luck subvert intentionality: Gitti's unexpected death brings Leni the money she cannot earn or borrow; the Beauchamp company decides not to relocate, but independently of Roswitha's efforts. Non sequiturs and narrative cul-de-sacs derail causal progress: characters appear suddenly without introduction and disappear without explanation. Kluge's cinematic time is malleable, not uniform. It can be speeded up, slowed down, interrupted, omitted, projected, and recalled. Transitions and temporal markers are largely absent. Does Anita's story take place over several months or several years? When the same shot of Leni Peickert is used near the beginning of *Artistes at the Top of the Big Top: Disoriented* and again near the end, notions of simultaneity and duration lose their utility. Gaps in time are not smoothed over; dreams and memories are not clearly designated. Locations change without warning or explanation. Anita moves from city to city without any clarification of her itinerary or timetable. Kluge's abandonment of illusionistic, invisible narration results in a more chaotic, jarring reflexivity—a modernist emphasis on artifice and arbitrariness.

In all Kluge's films, further fragmentation of the narrative cohesion occurs through the use of multiple stories. In the later films, these stories no longer share a single diegetic world, but break into mininarratives with no large narrative to organize them. Rather than stretching the limits of the feature-film format, Kluge begins to invent a new format in which the totality of the narrative disintegrates.

However, this narrative disintegration is somewhat contained by the author's presence as voice: shifting and subtle, but also reassuring. The familiarity of Kluge's voice and the information it provides is in tension with the multiplication and fragmentation of the narrative. It reasserts the existence of meaning, of an organizing intelligence behind the apparent chaos.

Kluge's modernist style is evident also in his shooting and editing styles. His loose, cinema-verité style of shooting probes the profilmic situation rather than controlling it or simply reproducing its appearance. The camera reveals hidden reality by looking for the unusual point of view, the fresh image. The random and the haphazard are harnessed to a political agenda that wants to change reality and the audience's relationship to it. This can only be accomplished by direct confrontation with reality—which is a complex of relationships, contexts, and functions—not through an imitation of reality that relies solely on dramaturgic artifice.

Montage is a key element in this process: a method for depicting connections and similarities, for shocking our expectations, for dialectical thinking, and for visualizing the invisible. Lyotard defines as "modern" the art that uses its technical means "to present the fact that the unpresentable exists. To make visible that there is something which can be conceived and which can neither be seen nor made visible."[2] Kluge speaks similarly of the potential of montage: "Since a relation exists between two images and the movement (the so-called filmic) remains between the two, information is hidden in this cut, which could not be captured in photographing a shot. That means that montage is concerned with something totally different than is a film, which consists only of raw material."[3] Kluge's editing maintains a tension between two different modernist montage styles: associative and dialectical. Montage is also a key method of reflexivity—by rejecting Hollywood's seamless editing style, Kluge emphasizes the constructedness (and thus the conditionality) of this work of art.

MODERNISM ON THE CHEAP

Kluge's style is not merely the product of an aesthetic program, it is a pragmatic solution to economic and organizational imperatives. Although the modernist sensibility may set certain general parameters, the particulars of Kluge's approach are shaped by his limited finances. The *Autor* must work cheaply and without the technical and human resources available to an industry director. A jack-of-all-trades—writer, director, producer—the *Autor* cannot afford to specialize in any one. Kluge claims proudly to be an amateur—both underpaid and inexpert. He contends that a lack of expertise contributes to the variance from dominant norms. According to the modernist logic of Adorno, one's incapacity to hide the signs of construction becomes a badge of pride rather than a sign of incompetence and fail-

ure. An eclectic approach using found materials is much more pragmatic than a systematic and pure form of modernist practice, which
would demand a rigorous and precise execution.

Kluge's eclecticism and opportunism are carried out like guerilla
warfare, seizing whatever is at hand to make art. This cultural jujitsu,
which turns the established institutions' own strengths against them,
anticipates strategies of subversion from within that have been undertaken by postmodern artists. Artistic autonomy comes not from physical distance, but from resistance in the midst of economic and cultural
contradictions. Private television and advertising can be exploited to
deliver critical programming to mass audiences.

THE EARLY POSTMODERNIST?

Despite Kluge's own pronouncements, some critics
might conclude that he is really a postmodernist in modernist clothing.[4] Four major aspects of his work would seem to support this
contention: his heterogenous style, his polysemic polyphony of voices,
his insistence on spectator autonomy and pleasure, and his utilization of mass media. For many commentators, heterogeneity of material and style, such as Kluge employs, are the hallmarks of postmodernism. Jim Collins asserts: "The issue of eclecticism becomes
perhaps the central issue in the debate over Post-Modernism, since it
is not only a matter of stylistics, but politics, in regard to both textual
practice and the critical approaches that have been brought to bear."[5]
Collins argues that high modernism, as characterized by the international style of architecture, sought only stylistic purity, ignoring "the
fragmentation and conflicted nature of contemporary culture."[6]

The stylistic analysis in chapter 4 argued that such heterogeneity
of form and materials characterizes almost all of Kluge's films. Kluge's
eclecticism and improvisation have caused him to juxtapose fictional
with documentary and instructional modes; to mix film, video, still
photos, and graphic media; to combine comedy, melodrama, and
crime genres; and to recycle his own and other images into a complex weave of intertextuality. The last half hour of *Odds and Ends* is a
good example: the "Summer 1986" sequence combines fast-action,
stills, and computer graphics; the shots of a NATO official are followed
by the fall-out shelter film; different genres as well as archival footage
are mixed in the story of Max and the African prostitute; and these

two characters have both appeared in the previous Kluge film (although Max's profession has changed). This form of parodic assemblage looks very similar to the pastiche and bricolage celebrated in postmodernism.

Another similarity to postmodernism is the way that Kluge's films present multiple points of view, variegated discourses, conflicting voices. Collins characterizes as "one of the fundamental tenets of Post-Modernism" the notion that "only by confronting the conflicting discourses we use to structure experience can we begin to understand what is actually at stake in the structuring process. Only then may we begin to see that no hierarchy of discourses or 'cultural orchestration' makes that process automatic in contemporary cultures."[7] *Artistes at the Top of the Big Top: Disoriented*, for example, is full of contrasting discourses: multiple narrators; nonfictional interviewed subjects; and the speech of the characters. These practices tend to decenter and disperse meaning. When combined with fragmented, open narrative structures, the result is a polysemic text: one that might equally be claimed as modernist or postmodernist. Kluge's parodic interviews and nonsensical dialogues not only suggest Joyce or Beckett but also the heteroglossia, the playful subversiveness, the knowing sophistication of Max Headroom.

Perhaps most important is Kluge's theoretical insistence on the primary role of the viewer. The concept of the "film in the head of the spectator" is wholly consonant with the decentralized notions of postmodernism. Meaning is not simply imposed from above, but results from the activity of the individual viewers, who make choices and organize their experiences. Collins elaborates: "Here the activity *of* the subject is as important as activity *on* the subject, whereas previous conceptions have emphasized only the latter. Due to the bombardment of conflicting messages the individual subject *must* be engaged in the process of selection and arrangement."[8] Kluge's practice of combining discussions with screenings indicates a responsiveness to users' needs that seemed lacking in many manifestations of high modernism.[9] Kluge also suggests different modes of reception and a variety of audience uses. In his acceptance of the pleasure-giving capacity of art, Kluge seems to move beyond the modernist dourness that Adorno displays in the following comment:

> At this point one cannot help realizing just how meager the concept of aesthetic enjoyment really is when we compare it with drunkenness— so meager, in fact, that what it stands for does not even seem worth

going after. . . . The concept of aesthetic enjoyment was a bad compromise between the social essence of art and the critical tendencies inherent in it. Underlying this compromise is a bourgeois mentality, which, after sternly noting how useless art is for the business of self-preservation, grudgingly concedes to art a place in society, provided it offers a kind of use-value modelled on the phenomenon of sensuous pleasure. This expectation perverts the nature of art as well as the nature of real sensuous pleasure for art is unable to provide it.[10]

For Kluge, experiencing art can constitute, among other things, sensuous pleasure. Art can also function as entertainment: "In its constitutive phase the cinema created a robust rule of thumb: films must have an experiential content and they must satisfy the spectator's interest in entertainment. . . . This pleasure is a reliable corrective: it is not a means of moral control."[11]

The confluence of all these postmodernist affinities is nowhere more evident than in Kluge's television productions, which resemble the programs that surround them in some ways. In addition to the fast-action clouds in the weather show, which seem like quotations from Kluge, the elliptical editing of the advertisements—sometimes with hand-held camera work—mimics Kluge's early narrative style. The heavy metal music program that often follows *10 vor 11* contains montage editing and electronic effects—solarization and polarization, alternation of black and white and color, the introduction of animation, multiple simultaneous images—similar to Kluge's techniques and in a similarly reflexive manner. In turn, Kluge's efforts to condense opera into mininarratives consciously imitates the narrativization of music that is occurring on MTV. Kluge's television-style announcer, who is present not only in many of his television shows but also in his last film, constitutes his mocking imitation of the medium that has itself learned so much from modernist practices.

THE LAST MODERNIST

Yet for all the similarities in Kluge's work to both mainstream television and to postmodern art in general, important differences remain. In categorizing Kluge's work as modernist or postmodernist, the presence of particular stylistic features, such as mixed genres and media, is less important than the system in which they operate and the functions that they serve. Eclecticism and heterogeneity are not postmodernist innovations, but have characterized many modernist works as well. It is a critical, political modernism that informs Kluge's productions. There is still a message—even in Kluge's refusal to communicate an unequivocal message—a nostalgic sadness in his comedy, and a purpose in his purposelessness. Traces of an Enlightenment mentality are ineradicable: "We quite agree with him [Habermas] about the necessity of the process of enlightenment, of the need for a new encyclopedia."[12] Although utilizing television, Kluge holds back from a full interaction with or integration into contemporary mass culture: "I can only influence a mass medium through a counter-mass medium. An entire public sphere through a counter-public sphere."[13] The popular culture artifacts that Kluge incorporates are largely historical rather than contemporary: the mass media are mediated, defamiliarized. Similarly, the station's announcers bracket off Kluge's program from the rest of the program flow as something different: "And now for our cultural broadcast." Kluge is culture written large—different and apart from the ordinary form of mass culture that surrounds it. His discussions with literary authors, social theorists, historians, astronomers, musicians, and classical scholars are not merely a plea for cultural diversity, but are designed to upgrade the medium. His programs bear the tradition of rationality; they constitute efforts to use a new medium to find solutions to social and intellectual problems. Although women are sometimes numbered among Kluge's guests, most are male and German, and almost all are white.[14] These are established figures within the intellectual community. The marginal, the minorities, and the young are much less represented.

Not only Kluge's interview programs, but even his more visually and acoustically attractive television programs, are distinguishable from the flow of programming that surrounds them. Kluge continues to play sophisticated games with his audiences: he suggests intentionality and the possibility of making sense of these images, yet his disruptive/associational style moves so quickly and combines so many diverse, unpredictable, and esoteric allusions that most viewers have difficulty making connections. Kluge provides sensory pleasures and yet teases or frustrates the intellect. He may have moved to the most "mass" medium, but he is still making high art according to modernist principles.

Ultimately, few rewards attend the effort to characterize particular elements of style as either modern or postmodern. Such an exercise was more useful in separating modernist art from either classical high art (realistic, representational) or from those popular media forms that carried narrative and representational forms into the modern period: radio, film, television, and the popular song. No longer are anti-representational and anti-illusionistic techniques necessary and sufficient to assure an artistic integrity and a political effect: MTV clips can employ any defamiliarizing techniques without necessarily overturning any social relations. Modernist forms and a new and widely used vocabulary capable of articulating many different kinds of messages are available to all.

As Collins himself has pointed out, the shock of these forms has largely worn off:

> For the avant-garde to be meaningful it must remain a relative term, yet those so desperate to label Post-Modernism as "neo-conservative" would de-relativize it by insisting that Modernism is the perpetual avant-garde, outside that field of tension [between tradition and innovation, mass culture and high art], resulting in a frozen set of stylistic features that are supposedly able to provide "the shock of the new" throughout infinity, when they actually remain as fresh as Miss Havisham and her wedding cake, attempting to step outside of time as the only alternative to having been rejected.[15]

But when one looks at the systems in which these forms operate, and at the purposes to which these systems are put, certain differences are still discernable. That is, if these forms are employed in a critical fashion, then they maintain a connection to the political modernist tradition.

The tension between modernism and postmodernism in Kluge's work can be located most clearly in his attitudes toward the mass media and the spectator. On the one hand, he retains the modernist skepticism toward the media; on the other, he sees them as a tremendous tool available to him. They attempt to enforce unanimity and univocal expression, yet they are susceptible to many different uses. If only in a warped way, they reflect needs and desires of the audience.

Kluge insists on his viewers' autonomy, and yet he has little confidence in their capacity to differentiate, to make their own meanings from all texts. Although Kluge himself as a spectator was able to use action films as a site for critical thought, in his own films he must prompt the spectator to thought through modernist alienation.[16] Implicit here is an acceptance of Adorno's notion of passive spectatorship as a norm that can only be surmounted by modernist production techniques. More than Adorno, Kluge sees the importance of different modes of viewing and embraces the possibility that media entertainment and pleasure are positive things—and yet he hesitates to provide the viewers with easy pleasures: he refuses them action, identification, and closure. Kluge insists that even their pleasures must be connected to intellectual processes: "The cinema is an institution of pleasure. Above all for the pleasures of ideas!" [17]

Many of the tensions and problematics in Kluge's work correspond to unresolved issues in postmodern theory and practice as well. Implicit, for example, in Collins's book, despite his intentions to the contrary, is a sense that serious art (by Laurie Anderson, Manuel Puig, Hans-Jürgen Syberberg) is more worthy of consideration than less self-conscious productions. Can and should postmodern art be critical without lapsing into modernism's binarisms? If there is no dominant culture, but simply many decentered cultures, then what is this art critical of—other than modernism? If there is no dominant culture, what contextual limits and constraints, if any, are imposed upon the producer and production? Can postmodern art be difficult or must it be engaging and accessible? If there is no place to stand outside of society, is there a place to stand within it?

Much of the polemical fervor in the debate between advocates of modernism and postmodernism has already diminished, and it will undoubtedly continue to do so. At a later date, it may be possible to distinguish more clearly both the continuities and differences between these two tendencies. No doubt many modernists will, like Charles Jencks, reemerge as postmodernists, carrying with them both wanted and unwanted remnants of modernism. Perhaps the elusive and unpredictable Kluge will proclaim in his next interview that he has been a postmodernist all along—but a particular kind of political, critical postmodernist. Or, more likely, Kluge and others will continue to defend modernism, while expanding that concept to fit changed texts and contexts. It is important to note that real battles are being fought here; but on any given issue, allies may be found in both camps. The complexity and contradictions within each concept must not be oversimplified, and neither should be used as the other's whipping boy. Rather, each should be seen as a useful antidote to the other, as a correction of the other's excesses and lacks. From Kluge, one can learn that "the only way to make no mistakes is to do nothing." One cannot remain aloof from the mass media so as to remain untainted. Much more so than high art, the mass media are the most important sites for the control of meaning today. We can also learn from Kluge that resistance can take place anywhere at any time—no consciousness is so industrialized that it cannot resist.

Nevertheless, Kluge has not been able to realize the full implications of his aesthetic program. If Kluge's engagement with popular culture were more intimate, if his productions were more playful and less difficult, if narrative and representation were less suspect, Kluge's impact on contemporary society would have been far more powerful and widely felt.

This study has attempted to apply a critical approach to the work of Alexander Kluge. Previous commentators, particularly Miriam Hansen, have provided excellent interpretations of Kluge's work, demonstrating interrelations between his films and his writings, between his practice and his theory. Such scholarship has won much wider audiences for his work in this country.

Building on such pioneering work, this book has attempted to examine Kluge's films closely, often from a production perspective, to understand how all aspects of his total praxis—filmic, theoretical, and political—have supported and sometimes contradicted one another. In particular, this examination has focused on certain tensions in his work, the relation between high and popular culture, between modernist and postmodernist practices. This analysis has tried to connect his work to both its sources and influences and to the new sensibilities and modes of expression that can be glimpsed in his solutions to modernist dilemmas. These solutions have been reached within significant economic constraints that have limited his choices and inflected his productions.

Much work remains to be done, particularly on the economic and political contexts of Kluge's production and on the aesthetic and political tensions within his texts. Moreover, Kluge's oeuvre is by no means complete. Not only are new works being constantly produced, but his theoretical perspective is constantly shifting. Kluge's eclecticism never rests. While he abandons little of the past, the addition of new vocabularies, new concepts, and new stories constantly reinterprets and rearranges his entire collection. As a subject of study, Kluge remains a lively, moving target. Kluge continues to be astonishingly productive both as a producer and as an interpreter of his work, two roles that the scholar must carefully distinguish. Neither Kluge's creative work nor his commentary about it should be viewed alone, and one cannot accept either—or their relation—uncritically.

This study also has some implications for future research in postwar German film as a whole. Kluge was not merely a midwife at the birth of New German Cinema—he continued to nurture it over the next twenty years. This activity was not purely altruistic. Kluge's own film practice was largely financed by the institutional relations—with federal, state, and local governments; television; and private industry—he helped establish. It is important to see the economic and pragmatic considerations that informed, and continue to inform, not just Kluge's work but that of the other independent directors who were his contemporaries and successors. Despite similarities of working conditions, however, the other New German directors did not necessarily share Kluge's utopian vision of film's potential, and they never really accepted the filmic style and polemic he promoted. Kluge intentionally created an impression of solidarity through his use of "we," his insistence on a united front, and his refusal to criticize his comrades even when their style, subject matter, and, later, their funding were much more similar to Hollywood industrial filmmaking than to his own.

Finally, this study suggests that modernism is neither dead nor hopelessly outdated, but that it continues to exercise significant influence, sometimes within and sometimes outside of postmodernism. Both concepts are sufficiently broad—covering matters of style, attitude, materials, and context—that many individual artists and art works arguably could be placed in either category. While many scholars are currently struggling to draw a clear line between the two, it may be more useful to posit a more complex relation of borrowing and reworking, as well as rejection. This is particularly true of late modernists, such as Alexander Kluge, who find themselves in the odd position of rearguard avant-gardists, defenders of a peculiar sort of tradition, one committed to iconoclasm and innovation.

Notes

Introduction

1. Andreas Kilb, "Der lange Abschied des Herrn K.," *Die Zeit* (Hamburg), 24 June 1988, 41. This and all other quotations from German sources have been translated by the author unless otherwise noted.

PART I: Surveying the Modernist Terrain

1. Ned J. Davison, *The Concept of Modernism in Hispanic Criticism* (Boulder, Colorado: Pruett Press, 1966), 6; quoted in Matei Calinescu, *Five Faces of Modernity* (Durham, N.C.: Duke University Press, 1987), 73.

2. Alexander Kluge, interview by author, Munich, January and July 1988.

3. Stuart Liebman, "On New German Cinema, Art, Enlightenment, and the Public Sphere: An Interview with Alexander Kluge," *October,* no. 46 (fall 1988): 57.

4. Kluge is perhaps also positioning himself with his friend Jürgen Habermas (another heir of the Frankfurt School) in his debate with Jean-François Lyotard about postmodernism. See Peter Dews's introduction to Habermas, *Autonomy and Solidarity: Interviews* (London: Verso, 1986), 1–34. The Frankfurt Institute for Social Research, which is commonly referred to as the Frankfurt School, included a number of scholars from different disciplines. In this book, the term primarily refers to the work of Theodor W. Adorno and, to a lesser extent, Max Horkheimer, the two central figures of the institute, whose book *Dialectic of Enlightenment* contains the seminal chapter, "The Culture Industry: Enlightenment as Mass Deception" (New York: Continuum, 1987).

Chapter 1: The Artist as Activist

1. Theodor W. Adorno, *Aesthetic Theory,* trans. C. Lenhardt, ed. Gretel Adorno and Rolf Tiedemann (London and New York: Routledge and Kegan Paul, 1984), 29.

2. Adorno was also an intimate of Schönberg and his Vienna circle of composers. Martin Jay, *Adorno* (Cambridge: Harvard University Press, 1984), 27.

3. Kluge first encountered Adorno in a reading room at the University of Frankfurt, the same hall depicted in Kluge's film *Abschied von gestern* (*Yesterday Girl,* 1965–

1966). Having read descriptions of Adorno, Kluge kept staring at him to ascertain whether this was really the man. Adorno came up to him, they started talking and became acquainted. Kluge was at the time working in the office of Hellmuth Becker and was able to do a favor for Adorno and their friendship grew.

4. Andreas Huyssen, *After the Great Divide* (Bloomington and Indianapolis: Indiana University Press, 1986), 217.

5. Alexander Kluge, *Gelegenheitsarbeit einer Sklavin: Zur realistischen Methode* (Frankfurt am Main: Suhrkamp, 1975), 222.

6. For example, Wolfgang Schivelbusch, *The Railway Journey: The Industrialization of Time and Space in the 19th Century* (Berkeley: University of California Press, 1986) and Georg Simmel's famous essay, "The Metropolis and Modern Life," in *Social Sciences III Selections and Selected Readings,* vol. 2, 14th ed. (Chicago: University of Chicago, 1948).

7. Even the Futurists or Constructivists, who were enthusiastic about the technological possibilities of modernization, showed an impatience with the status quo and an insistence on rapid social change.

8. See for example Lionel Trilling, *Beyond Culture* (New York: Viking, 1965), xiii ff.

9. Lionel Trilling, "On the Modern Element in Modern Literature," quoted in Malcolm Bradbury and James McFarlane, eds., *Modernism* (London: Penguin, 1976), 41.

10. Marshall Berman argues that this negativity is only one dimension of modernism. In the nineteenth century, the great modernists combined a radical critique of modernity and modernization with a more positive assertion of man's capacity to come to grips with industrialized society, to shape a new society that would serve rather than sacrifice mankind. Berman feels that twentieth-century modernist writers were more polarized: falling into either a futurist worshiping of the machine or a totalizing negativity that saw a crushing of human spirit by the forces of an administered society. The best modern art, Berman claims, has the critical edge of negativity combined dialectically with a vitality of optimism, in the face of despair. Marshall Berman, *All That Is Solid Melts into Air: The Experience of Modernity* (New York: Simon and Schuster, 1982), 24.

11. Ibid., 21.

12. Cf. Kluge, *Gelegenheitsarbeit einer Sklavin,* 220, 208.

13. Berman, *All That Is Solid Melts into Air,* 31.

14. Ibid.

15. Clement Greenberg, for one, has questioned the extent of this rupture with tradition: "But for the most part it remains only ostensibly a break, and only ostensibly radical. Actually, it's a dialectical turn that works to maintain or restore continuity: a most essential continuity: a continuity with the highest ethical standards of the past. It's not particular past styles, manners, or modes that are to be maintained or restored, but standards, levels of quality." Clement Greenberg, "Necessity of 'Formalism,'" *Lugano Review* (October 1972): 105. Moreover, individual modernists may find their own tradition or at least kindred spirits within the cultural tradition, such as the Surrealists' interest in Lautréamont for example.

16. Not all modernists were opposed to mass culture (e.g., the Surrealists). Not coincidentally, Surrealism was one of the strains of modernism to which Adorno was least sympathetic. Cf. Adorno, *Aesthetic Theory,* 44, or Jay, *Adorno,* 129.

17. Clement Greenberg, *Art and Culture* (Boston: Beacon Press, 1961), 10.

18. Adorno's dialectical analysis did, however, detect vestiges of resistance even in culture industry products: "The culture industry does retain a trace of something better in those features which bring it close to the circus, in the self-justifying and nonsensical skill of riders, acrobats and clowns, in the 'defense and justification of physical as against intellectual art.'" Horkheimer and Adorno, *Dialectic of Enlightenment,* 143. Similarly, even autonomous art is not completely exempt from the conditions of modern society.

19. Kluge, *Gelegenheitsarbeit einer Sklavin,* 196.

20. Adorno stresses the importance of autonomous art as the only valid aesthetic resistance to administered society: "The uncalculating autonomy of works which avoid popularization and adaptation to the market, involuntarily becomes an attack on them. The attack is not abstract, not a fixed attitude of all works of art to a world which will not forgive them for not bending totally to it. The distance these works maintain from reality is in itself partly mediated by that reality. The imagination of the artist is not a creation *ex nihilo;* only dilettanti and aesthetes believe it to be so. Works of art that react against empirical reality obey the forces of that reality, which reject intellectual creations and throw them back on themselves." Quoted in Ronald Taylor, ed., *Aesthetics and Politics* (London: NLB, 1977), 190.

21. Adorno, *Aesthetic Theory,* 334.

22. Alexander Kluge quoted in "Interview" by Ulrich Gregor, in *Herzog/Kluge/ Straub,* ed. Peter W. Jensen and Wolfram Schütte (Munich: Hanser, 1976), 158.

23. Frank Schirrmacher, "Angriff der Gegenwart auf die Zeit," *Frankfurter Allgemeine Zeitung,* 14 February 1992.

24. As Edward Lucie-Smith comments: "Modern art arose in an elitist context—it consciously addressed itself to the few. Art retreated from public Salons and Academies and passed into the hands of the private dealer. When modern art was seen in some conspicuously public place—for example, at the famous Armory Show in New York in 1913—the aim of the organizers seems to have been to shock the public as much as it was to inform them." Edward Lucie-Smith, *Art in the Seventies* (Ithaca, New York: Cornell University Press, 1980), 92.

25. In some cases, such as the surreptitious introduction of fake electrical outlets into the Museum of Modern Art, the game may be to *find* the art work.

26. Adorno, *Aesthetic Theory,* 35, 55.

27. Juan Marinello quoted in Calinescu, *Five Faces of Modernity,* 74.

28. Greenberg, *Art and Culture,* 6.

29. Hauser stresses both the technological nature of the medium and its social content and function. "The media of mass art are the products of the most up-to-date technical developments: its presentation is produced by mechanical means and is suited to the production of effects which can be reproduced under any circumstances at all. Of course every individual piece of music and every painting can be reproduced, but they are not conceived for this purpose. Works of mass art—on film, in radio, and in television—are on the other hand not only capable of being reproduced but created in the spirit of reproduction and made to be reproduced. They have the industrial character of consumer goods and can be taken care of in the category of business known as the 'entertainment industry.'" Arnold Hauser, *Sociology of Art,* trans. Kenneth J. Northcott (Chicago and London: University of Chicago Press, 1982), 597, 607.

30. Kluge has said that his work is an effort to confront contemporary reality

with opera, which represents for him both historical/cultural tradition and the "power station of emotion."

31. As Calinescu points out, this has been the case especially in the United States.

32. "At the same time, the avant-garde in the arts soon came to identify itself with the political avant-garde, and this identification was confirmed by the events of the First World War and the Russian Revolution. The abortive courtship between the Surrealist movement, led by Andre Breton, and the Russian and French Communist parties, is one of the dominant themes in the story of art in the period between the two world wars." Lucie-Smith, *Art in the Seventies,* 93. See also Greenberg, *Art and Culture,* 5.

33. Calinescu also distinguishes between these two avant-gardes. "The main difference between the political and artistic avant-gardes of the last one hundred years consists in the latter's insistence on the *independently* revolutionary potential of art, while the former tend to justify the opposite idea, namely that art should submit itself to the requirements and needs of the political revolutionists." Calinescu, *Five Faces of Modernity,* 104.

34. Ibid.

35. "The most prominent students of the avant-garde tend to agree that its appearance is historically connected with the moment when some socially 'alienated' artists felt the need to disrupt and completely overthrow the whole bourgeois system of values, with all its philistine pretensions to universality. So the avant-garde, seen as a spearhead of aesthetic modernity at large, is a recent reality." Ibid., 119.

Calinescu also quotes Roland Barthes who describes the avant-garde as the bourgeoisie's "violent protest turned against itself; initially by an esthetic violence against the philistines, then, with the increasing commitment, by an ethical violence, when it became the duty of a *life style* to contest the bourgeois order (among the surrealists, for example); but never by a political violence." Ibid., 120.

36. Although he gives examples of avant-garde artists, such as the Dadaists and Surrealists, Bürger never completely identifies those artists who fit his definition. For example, he does not refer to Brecht as a member of the historical avant-garde, although other commentators who seem to accept Bürger's distinctions, do explicitly include him. Peter Bürger, *Theory of the Avant-Garde* (Minneapolis: University of Minnesota Press, 1984).

37. Calinescu argues that the avant-garde succeeded too completely, that the notion of avant-garde became a part of everyday life after World War II and that its disruptive, shocking quality became merely amusing. Calinescu, *Five Faces of Modernity,* 122.

38. These productions have been regarded both as oppositional toward conventional practices and norms, and as forerunners of what will come to be standard practice. This is, in fact, often the case, where anomalous innovations become codified, integrated, and incorporated into Hollywood or, more recently, MTV productions.

39. Huyssen, *After the Great Divide,* xvii.

40. Ibid., ix. Huyssen thus goes even further than Bürger in evacuating important artists and movements from the modernist camp and turns much of his critique against "late" or "high" modernism.

41. I first saw *Krieg und Frieden* (*War and Peace,* 1982–1983) as a bootleg videotape in a small community club for teenagers; I was among an audience of about eight people in their teens and twenties. Similarly, my first opportunity to view *Der*

Kandidat (The Candidate, 1979–1980) occurred in the basement of a cafe/bar where six spectators sat on folding chairs. Both of these screenings took place in Berlin more than five years after the original release date of the films.

42. In fact, J. Hoberman has suggested that the work of Kluge, Werner Schroeter, Rainer Fassbinder, Hans-Jürgen Syberberg, Wim Wenders, and Werner Herzog "might be considered the seventies equivalent of a commercial avant-garde." He also regards Godard's films as functioning in a similar manner. J. Hoberman, "After Avant-garde Film," in *Art After Modernism: Rethinking Representation,* ed. Brian Wallis (New York: The New Museum of Contemporary Art, 1984), 68, 71.

43. Interview with the author, Munich, July 16, 1996.

44. Liebman, "On New German Cinema, Art, Enlightenment, and the Public Sphere," 57–58.

45. Jameson in Taylor, ed, *Aesthetics and Politics,* 206–8; Harvey, "Whose Brecht? Memories for the Eighties," *Screen* 23, no. 1 (May–June, 1982) 45–59.

46. D. N. Rodowick, *The Crisis of Political Modernism: Criticism and Ideology in Contemporary Film Theory* (Berkeley: University of California, 1984), vii–xxix.

47. Ibid., xxiii.

48. Ibid., xxvi.

49. Taylor, ed. *Aesthetics and Politics,* 204–5.

Chapter 2: The Armed Filmmaker

1. Klaus Eder and Alexander Kluge, *Ulmer Dramaturgien: Reibungsverluste* (Munich, Vienna: Carl Hanser, 1980), 85.

2. Hans Günter Pflaum, "Wir müssen gewissermaßen unterm Eis wegtauchen," *Frankfurter Rundschau,* 22 December 1976.

3. Ibid.

4. For example, his book *Ulmer Dramaturgien* has the subtitle "Reibungsverluste," or "frictional losses," which is a reference to the writings of Karl von Clausewitz. For Clausewitz, the term describes the difference between war on paper and war as it is actually fought. Kluge explains that film is not war, in so far as it does not seek the destruction of anybody's consciousness. "But film is nevertheless battle, partisan behavior. The essential part is the friction." Eder and Kluge, *Ulmer Dramaturgien,* 84.

5. This notion was explored most fully in the 1972 book on social theory which Kluge coauthored. Oskar Negt and Alexander Kluge, *Öffentlichkeit und Erfahrung: Zur Organisationsanalyse von bürgerlicher und proletarischer Öffentlichkeit* (Frankfurt am Main: Suhrkamp, 1972).

6. Timothy Corrigan, "The Commerce of Auteurism: A Voice Without Authority," *New German Critique,* no. 49 (winter 1990): 43.

7. Corrigan remarks:

> With Kluge one finds less a critical subversion of auteurism as a production strategy than a critical exploitation of auteurism as a category for reception. Indeed, the marked shift within auteurism as a way of viewing and receiving movies, rather than as a mode of production has been the central change in the meaning of auteurism from the sixties to the eighties. It is along these lines that Kluge has begun to make specific use of the commerce of his own singularity and subjectivity. (Ibid., 44)

In response it could be argued that for both the French New Wave and for Kluge, the concept of the auteur served the dual aims of production and reception. In France in the 1950s, auteurism served to lionize Hollywood directors and served as self-promotion for the New Wave directors. Even in the reception of his early work, Kluge presented himself as a source of interpretation—through the press and live appearances at theaters. The fact that Kluge has consistently disclaimed his willingness to interpret his films extratextually by no means changes the fact that he is constantly providing such extratextual interpretive clues and an interpretive coherence in his own (admittedly complex) persona. Although Corrigan's observations about the complexity of the auteur concept are well taken, his arguments regarding a particular historical development of the term with respect to Kluge are less convincing.

8. His father appears in *Ein Arzt aus Halberstadt* (A Doctor from Halberstadt, 1969–1970), his mother in *Besitzbürgerin, Jahrgang 1908* (A Woman of Means, Class of 1908, 1973), his grandmother in *Frau Blackburn, geb. 5 Jan. 1872, wird gefilmt* (Frau Blackburn, Born January 5, 1872, Is Filmed, 1967), and his sister in *Feuerlöscher E. A. Winterstein* (Fireman E. A. Winterstein, 1968). Alexandra also acted in three of his feature films (cf. infra).

9. Rainer Lewandowski, *Alexander Kluge* (Munich: C. H. Beck, 1980), 7.

10. Unmarked Pressbook, in Kluge files, Deutsches Institut für Filmkunde, Frankfurt am Main.

11. The most notable instance occurs in "Heft 2: Der Luftangriff auf Halberstadt am 8. April, 1945," in Alexander Kluge, *Neue Geschichten, Hefte 1–18: "Unheimlichkeit der Zeit"* (Frankfurt am Main: Suhrkamp, 1977), 33–106. An English translation of this article is available as "The Air Raid on Halberstadt, 8 April 1945," trans. Reinhard Mayer, *Semiotext* 4, no. 2 (1982): 306–15.

12. Rainer Lewandowski, *Die Filme von Alexander Kluge* (Hildesheim, New York: Olms, 1980), 347, 331.

13. Ibid., 347.

14. Karsten Peters, "Filme zum Träumen: Gespräch mit Alexander und Alexandra Kluge," *Abendzeitung* (Munich), 5 October 1966.

15. Ibid.

16. Thomas Böhm-Christl, ed., *Alexander Kluge* (Frankfurt am Main: Suhrkamp, 1983), 323. Klaus Lackschéwitz, "Junger Deutscher Film: Porträt eines Autors und Regisseurs," *Film-Telegramm* 19, no. 4 (24 January 1967): 9.

17. Rainer Werner Fassbinder, "Alexander Kluge soll Geburtstag gehabt haben," in *Filme befreien den Kopf,* ed. Michael Töteberg (Frankfurt am Main: Fischer, 1986), 115.

18. Lewandowski, *Die Filme von Alexander Kluge,* 347.

19. Collaboration had many benefits for Kluge. In some cases, it enabled him to work with individuals who had more expertise in a particular area (Edgar Reitz as film expert, Oskar Negt as social theorist), multiply his productivity (jointly authored publications in media theory), and provide more diversity, legitimacy, and public interest (the collaborative films with Schlöndorff, Fassbinder and others). Collaboration was an operational principle that corresponded to central theoretical concepts and had as well a pragmatic efficacy. These collaborations, however, were not always unproblematic or egalitarian.

20. Lewandowski, *Alexander Kluge,* 9. Kluge reminisces about Adorno in Eder and Kluge, *Ulmer Dramaturgien,* 47–48.

21. Eder and Kluge, *Ulmer Dramaturgien,* 102, 27.

22. Alexander Kluge, *Lebensläufe: Anwesenheitsliste für eine Beerdigung* (Stuttgart: Goverts, 1962). The translation published in the United States as Alexander

Kluge, *Attendance List for a Funeral,* trans. Leila Vennewitz (New York: McGraw-Hill, 1966), included two additional stories, most notably the one used as the English title.

23. Lackschéwitz, "Junger Deutscher Film," 9.

24. Schamoni and Kluge share credit as director, and Wirth, who shot several films for the young German directors, was the cameraman. Throughout his career, Kluge showed little fascination for the technical side of production and was never credited with camera or sound work. In only one instance, *Lehrer im Wandel* (Teachers through Change, 1962–1963), is he credited as the editor. Lewandowski, *Die Filme von Alexander Kluge,* Appendix.

25. "Wir wollen den neuen deutschen Film machen," *Süddeutsche Zeitung* (Munich), 10 March 1962.

26. Documentaries include films like *Rennen* (Racing, 1961), *Lehrer im Wandel,* and *Porträt einer Bewährung* (Proven Competence Portrayed, 1964). Quasi-documentaries like *Frau Blackburn, geb. 5 Jan. 1872, wird gefilmt,* and *Besitzbürgerin, Jahrgang 1908* contain both documentary and fictional material. Pseudodocumentaries such as *Feuerlöscher E. A. Winterstein* seem to be portraits of real people but are scripted.

27. "Wir wollen den neuen deutschen Film machen."

28. In several interviews and articles in 1962, Kluge indicated a desire to elevate German film to the status of literature (e.g., Alexander Kluge, "Was wollen die 'Oberhausener?'" *Kirche und Film,* no. 11 (November 1962): 2–4). He mentioned parallels and possible ties between young filmmakers and Group 47, an organization of leftist writers in Germany. Ibid. and "Der junge deutsche Film," *Dokumentation zu einer Ausstellung der Constantin-Film* (Opened March 30, 1967).

29. Lewandowski, *Die Filme von Alexander Kluge,* 348.

30. Lewandowski, *Alexander Kluge,* 12.

31. This prize retains a slightly political flavor. It is traditionally awarded on March 18, the anniversary of the 1948 revolution. "Berliner Fontane-Preis für A. Kluge," *Süddeutsche Zeitung,* 19 March 1979.

32. Although never a fully developed theory of cinema, the *politique des auteurs* emphasized the director as the author or creative force in film production. Cf. Ed Buscomb, "Ideas of Authorship," *Screen* 14, no. 3 (autumn 1973): 75–85. Thomas Elsaesser argues that

> the concept of *Autorenfilm* had primarily a strategic function, and the book [Elsaesser's New German Cinema] tries to contextualize the often heroic self-representation of the filmmakers, by showing how the star directors were part of a broadly-based movement inside Germany to win new audiences as well as representing a unique marketing asset internationally. Such a view does not mean the heroes have to be toppled from their pedestals—although the image of a solitary, persecuted, or even a collective and triumphant struggle has to be seen for what it is: a discourse, a stance, a necessary fiction to enable and motivate productivity. (*New German Cinema: A History* [New Brunswick, New Jersey: Rutgers University Press, 1989], 2–3)

33. The *Cahiers du Cinéma* critics who promoted this theory could find a unique personal style even in Hollywood films. See, for example, Eric Rohmer's discussion of Nicholas Ray in "Ajax or the Cid," trans. Liz Heron, in *"Cahiers du Cinéma," The 1950s: Neo-Realism, Hollywood, New Wave,* ed. Jim Hillier (Cambridge, Massachusetts: Harvard University Press, 1985), 111.

34. Born in France, Straub worked for five French directors in the 1950s, including Robert Bresson, who strongly influenced his style. 1n 1958, Straub moved to

Germany, where he worked until moving to Italy in 1969. John Sandford, *The New German Cinema* (New York: DeCapo, 1982), 27.

35. Eder and Kluge, *Ulmer Dramaturgien,* 102. He also has mentioned François Truffaut's *The 400 Blows* (1959), Eric Rohmer's *The Sign of Leo* (1959), Chris Marker's *Letter from Siberia* (1957), and the films of Robert Bresson: "You learn from these as if at school." "Wir wollen den neuen deutschen Film machen."

36. His later association with Oskar Negt and his experiences as an educator at Ulm and Frankfurt augmented these credentials over the years.

37. Kluge, "Was wollen die 'Oberhausener?'" 2.

38. The financial plight of the German film industry was in large part the result of the American occupation policy which favored Hollywood firms over German and insisted on decentralization of the German film production, to prevent its future use as a propaganda tool. "By licensing a host of small independent production companies, the [Allied] Control Commission bequeathed to the post-war film industry its most persistent problems, namely chronic liquidity crises, under-capitalisation, and a narrow-based home market orientation." Elsaesser, *New German Cinema,* 11.

39. Rainer Lewandowski, "Der Wunsch, etwas zu verändern," *Medium,* no. 4 (April 1982): 13.

40. Eric Rentschler, ed., *West German Filmmakers on Film: Visions and Voices* (New York: Holmes and Meier, 1988), 2.

41. The signatories were all male, and, despite the emphasis on their youth, none was younger than twenty-seven and the oldest was thirty-nine. "Die Krise," *Cinema* (Zurich) 8, no. 3 (autumn 1962): 395.

42. The film critic Joe Hembus had anticipated this denunciation in a collection of essays ironically titled "The German Film Couldn't Be Any Better" (*Der deutsche Film kann gar nicht besser sein* [Bremen: Carl Schuenemann, 1961]). Hembus cited five reasons for the sorry state of German postwar cinema: the forced emigration of creative talent in the 1920s and 1930s; the derogation of creativity in favor of stars and production values; the exclusion of the young generation; repetition of formulas and standardization; and the refusal to deal seriously with historical and political questions (see "Die Krise," 390). The same year another critic, Walther Schmieding, wrote a book called "Art or Box Office: Always Annoyed by German Film" (*Kunst oder Kasse: Der Ärger mit dem deutschen Film* [Hamburg: Rütten und Loening, 1961]).

43. Raymond Williams, *The Politics of Modernism* (London and New York: Verso, 1989), 33.

44. Kluge, "Was wollen die 'Oberhausener?'" 2.

45. Sandford, *The New German Cinema,* 13.

46. Herbert Hegedo, "'Oberhausener' im Winterschlaf," *Hamburger Abendblatt,* 13 April 1963.

47. Over 300 Heimat films were produced in the 1950s, including one of the decade's most popular films, *Grün ist der Heide* (*Green is the Heath,* 1951). Anton Kaes, *From Hitler to Heimat: The Return of History as Film* (Cambridge, Massachusetts: Harvard University Press, 1989), 15.

48. The denazification program of the Allies ended in the early 1950s. Few Germans who had emigrated to Hollywood during the 1940s and 1950s returned to work in the postwar German film industry. Those who did found the industry controlled by individuals who had been active in the Nazi era and who were not enthusiastic about the émigrés' return. Elsaesser, *New German Cinema,* 13–14.

49. This is not to say that the Oberhauseners identified completely with the student movement or vice-versa. It must be remembered that these filmmakers were about ten years older than the students who were just beginning their activism in the early 1960s. By the late 1960s, many of these filmmakers were themselves seen as "established." See Lewandowski, *Alexander Kluge,* 13–14.

50. Kluge, "Was wollen die 'Oberhausener?'" 2.

51. The others were attorney Norbert Kückelmann and Hans Rolf Strobel. Eder and Kluge, *Ulmer Dramaturgien,* 32.

52. Lackschéwitz, "Junger deutscher Film," 9. Reitz, Haro Senft, Strobel, Heinz Tichawsky, Hans-Jürgen Pohland, and Peter Schamoni's brother Thomas also received funding from the Kuratorium, although most of the Oberhauseners did not. A number of other important directors of the New German Cinema who were not Oberhausen signatories were also subsidized on their first features: Jean-Marie Straub, Werner Herzog, and Vlado Kristl. Recipients of funding also included two of Kluge's students at the Ulm film school: Reinhard Kahn and Ula Stöckl. Hans Rolf Strobel, "Kein fröhlicher Rückblick—kein trauriger Ausblick," *Medium* 12, no. 4 (April 1982): 3–5.

53. Unless otherwise noted, most of the information on the Ulm Institute is derived from three sources: Eder and Kluge, *Ulmer Dramaturgien;* Herbert Lindinger, ed., *Die Moral der Gegenstände* (Berlin: Internationales Design Zentrum Berlin, 1987); or Klaus Eder et al., *Anschauung und Begriff: Die Arbeiten des Instituts für Filmgestaltung Ulm 1962 bis 1995* (Ulm: Institut für Filmgestaltung, 1995).

54. Prior to the Oberhausen Manifesto in 1962, at least six of the Oberhausen signatories had served as film instructors or advisors: Schleiermacher, Herbert Vesely, Ferdinand Khittl, Raimond Ruehl, Senft and Franz Josef Spieker. Although most accounts of the Film Department indicate that it was established after Oberhausen, according to contemporary records of the *Hochschule* itself, the department was functioning as an adjunct to the Department of Visual Communication already in the first quarter of the 1961–62 school year (beginning in October, 1961). Under the Kluge/Schleiermacher/Reitz regime, various other filmmakers served on the faculty from time to time, including Vlado Kristl, who apparently encouraged some student upheavals, and Beate Mainka (later Mainka-Jellinghaus), who edited many of the films of Kluge and Herzog. Eder and Kluge, *Ulmer Dramaturgien,* 33–34. At the time of his appointment, as Michael Koetzle points out, Kluge had produced only 2 short films totaling 21 minutes running time. The second of these, *Rennen,* was simply an edit of found footage. Michael Koetzle, "In Gefahr und grösster Not . . . ," *Text + Kritik* (Heft 85–86) (January 1985): 113.

55. Detten Schleiermacher quoted in Lindinger, ed., *Die Moral der Gegenstände,* 182–3.

56. The instruction, which consisted of both seminars and working groups, was apparently rather flexible. A catalog from 1967 indicates that a course of study could vary between two and five years. Lindinger, ed., *Die Moral der Gegenstände,* 189. The curriculum of the film school was developed by members of the Oberhausen group (Bernhard Dörries, Reitz, Schleiermacher, Senft, Strobel, and Kluge) and film critics from the magazine *Filmkritik* (Ulrich Gregor, Theodor Kotulla, Enno Patalas).

57. Eder and Kluge, *Ulmer Dramaturgien,* 37.

58. Lindinger, ed., *Die Moral der Gegenstände,* 190.

59. Eder and Kluge, *Ulmer Dramaturgien,* 5.

60. "The false model of the priority of the picture over the word rests upon this

tranquil-purist thought that is only secondarily interested in the expression or the content of a film and leads ultimately to formalism." Edgar Reitz, Alexander Kluge, Wilfried Reinke, "Wort und Film," in Eder and Kluge, *Ulmer Dramaturgien*, 15.

61. Lindinger, ed., *Die Moral der Gegenstände*, 182–84.

62. Ibid.

63. Kluge divides the Ulm Institute's history into five phases: 1) 1962–1967, Film Education; 2) 1973–1977, Reform of Film Politics; 3) 1978–1983, The Great Cinema Crisis; 4) 1987–1993, Further Development of Film in Television and in the New Digital Media; and 5) 1995, New Orientation. He also provides an extensive list of Institute publications and productions. Eder et al., *Anschauung und Begriff*, 136–41. Two interesting publications on film theory have appeared under the Institute's aegis: *Ulmer Dramaturgien: Reibungsverluste* and *Bestandsaufnahme: Utopie Film* (Frankfurt am main: Zweitavsendeins, 1983).

64. Eder and Kluge, *Ulmer Dramaturgien*, 75–76. Joe Hembus has spoken rather caustically about the achievements of

> the "Ulm Institute for Film Design," also called Dr. Kluge's Country School or Academy for Claustrophobic Masochism. . . . Ulm has never been a home town for German experimental film or a catalyst for contact with the narrative cinema. . . . There has never been a single major theory that has impacted on the film world. Still I have the feeling that Ulm also has not enriched German film with even a single significant filmmaker (I speak of course of the students, not of the teachers Kluge and Reitz)! (*Der deutsche Film kann gar nicht besser sein: Ein Pamphlet von gestern, eine Abrechnung von heute* [Munich: Rogner & Bernhard, 1981], 189)

65. Cf. Koetzle, "In Gefahr und grösster Not . . . ," 122.

66. Alexander Kluge from Eder and Kluge, *Ulmer Dramaturgien*, 5.

67. In 1978, Kluge threatened to sue a conservative magazine for misquoting him. "Alexander Kluge: Das habe ich nicht gesagt," *Film-Telegramm* 30, no. 9 (24 April 1978): 1.

68. Already in 1962, Kluge suggests that what is needed is a structural change in the German film industry and points to a new institution founded by some of the Oberhauseners: Junger deutscher Film, Gemeinnützige G.m.b.H. "Die Krise," 393.

69. Lewandowski notes: "Kairos is the god of the favorable moment (Greek: 'the just, favorable point of time' for an undertaking) who was cultically honored in Olympia. He was portrayed there with wings, carrying scales." Lewandowski, *Alexander Kluge*, 176.

70. Elsaesser suggests two downsides to this brand of auteurism. First, it forced a lot of creative people to spend much of their time looking for funding and dealing with finances rather than making films. Secondly, the valorization of the director encouraged many competent writers, cameramen, and other talented film people to become directors even when their talents lay in other directions. The result was a proliferation of less-talented directors, because that was the only way to obtain funding. Elsaesser, *New German Cinema*, 103ff, 312ff.

71. Liebman, "On New German Cinema, Art, Enlightenment, and the Public Sphere," 25.

72. Strobel, "Kein fröhlicher Rückblick—kein trauriger Ausblick," 4.

73. Liebman, "On New German Cinema, Art, Enlightenment, and the Public Sphere," 23.

74. Despite an initial hesitancy about the organization, Kluge soon began to play a central role. Although he refused any official title, he served on the board and was consulted about every move. "Der deutsche Film hat 1967 eine Chance," *Starpress*

(Hamburg) 14, nos. 80–81 (20 December 1966): 6. Lackschéwitz, "Junger Deutscher Film," 11. Lewandowski, *Alexander Kluge,* 176.

75. See for example Hans-Günter Pflaum's interview with Kluge in 1976, "Wir müssen gewissermaßen unterm Eis wegtauchen."

76. Lewandowski, *Alexander Kluge,* 176.

77. An extensive discussion of these institutions is included in chapter 6.

78. In 1962, Pohland spoke of "being able to make artistic films in Germany that meet international standards." "Die Krise," 393.

79. "Der deutsche Film hat 1967 eine Chance," 6.

80. The figure fifteen includes all of Kluge's collaborative films and *"Zu böser Schlacht schleich ich heut nacht so bang—."* ("Into This Evil Fight Tonight I Am Afraid to Creep . . . ," 1977), which was a reedit of *Willi Tobler und der Untergang der 6. Flotte* (*Willi Tobler and the Wreck of the Sixth Fleet,* 1969–1971). Kluge's awards have included:

1961	*Brutalität in Stein*	Oberhausen Main Prize (1 of 6)
1964	*Lebensläufe*	Berlin Art Prize—Young Generation
1965	*Porträt einer Bewährung*	Oberhausen Main Prize (1 of 4)
1966	*Schlachtbeschreibung*	Bavarian State Prize for Literature
	Abschied von gestern	Venice Silver Lion
		Int'l Catholic Film Office Prize
		Italian Film Club Prize
		Spanish Critics' Luis Buñuel Prize
1967	*Abschied von gestern*	Federal Film Prize (Gold)
1968	*Die Artisten in der Zirkuskuppel*	Venice Golden Lion
1969	*Die Artisten in der Zirkuskuppel*	Federal Film Prize (Gold)
1972	*Gelegenheitsarbeit einer Sklavin*	Sorrento Main Prize
1976	*Der starke Ferdinand*	Cannes International Film Critics' Prize
		Naples Special Prize
1979	*Die Patriotin*	Federal Film Prize (Silver)
1983	*Die Macht der Gefühle*	Venice Critics' Prize

Lewandowski, *Die Filme von Alexander Kluge,* 347–50.

81. Those producers whose earlier films had grossed more than 500,000 DM could apply to a new committee, the *Filmförderungsanstalt* (Film Subsidy Board known as FFA), for funding for a new project. Amounts of up to 250,000 DM could be awarded, and the new films were not required to employ the same director as the successful one. Sandford, *The New German Cinema,* 14.

82. Some limited theatrical distribution was, however, provided for Kluge and a few other Young German directors by established companies like Gloria and Constantin. Eder and Kluge, *Ulmer Dramaturgien,* 103.

83. See, for example, Elsaesser, *New German Cinema,* 20–27.

84. Sandford, *The New German Cinema,* 15.

85. *ARD-Jahrbuch 75* (Hamburg: Hans Bredow Institut, 1975), 347. *Filmförderung 1974–1979: Der Deutsche Film und das Fernsehen* (Frankfurt: ZDF, 1980), 40.

86. In 1978, Kluge relinquished his seats on several of these boards to Bernhard Sinkel, another NGC director, in protest over the continuing subsidization of the commercial film producers. Florian Hopf, "Alexander Kluge legt FFA-Ämter nieder," *Filmreport,* 10 April 1977.

87. Elsaesser, *New German Cinema,* 40ff.

88. Kluge has attacked the Subsidy Board for favoring "big budgets and big names," for overemphasizing scripts (especially literary adaptations), and for avoiding

fantasy and politics. Vivian Naefe, "Wir müssen uns Nebenbuhler suchen," *Abendzeitung* (Munich), 3 January 1979.

89. "Die Verantwortung der Filmwirtschaft," *Medium,* no. 4 (April 1982): 2.

90. Naefe, "Wir müssen uns Nebenbuhler suchen."

91. The filmmaker Helke Sander has commented on several occasions how difficult it is to argue with Kluge or get angry with him, even when one disagrees vehemently with him. "I was taken in by Kluge's charm, his intelligence, as well as his wit (which to me is irresistible); by his ability to correlate unusual facts, one with the other; and by his generosity." Helke Sander, "'You can't always get what you want': The Films of Alexander Kluge," *October,* no. 49 (fall 1988): 62.

92. For example, in a 1965 interview he praised Günter Grass for his involvement in politics, but dismissed any such activity on his own part because of lack of aptitude: "I am no showman." "Dichter in der Arena," *Abendzeitung* (Munich), 30 July 1965.

93. An example of this would be the interviews he gave before the release of his film *Artisten* at the Venice biennale in 1968. By suggesting that the film was a metaphor for the state of German film culture, he gave critics and judges a handle for interpreting a somewhat difficult film, and no doubt contributed to the film's success at the festival.

94. See, for example, Herbert Hegedo, "'Oberhausener' im Winterschlaf"; Brigitte Jeremias, "Alexander und Alexandra," *Frankfurter Allgemeine Zeitung,* 14 October 1966; and Lackschéwitz, "Junger Deutscher Film," 9–11.

95. Alexander Kluge, *Der Angriff der Gegenwart auf die übrige Zeit* (Frankfurt am Main: Syndikat, 1985), 12. Kluge has substantially revised and rereleased a number of his works through the years, including *Attendance List for a Funeral, The Battle,* and the film *Strongman Ferdinand.*

96. See, for example, Kluge, "Was wollen die 'Oberhausener?'" and Hegedo, "'Oberhausener' im Winterschlaf," where he is identified in the text as both a doctor and an attorney (and the caption to the accompanying photo reads "Dr. Kluge").

97. Timothy Corrigan, "The Commerce of Auteurism," 54.

98. Yvonne Rainer and Ernest Larsen, "'We are Demolition Artists': An Interview with Alexander Kluge," *The Independent* (June 1989): 21; quoted in Corrigan, "The Commerce of Auteurism," 52. Kluge also uses this metaphor to defend his aesthetics of fantasy in Kluge, *Gelegenheitsarbeit einer Sklavin,* 249.

99. Corrigan, "The Commerce of Auteurism," 53. Corrigan goes on to point out that Kluge shifts the emphasis from the director to the public as the filmic auteur. This is an often-repeated move by Kluge, asserting the importance of the audience in the making of meaning. He in no way diminishes his own artistic status with this assertion, however; in fact, it serves to distinguish him from most of the auteur-stars.

100. To some, Kluge appeared rather coldly calculating and was resented by some of his peers for getting on too well. Lackschéwitz, "Junger Deutscher Film," 10.

101. Most conspicuous among the projects that did not receive public funding were the extremely controversial and primarily documentary collaborative films: *Deutschland im Herbst* (*Germany in Autumn,* 1977–1978), which was funded by the owner of *Der Spiegel,* Rudolf Augstein, and *Der Kandidat* (*The Candidate,* 1979–1980).

Chapter 3: Telling, Condensing, Interpreting

1. Alexander Kluge, *Die Patriotin: Texte, Bilder 1–6* (Frankfurt am Main: Zweitausendeins, 1979), 40.

2. Walter Benjamin, *Charles Baudelaire: A Lyric Poet in the Era of High Capitalism* (London: Verso, 1983), 113.

3. On the other hand, Kluge's more theoretical texts are often interrupted by stories (sometimes graphically isolated in boxes or with different fonts) which function as exemplars or parallel texts. This would argue for the centrality of particular real-life experiences (i.e., narratives) in Kluge's theory.

4. Adorno, *Aesthetic Theory*, 150–51.

5. *Der grosse Verhau* (*The Big Mess*, 1969–1971) will be discussed with Kluge's other early work, but its narrative structure bears more similarities to his later work.

6. The more mainstream style of the film was buttressed by a relatively high budget (for a Kluge film) and resulted in higher production values than most of his films. For example, this film was awarded 650,000 DM from ZDF in contrast to only 200,000 DM for his previous film. *Filmförderung 1974–1979,* 18. This film began as a collaboration with Reitz, but early in the filming the two codirectors had a falling out and Reitz left the project.

7. *Ein Herz und eine Seele.* In addition to his mass media popularity, Schubert also was well established in the high art realm of theater. A former member of the Berlin Brecht ensemble and the Munich Kammerspiele, he had been, at the time of *Strongman Ferdinand*'s release, part of the troupe of the Hamburg Schauspielhaus. *Der starke Ferdinand Pressbook,* Constantin Film, 18–9, Deutsche Film und Fernsehen Bibliothek, Berlin.

8. This film won the International Film Critics' Prize at Cannes and Special Prize at Naples, and might also have done very well in German cinemas. As it was, newspaper advertising, film reviews, and promotional interviews could not be published at the critical moment of release, and the film was withdrawn from theaters in the major cities before the strike was ended. Kluge is said to have disliked the film, and, after limited screenings, he recut it to make it more similar to his other productions. Subsequently, he claimed to like it very well. Horst Wiedemann, "Filmpolitik und Der starke Ferdinand," *Film und Ton* 24, no. 1 (1978): 56.

9. Both *The Big Mess* and *Willi Tobler* warrant some special comment. These two science fiction films were both shot at about the same time (between January 1969 and April 1970) in Ulm. Some of the same actors were involved in both, and the locale and time frame for both films is approximately the same. They were apparently envisioned as a single film, in so far as a clear conception existed prior to filming. Lewandowski asserts that there was no firm shooting plan and that large portions of the films were improvised. Kluge has confirmed the tentative nature of the project, which had two main goals: to make a film and to develop new special effects techniques. "When the films were finished, then we knew what films we should have made." Lewandowski, *Die Filme von Alexander Kluge* 160.

Neither of these films obtained a theatrical release, nor did the 1977 reedited version of *Willi Tobler*, "*Zu böser Schlacht schleich ich heut nacht so bang—.*" Both films are attempts to create something coherent out of rather inchoate footage. They can, perhaps, be viewed as extreme examples of Kluge's episodic technique. Here, his flexibility and adaptiveness to particular shooting conditions and opportunities were not limited by an overarching plan for the film as a whole. *The Big Mess* anticipates the bifurcated narrative of *The Middle of the Road Is a Very Dead End,* but it does not intercut between two plotlines as the latter does.

10. Each of these episodes is a kind of mininarrative, and within each narrative the same ellipses of time and space, and of motivation and causality, are present. Some-

times there is a climax—a confrontation between Anita and a landlady or Anita and a boss—at other times the key scenes are not shown; in other places, she just moves on with no specific explanation.

11. In contrast to this film, the short story upon which it is based is much more coherent. Not only are spatial and temporal transitions spelled out, incidents are less ambiguous and motivations are articulated. It is difficult to determine whether the film is more experimental than the short story or is simply less controlled. Whatever case, the former is considerably more difficult to comprehend than the latter.

12. Kluge indicates that many of the problems in the film resulted from the collaborative nature of the project and the inadequacy of the financing. *Herzog/Kluge/Straub,* 172–73.

13. As in his contemporaneous book *Learning Processes with a Deadly Outcome,* Kluge uses the science fiction genre in these two films as a site for working through issues raised by the battle of Stalingrad, which itself is Kluge's microcosm for the German experience of World War II.

14. *The Big Mess* and *Willi Tobler* in particular did very badly. Neither had a regular theatrical release. *The Big Mess* was booed when it played at the Moscow Film Festival in 1971, and many negative responses greeted the showing of *Willi Tobler* on ZDF several months later. In both cases, the science fiction was very crudely mounted. The *New York Times* reviewer, Thomas Curtiss, suggested that it was like Méliès trying to do *2001.* The parody was often amusing—in particular the portrait of the Bavarian couple with a spaceship furnished like a Bavarian living room—but it occasionally bordered on slapstick. Both films depend heavily on intertitles, not simply for commentary but for narrative coherence and intelligibility. American critics at Venice, where *The Big Mess* was screened, commented that "the action of the motion picture is confused" (Thomas Quinn Curtiss, *New York Times,* 4 September 1971) and that "chances for the regular market are practically zero" (*Variety,* 22 September 1971). *Variety* also added, "The director called his film an experiment which he would not like to repeat in this form—perhaps a wise decision." Nevertheless, Kluge proceeded with its doppelgänger: *Willi Tobler.*

15. The teams included the following members: Heinrich Böll, Alf Brustellin, Hans Peter Cloos, Rainer Werner Fassbinder, Alexander Kluge, Maximiliane Mainka, Beate Mainka-Jellinghaus, Edgar Reitz, Katja Rupé, Volker Schlöndorff, Peter Schubert, Bernhard Sinkel, and Alexander von Eschwege. Kluge, *Die Patriotin: Texte/Bilder 1–6,* 20–22. Miriam Hansen, "Cooperative Auteur Cinema and Oppositional Public Sphere: Alexander Kluge's Contribution to *Germany in Autumn,*" *New German Critique,* nos. 24–25 (fall–winter 1981–2): 36–56.

16. Attendance in Germany for this film approached 400,000 viewers, by far the largest domestic theatrical audience for any of Kluge's films.

17. Three articles in particular take up this theme, all included in the Kluge issue of *October,* no. 46 (fall 1988): Miriam B. Hansen, "Reinventing the Nickelodeon: Notes on Kluge and Early Cinema," 190–93; Stuart Liebman, "Why Kluge?" 6; Heide Schlüpmann, "What Is Different Is Good," 135.

18. Alexander Kluge, *Die Macht der Gefühle* (Frankfurt am Main: Zweitausendeins, 1984), 66.

19. In this number are included the two fictionalized interviews; "The Shot" trial; the rape; the single shot of a woman with a bruise, Frau Bärlamm, which has several episodes; the burning of the opera house; and the story of Betty, Mäxchen, Manfred, and Kurt, which also has several parts.

20. Kluge has used the film-within-a-film technique before, but in a more straightforward manner: Roswitha in *Occasional Work of a Female Slave* attends a screening of the film *Chapayev,* from which she draws inspiration for political struggle; and in *Germany in Autumn,* the TV producers watch a scene from the proposed Antigone production. *The Blind Director* sequence is, however, the first time that a film-within-a-film is revealed as such retrospectively. This shifting of ontological status foregrounds the process of narrative construction.

21. Enno Patalas in the "Protokoll" for *Yesterday Girl* identifies the source of this quotation as *Crime and Punishment;* he also attributes several others to Karl Jaspers and Reinhard Baumgart. *Abschied von gestern: Protokoll,* ed. Enno Patalas (Frankfurt am Main: Filmkritik, n.d.), 7, 58, 94.

22. Miriam B. Hansen, "Alexander Kluge, Cinema and the Public Sphere: The Construction Site of Counter-History," *Discourse,* no. 6 (fall 1983): 65.

23. B. Ruby Rich, "She Says, He Says: The Power of the Narrator in Modernist Film Politics," *Discourse,* no. 6 (fall 1983): 38.

24. Hansen, "Alexander Kluge, Cinema and the Public Sphere," 67.

25. Ibid., 64–65.

26. "I believe that everything which happens in this world, which moves, is put in motion ultimately by emotions, but that they have no institutional power. 'They are everywhere, only one doesn't see them.'" Kluge, *Die Macht der Gefühle,* 44.

27. Hansen, "Alexander Kluge, Cinema and the Public Sphere," 66.

28. Rich, "She Says, He Says," 38.

29. Bertolt Brecht, "The Film, the Novel and Epic Theater," *Brecht on Theatre,* ed. and trans. John Willett (New York: Hill and Wang, 1964), 48.

30. Anton Kaes, *From Hitler to Heimat: The Return of History as Film* (Cambridge, Massachusetts: Harvard University Press, 1989), 115–16.

31. Some sequences may have been conceived as illustrations of characters' thoughts, but Kluge refuses to follow Hollywood's practice of clearly marking them as such. In *Yesterday Girl,* for example, it could be that the Jewish cemetery, the photograph of the family, and the surreal chase are all subjective, all imagined.

32. After *Yesterday Girl,* almost all montage sequences in Kluge's films are not narratively motivated. As Kluge felt increasingly comfortable about inserting non-narrative or at least nonenacted material into his films, any diegetic motivation for montage sequences became unnecessary and, from his standpoint, perhaps counterproductive. He did not want us inside the characters' heads.

33. Andreas Huyssen, "An Analytic Storyteller in the Course of Time," *October,* no. 46 (fall 1988): 123.

34. In the foreword to his first collection of stories, he conveys this feeling: "The stories in this volume question tradition from a number of very different aspects. They are case histories, some invented, some not invented; together they present a sad chronicle." Alexander Kluge, foreword to *Attendance List for a Funeral: Eleven Stories by Alexander Kluge,* trans. Leila Vennewitz (New York: McGraw-Hill, 1966).

35. Liebman, "Why Kluge?" 6.

36. Hansen, "Alexander Kluge, Cinema and the Public Sphere," 68. Hansen has rightly emphasized that much of the dialogue in Kluge's films is developed by the actors themselves. She argues that this increases the "figurative complexity of character conception" (ibid.). To a certain extent, this direct expression by the actors does counter the dominance of the narrator's voice. Most of the time, however, the characters are silent, and their dialogues tend to be set pieces with narrow objectives. Al-

though the actors' words are their own, the meaning is constrained by the ironic situation that Kluge has set up. Thus, while there is a certain measure of spontaneity and a tension between the narrator and the actor, it is the narrator/filmmaker who has the last word, contextualizing and commenting on the dialogue in the postproduction process.

37. Hansen's comments can be seen as a part of an ongoing debate about the depiction of women in Kluge's films. This will be discussed in chapter 5.

38. Bertolt Brecht, "Short Description of a New Technique of Acting which Produces an Alienation Effect," *Brecht on Theatre*, 136.

39. Although Kluge's collaborative documentaries did comparatively well at the box office, none surpassed 400,000 theater viewers—this in a country of about 60 million people. Information was obtained from Kluge's distributor, Filmverlag der Autoren, Munich, as of July 1988.

40. Huyssen, "An Analytic Storyteller in the Course of Time," 118. Huyssen argues that his books of stories are even less attractive because of their length than are his films. He claims that the former also lack the authorial commentary which is ubiquitous, if ambiguous, in the films.

> The basic paradox and difficulty of these texts by Kluge is that they rely on knowledges, abilities, and desires which, according to his own theoretical analyses of contemporary mass media culture, are on the wane because of the pervasive growth during the period of late capitalism of what he and Negt describe in *Öffentlichkeit und Erfahrung* (*The Public Sphere and Experience*) as the public spheres of production. But even if the reader's ability to produce new social experience is not blocked, even if the reader brings along enough basic knowledge of political economy, social theory, and psychoanalysis to decipher Kluge's stenographic, dialectical constructions of aesthetic image and theoretical concept, the first reaction to the labyrinths of Kluge's story collections, particularly those published during the 1970s, is likely to be frustration and irritation. (ibid.)

41. Although Kluge received funding from ZDF for an additional film, *Neues vom Tage* (News of the Day, 1990), it was not intended for theatrical distribution and received none. *Neues vom Tage* does not announce itself the work of Alexander Kluge, but is credited to Werkstatt Film/Fernsehen, apparently an organization constructed by Kluge ad hoc. Kluge's heavy work load in television has precluded any new cinematic projects in the last decade.

Chapter 4: Cinema Impure

1. Benjamin, *Charles Baudelaire: A Lyric Poet in the Era of High Capitalism*, 79.

2. Eric Rentschler discussed this ragpicker metaphor with the author in Berlin in August 1988. See his 1990 article, Eric Rentschler, "Remembering Not to Forget: A Retrospective Reading of Kluge's *Brutality in Stone*," *New German Critique*, no. 49 (winter 1990): 23.

3. Russell Berman, *Modern Culture and Critical Theory: Art, Politics and the Legacy of the Frankfurt School* (Madison: University of Wisconsin Press, 1989), 74.

4. Frederick R. Karl, *Modern and Modernism: The Sovereignty of the Artist 1885–1925* (New York: Atheneum, 1985), 281.

5. Peter Kremski, "Geschichten zur Geschichte," *Filmbulletin* 29, no. 5 (October–November 1987): 47–48.

6. Liebman, "Why Kluge?" 7. In a similar vein, Noël Carroll has spoken of the "modernist aesthetic" evident in these structuralist films. Noël Carroll, "Film," in Stan-

ley Trachtenberg, ed., *The Postmodern Moment: A Handbook of Contemporary Innovation in the Arts* (Westport, Connecticut: Greenwood Press, 1985), 127.

7. Quoted in Bion Steinborn, "Cinema Pure, Cinema Impure," *Filmfaust* 7, no. 26 (February–March 1982): 32.

8. The respite from motion in these images may fulfill Kluge's avowed aim of providing pauses for the viewer during the course of the film. This is discussed further in the Montage section below.

9. As discussed in the previous chapter, voice-over narration has a similar aesthetic/economic function, and these two stylistic devices are often used in conjunction.

10. Quoted in Steinborn, "Cinema Pure, Cinema Impure," 48.

11. Ibid. Kluge's attentiveness during the creative process to the fortuitous accident is an aesthetic parallel to the social and political opportunism—symbolized by *kairos* (discussed earlier)—that he has practiced.

12. The clips from sound films often have a primitive acoustic quality, and both the pictures and soundtracks often show deterioration from age. These marks of aging provide yet another contrast in texture and tone of the materials.

13. "Red Roses for a Blue Lady" is heard in *Yesterday Girl,* a Spanish version of the Beatles' song "Yesterday" is heard in *Artistes at the Top of the Big Top: Disoriented,* and snippets of several pop songs are heard in *Occasional Work of a Female Slave.*

14. In this respect again, Kluge seems to distance himself from a postmodern strategy that might erase the distinction between popular and high art.

15. Steinborn, "Cinema Pure, Cinema Impure," 48.

16. In discussing film dialogue, Adorno remarks, "Film, therefore, must search for other means of conveying immediacy: improvisation which systematically surrenders itself to unguided chance should rank high among possible alternatives." Theodor W. Adorno, "Transparencies on Film," *New German Critique,* nos. 24–25 (fall–winter 1982): 199–200.

17. In all but one of his features, Kluge employed at least two different cinematographers—and on *The Patriot* he used seven. This was necessary because the episodic shooting schedules stretched over months or years and often took place in several different cities.

18. *Herzog/Kluge/Straub,* 169. In other instances, this jerkiness—which is reminiscent of silent films—is more obviously satirical. For instance, in *Yesterday Girl,* accelerated footage of a police drill exhibition makes the policemen and their cars look like wind-up toys (Keystone cops).

19. Eder and Kluge, *Ulmer Dramaturgien,* 42.

20. As suggested previously, Kluge's characters are often loners, and he does not attempt to reveal their psychological motivations through dialogue and action.

21. "Finally we should not neglect the simultaneous poem, in which Tzara, Huelsenbeck and Janco simultaneously read their banal poems in German, French and English, at the top of their voices. . . . Simultaneism and bruitism (noise-ism) were legacies from the futurists." Karl, *Modern and Modernism,* 352.

22. Arnold Hauser, *Sociology of Art* (Chicago and London: University of Chicago Press, 1982), 624.

23. In several instances, in fact, Kluge has given joint authorship credits to his editors: Beate Mainka-Jellinghaus, for *Odds and Ends,* and to her sister, Maximiliane Mainka, for *"Zu böser Schlacht schleich ich heut nacht so bang—."*

24. Hansen, "Reinventing the Nickelodeon," 195.

25. One might also argue that after looking for a pattern and not finding one, the viewer begins to ignore this difference between shots since it appears to lack meaning.

26. In 1984, shortly after the release of the film *Die Macht der Gefühle,* Kluge published a book of the same name; it contains his commentary on the film, an annotated text list for the film, Kluge's thoughts on two collaborative films (*The Candidate* and *War and Peace*), and many new short stories. Kluge, *Die Macht der Gefühle,* 172.

27. *Yesterday Girl, Occasional Work of a Female Slave,* and *The Middle of the Road Is a Very Dead End* were shot entirely in black and white, while *Strongman Ferdinand* is shot entirely in color. All of Kluge's other features include some footage of both kinds.

28. Quoted in Steinborn, "Cinema Pure, Cinema Impure," 40.

29. Ibid.

30. In *Strongman Ferdinand* both opening and end titles are inserted into the body of the film, serving as intertitles.

31. Harvey Gross, "Parody, Reminiscence, Critique: Aspects of Modernist Style," in *Modernism, Challenges and Perspectives,* ed. Monique Chefdor, Ricardo Quinones, and Albert Wachtel (Urbana and Chicago: University of Illinois Press, 1986), 130.

32. Brecht explained the use of written words in his drama as follows: "Equally important were the spoken word and the written word (of the titles). Reading seems to encourage the audience to adopt the most natural attitude towards the work." Bertolt Brecht, "The Modern Theater Is the Epic Theater," *Brecht on Theatre,* 38. Benjamin refers to this as the "literarizing" technique: "The literarization of theatre by means of verbal formulas, posters, captions, is intended to, and will, 'make what is shown on the stage unsensational.'" Walter Benjamin, "What Is Epic Theatre?" *Understanding Brecht* (London: Verso, 1983), 7.

33. Eckart Schmidt, "Das Publikum soll zufrieden sein," *Die Welt* (Bonn), 19 March 1966. Obviously, Kluge became less concerned about plot interruptions in his later films.

34. As mentioned in the previous chapter, the intertitles in *The Big Mess* and *Willi Tobler* are quite numerous and varied in color and design style, and most have a "home-made" quality about them.

35. In *The Patriot,* the titles are similar except that the main title is white on red. The intertitles in *The Candidate* vary even further from Kluge's normal style: they employ several typefaces mounted on differently colored backgrounds.

36. "Hell lesen wir am Nebelhimmel wie dick die Wintertage sind. Langsames leben ist lang."

37. "Je näher man ein Wort ansieht, desto ferner sieht es zurück."

38. "Tausend Jahre fiel der Tau. Morgen bleibt er aus. Sterne treten ungenau in ein neues Haus."

39. Brecht quoted in Benjamin, *Understanding Brecht,* 7.

40. Quoted in Liebman, "Why Kluge?" 13.

41. In *Strongman Ferdinand,* for example, there are three shots in a row of his car and camper headed toward Brussels. All three are head-on long shots, with slight differences in distance from the camera. This may be a way of emphasizing both the length of the journey and the abrupt decisiveness of Ferdinand's action.

42. Two similar examples occur in *The Power of Emotion.* A young woman climbs a stairway, walks right up to the camera, pauses while the narrator comments on the bruise above her eyebrow, then walks away. Schleich stands on the sidewalk staring at the camera while the narrator introduces him, then walks out of the shot.

43. "Dramatized sequences" refers to those narratives that Kluge has himself filmed using actors.

44. *Herzog/Kluge/Straub*, 163.

45. Edgar Reitz, Alexander Kluge, and Wilfried Reinke, "Wort und Film," *Sprache im technischen Zeitalter*, no. 13 (January–March, 1965): 1016.

46. The use of diegetic music in Kluge is rather infrequent. In most cases it consists of characters singing. For example, in *Yesterday Girl*, Anita sings the Hans Eisler version of the "*Deutschlandlied*" and then is taught to sing an aria. In *The Patriot*, Gabi Teichert and her friends puzzle over the words of the "Ode to Joy" while listening to Beethoven's Ninth. In most of these cases, such diegetic performance is characterized as a learning process, a dissection of the construction of the music.

47. For example, a firestorm bombing in *The Power of Emotion* is composed of news footage of fires and magazine illustrations as well as enacted shots. These are all held together by the sounds of bombs and sirens.

48. This segmentation is very similar to the breakdown Kluge published in his book, *Die Macht der Gefühle*, 74–81. The only major difference is that he combines segments 13 through 17 into one unit. Kluge's commentary will be discussed at the end of the analysis.

49. Kluge identifies this as a clip from the 1941 film *Stukas* directed by Karl Ritter. Kluge, *Die Macht der Gefühle*, 171–72.

50. Kluge identifies the train shots as an excerpt from the 1933 film *Morgenrot* by Gustav Ucicky, the first film seen by Hitler after assuming the chancellorship. Ibid., 170–71.

51. The funeral footage is a memorial service for Hessian minister Heinz Herbert Karry, who was murdered. Kluge does not identify the deceased in the book or interviews at the time of the film's release.

52. Kluge, *Die Macht der Gefühle*, 176.

53. Kluge is not always predictable in this respect, however. For example, in the *Aida* sequence of this film, Kluge shows several close-ups of the lovers; at one point, however, he injects a single brief shot of Siegfried and Kriemhild. This is clearly a way of establishing a parallel between the two tragic love stories, but it happens so quickly that few spectators would notice it on first viewing. It might very well register subconsciously, however.

54. Kluge's book, *Die Macht der Gefühle*, provides much additional information about the sequence just analyzed and characterizes it as the tragedy of the fifth act. He describes both the content and the original context of the clips and suggests parallels and relations both within the sequence and historically. Although this detailed commentary reveals the rich resonance of Kluge's montage, it also unintentionally demonstrates that the average viewer's experience is much more limited. Ibid., 74–80, 179.

55. David Bordwell has pointed out that these two distinct phases in Eisenstein's montage practice correspond to an epistemological shift in his film theory. The earlier, dialectical practice is based on a more materialist, behaviorist notion of knowledge, while the later associational montage is rooted in more organic conceptions. David Bordwell, "Eisenstein's Epistemological Shift," *Screen* 15, no. 4 (winter 1974–5): 32.

56. One significant similarity between the two directors' montage style is the frequent use of metaphor. For Kluge, a shot of fire is associated with emotions because "One speaks of burning passions, not cooling ones." Yet for Eisenstein, the use of metaphor (such as the peacock juxtaposed with Kerensky) is much more direct and unambiguous than most of Kluge's montage. The shot of the peacock immediately fol-

lows a shot of Kerensky. In Kluge's film, the burning buildings are part of their own sequence and are not, for example, inserted immediately next to a shot of a smitten suitor. Although Eisenstein's overtonal montage was often subtle, his tonal montage was readily accessible even to uneducated audiences.

57. Kluge's favorite phrase, "the film in the viewer's head," occurs in many interviews and writings. One instance is in *Herzog/Kluge/Straub*, 157–58. Eisenstein discusses "inner monologue" and "inner speech" in Sergei Eisenstein, *Film Form* (Cleveland: World Publishing Company, 1957), 103–7, 129–30.

58. "Watching the pictures which came from the West and from America . . . I come to the following conclusion: *Verdict of death, decreed by the Kinoks in 1919, to all motion pictures without exception, is in effect to this day.*" Dziga Vertov quoted in Harry M. Geduld, *Filmmakers on Filmmaking* (Bloomington: Indiana University Press, 1967), 82.

59. "The 'Kino-eye,' which has set for itself the task: 'To combine science with cinematic depiction in the struggle to reveal truth . . . to decipher reality,' was born in dozens and hundreds of experiments." Ibid., 90.

60. Ibid., 104.

61. For Kluge, these spaces are the time for the viewer to make his own associations and connections. This sounds better in theory than in practice. When one has only a forty-eighth of a second between shots—the amount of time it takes for one frame to be replaced by the next—there is not a lot of time to process the preceding information, situate it in relation to already accumulated information, and draw conclusions and parallels.

62. This difference between the Russians and Kluge can be accounted for, at least in part, by their different social contexts. The Russians, after the Revolution, were attempting to unify the audience to become emotionally committed to the construction of the new society. In contrast, Kluge is in a prerevolutionary capitalist society and is not rallying support for a particular political program; he is attempting to encourage skepticism about the ideological component of all cultural products. Kluge tries to foster democratic counterinstitutions rather than conformity to a new social order.

63. "Eisenstein never saw montage as the deliberate promotion of the heterogeneity itself for aesthetic and political effect, which is what it always meant for the German practitioners of montage, and for Brecht in particular." Ben Brewster, "Editorial Note," *Screen* 15, no. 4 (winter 1974–5): 32.

64. Benjamin writes of Brecht's formal methods: "Here then—that is to say with the principle of interruption—the epic theater adopts a technique which has become familiar to you in recent years through film and radio, photography and the press. I speak of the technique of montage, for montage interrupts the context into which it is inserted. . . . The interrupting of the action, the technique which entitles Brecht to describe his theater as *epic*, always works against creating an illusion in the audience." Benjamin, *Understanding Brecht,* 99. See also the description of Brecht's aesthetic of estrangement in Eugene Lunn, *Marxism and Modernism: An Historical Study of Lukács, Brecht, Benjamin and Adorno* (Berkeley: University of California Press, 1982), 103.

65. "Montage is a theory of relationships (contexts). In filmmaking I am always faced with the problem that whatever I can see does not actually contain reality. . . . If I understand realism as a knowledge of relationships, then I must set a cipher for that which I cannot show in a film, for that which the camera can not shoot. This cipher is called the contrast between two shots; that is another word for montage." Eder and Kluge, *Ulmer Dramaturgien,* 97–98.

66. One example of Kluge's populist claims is the following: "While the classical arts: music, literature, pictorial arts, have originated in the needs of a small, educated upper stratum, and in this narrow context have developed standards of quality, film is connected to the plebeian needs of an urban lower stratum—in this respect more closely related to the circus or to the annual fairs." Dost, Hopf, and Kluge, *Filmwirtschaft in der BRD und Europa,* 65.

PART II: Excursus into an Altered Landscape

1. Jean-François Lyotard, *The Postmodern Condition* (Minneapolis: University of Minnesota Press, 1984), 79.

2. Jameson describes the salient aspects of this new society as follows:

New types of consumption; planned obsolescence; an ever more rapid rhythm of fashion and styling changes; the penetration of advertising, television and the media generally to a hitherto unparalleled degree throughout society; the replacement of the old tension between city and country, center and province, by the suburb and by universal standardization; the growth of the great networks of superhighways and the arrival of automobile culture—these are some of the features which would seem to mark a radical break with that older prewar society in which high modernism was still an underground force.

Fredric Jameson, "Postmodernism and Consumer Society," in *Postmodernism and Its Discontents,* ed. E. Ann Kaplan (London, New York: Verso, 1988), 28. To Jameson's list could be added other inventions and structural changes geared toward portability (transistor radios, portable TVs, boomboxes, cellular phones), reproducibility (Xerox, fax machines, super-8 movies, audio and video recorders), instantaneity (Polaroids, fast foods, microwave ovens), and the shrinking of distances (airplane travel, satellite communication). Characteristic of this social organization is the replacement of manufacturing by information and service industries, condensation of time and space, and instantaneous global communication.

3. Todd Gitlin, "Postmodernism defined, at last," *Utne Reader* (July–August 1989): 52. This article first appeared in *Dissent.*

4. List reproduced in David Harvey, *The Condition of Postmodernity* (Oxford: Blackwell, 1989), 43.

5. Gitlin, "Postmodernism defined, at last," 52.

6. Huyssen, *After the Great Divide,* 196–97. Huyssen points out that

The situation in the 1970s seems to be characterized rather by an ever wider dispersal and dissemination of artistic practices all working out of the ruins of the modernist edifice, raiding it for ideas, plundering its vocabulary and supplementing it with randomly chosen images and motifs from pre-modern and non-modern culture as well as from contemporary mass culture. Modernist styles have actually not been abolished, but, as one art critic recently observed, continue "to enjoy a kind of half-life in mass culture."

Ibid., 196, quoting Lucie-Smith, *Art in the Seventies,* 11.

7. For example, Hassan's binary list (itself modernist or postmodernist?), which contrasts the qualities of the two sensibilities, begins with an opposition between Symbolism (modernist) and Dadaism (postmodernist). Many critics would argue that the latter movement belongs squarely in modernism, both historically and stylistically, and that Hassan's claims are too broad.

8. For example, Robert Stam looks to Bakhtin for the vision of "a fundamentally non-unitary, constantly shifting cultural field in which the most varied discourses ex-

ist in shifting, multivalenced oppositional relationships." Robert Stam, "Bakhtin and Left Cultural Critique," in Kaplan, *Postmodernism and Its Discontents,* 142.

Another instance:

> The representational systems of the West admit only one vision—that of the constitutive male subject—or, rather, they posit the subject of the representation as absolutely centered, unitary, masculine. . . . It is precisely at the legislative frontier between what can be represented and what cannot that the postmodernist operation is being staged—not in order to transcend representation, but in order to expose that system of power that authorizes certain representations while blocking, prohibiting or invalidating others. Among those prohibited from Western representation, whose representations are denied all legitimacy, are women. . . . This prohibition bears primarily on woman as the subject, and rarely as the object of representation. (Craig Owens, "The Discourse of Others: Feminists and Postmodernism," in Hal Foster, ed., *The Anti-Aesthetic: Essays on Postmodern Culture* [Port Townsend, Washington: Bay Press, 1983], 59)

Or again: "Postmodern knowledge is not simply an instrument of power. It refines our sensitivity to differences and increases our tolerance of incommensurability." Lyotard, *The Postmodern Condition,* 55.

9. Kaplan, *Postmodernism and Its Discontents,* 3–5. Huyssen talks of both "affirmative" and "critical moments of postmodernism." Huyssen, *After the Great Divide,* xii. Hal Foster talks of a "postmodernism of reaction" and a "postmodernism of resistance." Hal Foster, "Postmodernism: A Preface," in Foster, *The Anti-Aesthetic,* xii.

10. "It is easy to find a public for eclectic works. By becoming kitsch, art panders to the confusion which reigns in the 'taste' of the patrons. Artists, gallery owners, critics and public wallow together in the 'anything goes,' and the epoch is one of slackening. But this realism of the 'anything goes' is in fact the realism of money; in the absence of aesthetic criteria, it remains possible and useful to assess the value of works of art according to the profits they yield. Such realism accommodates all tendencies, just as capital accommodates all 'needs,' providing that the tendencies and needs have purchasing power." Lyotard, *The Postmodern Condition,* 76.

11. Manas Ray, *Postmodernism / Engagement with History: The Cinema of Alexander Kluge* (Queensland, Australia: Griffith University, n.d.), 4. Note that this reference is to an undated first draft of this book.

12. Ibid., 5.

13. Ibid., 16.

Chapter 5: The Film in the Auteur's Head

1. Kluge, *Der Angriff der Gegenwart auf die übrige Zeit,* 12. It is interesting to note that this *Drehbuch* or "script" was published before the film was released and differs from the release print in many ways. Perhaps half of what is in the script shows up in this film. A more detailed discussion of these differences follows on pages 148 and 165 below.

2. He has written that "film must be able to attend to social documentation, political questions, educational questions and new filmic developments, which under the previous requirements of film work were possible only in a very limited way." Kluge, "Was Wollen die 'Oberhausener?'" 2.

3. He did, of course, adapt many of his own published stories.

4. Kluge quoted in Steinborn, "Cinema Pure, Cinema Impure," 42–43.

5. Kluge emphasizes the importance of the experiences brought to the film by each spectator. These must be utilized in interpreting the work, producing meaning.

6. Kluge, *Gelegenheitsarbeit einer Sklavin,* 216.

7. Quoted in Liebman, "On New German Cinema, Art, Enlightenment, and the Public Sphere," 40.

8. Gertrude Koch, "Alexander Kluge's Phantom of the Opera," *New German Critique,* no. 49 (fall 1990): 87.

9. In the book about this film, Kluge states that other possible titles for the film included: "Das Geheimnis der letzten Stunde" (Last-moment-details) or "Das Kino und die Illusion der Stadt." Kluge, *Der Angriff der Gegenwart auf die übrige Zeit,* 8.

10. The title is provocative in a way similar to that of the previous film, *The Power of Emotion,* in so far as it anthropomorphizes an abstract concept.

11. Raymond Williams, for example, argues that the shift from the city to the metropolis was the key factor in the development of modernism. The metropolis embodied not only the negative social conditions against which artists rebelled, but also provided the conditions that made the new art possible: immigrant observers, whose physical uprooting freed them from cultural traditions; a more open intellectual milieu with more complex and fluid social relations; and new sources of patronage, both private and institutional. Williams, *The Politics of Modernism,* 37–47.

12. Kluge, *Der Angriff der Gegenwart auf die übrige Zeit,* 10.

13. This critique is not from some Rousseauian rustic, but from an urbane devotee of city life. Kluge has spent most of his life in Berlin, Frankfurt, and Munich. On several occasions he has professed his great affection for Frankfurt, the most modern metropolis in Germany, yet even this city now suffers from certain excesses of overdevelopment.

14. Unorthodox sexual practices have positive consequences in a number of Kluge's films. In *The Power of Emotion,* a rapist brings an almost dead woman back to life. In *The Patriot,* a peeping tom is befriended and given vision tips by his victim. Leni Peickert, in *Artistes at the Top of the Bigtop: Disoriented,* seems most at ease with the man who seduced her as a child. Only by breaking with social norms does sexuality seem to be reinvested with a healing or creative power.

15. Miriam Hansen, "Introduction," *New German Critique,* no. 49 (fall 1990): 7–8.

16. Heide Schlüpmann, "'What is different is good,'" 150.

17. Kluge, *Gelgenheitsarbeit einer Sklavin,* 220.

18. It is interesting to note that cinema's rival, television, is curiously absent from the film. No images of the television are shown. The narrator does refer to Gerlach, a man who, while interested in producing television programming, is nonetheless too busy to watch television. Kluge himself is said to watch almost no television.

19. Georg Simmel, "The Metropolis and Mental Life," in *The Sociology of Georg Simmel,* trans. and ed. Kurt H. Wolff (Glencoe, Illinois: Free Press, 1950), 409.

20. Max Horkheimer and Theodor W. Adorno, *Dialectic of Enlightenment* (New York: Continuum, 1987), 120–21.

21. Quoted in *Der Angriff der Gegenwart auf die übrige Zeit Pressbook,* 5.

22. Kluge, *Der Angriff der Gegenwart auf die übrige Zeit,* 10–11.

23. The question of *Zusammmenhang* in Kluge's work has been raised by many commentators. David Wellbery has claimed that Kluge's affinities with Postmodernism stem from the way he has problematized the whole notion of *Zusammenhang.* In my view, this is a key argument for seeing his connection to the modernist tradition. How

things interconnect is a major question for Kluge, but he never questions the possibility of Zusammenhang or its centrality for making meaning and as a principle of artistic construction. David E. Wellbery, "Postmodernism in Europe: On Recent German Writing," in The Postmodern Moment: A Handbook of Contemporary Innovation in the Arts, ed. Stanley Trachtenberg (Westport, Connecticut: Greenwood Press, 1985), 238. Wellbery remarks in a footnote that Kluge's and Negt's Geschichte und Eigensinn "might well be considered the most significant postmodernist theoretical work produced in Germany." Ibid., 244.

24. In the screenplay, Kluge remarks that this is a film about film. He refers to the cinema as the "power station of emotion" in the twentieth century, but fears that it may not survive much longer: "I would not be prepared to divorce myself from the illusion that the cinema, to which I have dedicated so much of my work time, will move victoriously into the 21st century. This notion allows me to deal realistically with the dangers that threaten film, the phenomenon of the so-called new media. One abandons an old illusion as one constructs a new one." Kluge, Der Angriff der Gegenwart auf die übrige Zeit, 13. As his penultimate film—and, some would argue, his last fully realized film—it may also represent his personal farewell to involvement in the medium.

25. Schmidt, "Das Publikum soll zufrieden sein," vi. Renate Schramm, "Oft geht Kluge zweimal pro Tag ins Kino," Abendzeitung, 14–15 September 1968. Oddly enough, he claims that it doesn't matter whether the films he sees are bad, because he can make them better in his thoughts. This seems an oddly elitist argument. He finds films thought-provoking even when they are bad, but he must make different, presumably better films, so that other spectators will be able to think.

26. Franz Schöler, "'Man muß zärtlich sein,'" Handelsblatt, 24 September 1966.

27. Kluge, Gelegenheitsarbeit einer Sklavin, 196.

28. Gert Gliewe, "Kino als Kraftwerk der Gefühle: AZ-Gespräch mit Alexander Kluge über seinen neuen Film," Abendzeitung (Munich), 21 September 1985.

29. Kluge suggests that such experience is not only unfilmed, but unfilmable, at least in traditional narrative. This is not necessarily the case, however. The experiments in the 1970s with the Arbeiterfilm showed not only that these subjects can be filmed, but that large audiences are interested in seeing fictional films that take up everyday concerns from a nondominant point of view. These films were in fact so effective that they became political liabilities for Westdeutscher Rundfunk, which was commissioning them. See Richard Collins and Vincent Porter, WDR and the Arbeiterfilm: Fassbinder, Ziewer and others (London: British Film Institute, 1981).

30. Kluge, Der Angriff der Gegenwart auf die übrige Zeit, 12.

31. Alexander Kluge, "On Film and the Public Sphere," trans. Thomas Y. Levin and Miriam Hansen, New German Critique, nos. 24–25 (fall–winter 1981–2): 218.

32. Helke Sander, "'You Can't Always Get What You Want,'" 61.

33. "Kluge—doppelt gesehen," Film-Echo/Film Woche 22, no. 96 (30 November 68): 4.

34. Alexander Kluge, Theodor Fontane, Heinrich von Kleist und Anna Wilde: Zur Grammatik der Zeit (Berlin: Klaus Wagenbach, 1987), 51.

35. Mädi Kemper, "Zu Kluges 'Gelegenheitsarbeit einer Sklavin,'" Frauen und Film, no. 3 (November 1974): 23–24.

36. Norbert Jochum, "Alexander-Schlacht," Die Zeit (Hamburg), 23 August 1985.

37. As mentioned in the previous chapter, Enno Patalas, a friend of Kluge's and curator of the Munich Film Museum, did supplement the *Abschied* script slightly by identifying some of the quotations and images that were not identified in the film itself.

38. Given the short runs that Kluge's films often have, and the fact that his films are not available commercially on videotape, the screenplay is a much more valuable resource than it would be for most commercial films.

39. Kluge, *Der Angriff der Gegenwart auf die übrige Zeit*, 8.

40. Liebman, "On New German Cinema, Art, Enlightenment, and the Public Sphere," 35.

41. Kluge might be happy to agree that he does not impose some preexisting concepts on reality, that he takes the world as he finds it. He might then quote Marx: "In order to make petrified objects dance, you must play them their own tune." Yet, is not even this an *a priori* theoretical position dictating a particular attitude toward reality and a specific approach to filmmaking? Kluge either ignores or celebrates such paradoxes; he resolves them, if ever, only by his pragmatic production practice, in which he simply gets what he can on film.

42. Jochum, "Alexander-Schlacht."

43. Ibid.

44. Kluge, *Gelegenheitsarbeit einer Sklavin*, 208.

45. For example:

> [The spectator] should rely on his fantasy and not seek a pre-digested red thread. If the spectator relaxes and observes precisely, the film cannot confuse him. If however he brings along the normal swimming habits from the German crime film and the five Angelique films, then he will have difficulties. There are two kinds of viewers. The one kind uses the cinema only as something to consume and are correspondingly used by the cinema. But in my opinion there are many more people, who also want to encounter real experiences in the cinema and who possess an active fantasy. They, and not some elite group, are the ones for whom I have made the film.

Alexander Kluge quoted in Franz Schöler, "Mit Phantasie die Welt beflügeln," *Die Welt* (Bonn), 14 September 1968.

46. Kluge quoted in Schöler, "Man muß zärtlich sein."

47. Schöler, "Das Publikum soll zufrieden sein."

48. Kluge, "On Film and the Public Sphere," 210–11.

49. In an interview with Liebman, Kluge criticized Eisenstein's film practice as too controlling and characterized it as an "intentionalist pathos." Liebman, "On New German Cinema, Art, Enlightenment, and the Public Sphere," 49.

50. Liebman, "Why Kluge?" 6.

51. Steinborn, "Cinema Pure, Cinema Impure," 48.

52. Liebman, "On New German Cinema, Art, Enlightenment, and the Public Sphere," 55.

53. Ibid., 55.

54. Sander, "'You Can't Always Get What You Want,'" 61.

55. Kluge, *Gelegenheitsarbeit einer Sklavin*, 196.

56. Miriam Hansen, "Cooperative Auteur Cinema and Oppositional Public Sphere: Alexander Kluge's contribution to *Germany in Autumn*," 54.

57. See, for example, his metaphorization and diminution of Gabi Teichert's activities in *The Patriot*.

58. Maxim Biller, "Im Dunkel der Köpfe," *Der Spiegel* 39, no. 44, (28 October 1985), 271.

59. The more political collaborative films have side-stepped the politics of public funding by obtaining private funders (among them Rudolf Augstein, the owner of *Der Spiegel*).

60. "The crucial point is that a writer's production must have the character of a model: it must be able to instruct other writers in their production and, secondly, it must be able to place an improved apparatus at their disposal. This apparatus will be the better, the more consumers it brings in contact with the production process—in short the more readers or spectators it turns into collaborators." This program for structural change sounds very much like Kluge's. Both concepts owe much to Brecht's epic theater. Benjamin, *Understanding Brecht*, 98.

61. Harvey Gross, "Parody, Reminiscence, Critique: Aspects of the Modernist Style," in *Modernism: Challenges and Perspectives*, ed. Monique Chefdor, Ricardo Quinones, and Albert Wachtel (Urbana and Chicago: University of Illinois Press, 1986), 140.

62. Kluge's films also often incorporate inside jokes, which are both distancing and esoteric. For example, in *Occasional Work of a Female Slave*, Bion Steinborn, Alexandra Kluge's husband at that time, plays her fictional husband, Franz Bronski. In the credits he is identified only as Bronski and she as Kluge. In *The Power of Emotion*, the reporter played by Alexandra is identified as Frau Pichota. Pichota is also the name of the married man that got Anita G. (also played by Alexandra) pregnant in *Yesterday Girl*. It is as if, years later, she has finally married him. Kluge's films are full of such intertextual connections—shots repeated in different films, characters with the same or similar names, etc.—which present teasing riddles to the cognoscenti.

63. Quoted in B. Ruby Rich, "She Says, He Says," 31.

64. Sander, "'You Can't Always Get What You Want'" 64.

65. Hansen, "Cooperative Auteur Cinema and Oppositional Public Sphere," 55.

66. Hansen, "Introduction," 7.

67. Hansen, "Reinventing the Nickelodeon," 194.

68. Mirian Hansen, "Alexander Kluge Cinema and the Public Sphere: The Construction Site of Counter-History," *Discourse*, no. 6 (fall 1983): 67.

69. Ibid., 68.

70. Kluge's evaluation of his sister's contributions to the film were not always consistent. In one interview he suggested that her insistence that Roswitha move outside the family was perhaps a mistake. He felt that the issues should be resolved there and, until they were, she would not be able to function effectively out of the family. "She wants to turn to politics. Now such a decision is first of all abstract. If one goes out of the family into the public sphere, into the city and searches through the city for opportunities for struggle, then one will never come upon really concrete struggles. Because one does not bring one's own interests out of the family with one." "Fürsorge und was weiter," *Filmreport*, nos. 23–24 (31 December 1973): 29. In other interviews he softened his position to say that she insisted on political activity in the public sphere and that this was correct. "This production power alone in the family does not earn anything, only on the larger social plane does it lead to dividends for the fantasy." Barbara Bronnen, "Roswitha ist so listig," *Abendzeitung* (Munich), 7 December 1973. In this same article, Kluge also blamed his sister for the lack of warmth in the characterization.

71. In *The Blind Director*'s story of the superfluous doctor, Kluge narrates

1. She is a doctor. She goes on vacation.
2. That was her office.
3. During her vacation her boss, whose practice she has developed for years, hires a young doctor fresh from a university clinic.
4. The two hundred thousand mark machine, with which the young colleague has bought his way into the practice.
5. He gets her room.
6. The staff shows the problem.
7. Superfluous.
8. The colleague is ambitious.
9. She has received a new workplace in the basement.
10. Professor Wederhoff has gotten old.
11. He's sorry.
12. They have worked together fifteen years.
13. She has resigned without notice.
14. She has been standing here now for two hours.
15. The admission ticket, unused.
16. For a moment she thought that she was needed here.
17. A person who loses his job, doesn't take the next best but rather the sixth worst, provided that it is professorial.
18. She behaves professorially. For a hundred years people have constrained their lives professorially, because otherwise they could not survive.
19. The present expands itself.

Most of these comments are straightforward and factual. There is a touch of irony in their brevity and abruptness, but they do not question the authority of the narrator. Comments 17 through 19 are less factual and more reflective. All three of them include sweeping statements that, while suggestive, are ambiguous or vague. They sound profound, but may or may not contain any useful or valid insights. Although there is certainly a shift in the discourse here, this does not constitute a significant shift in the point of view or the authority of the narrator. If anything, the last three comments simply deepen the sense of the narrator's omniscience.

72. Rich, "She Says, He Says," 32.

73. Ibid.

74. Ibid.

75. Rich points to three instances in which the narration undermines Roswitha's actions. The first is the title that informs us that the factory is going to be moved. We learn the fact easily, but Roswitha must expend a lot of energy to ascertain this. The second is the title that informs us that the company decided not to relocate—"independently of Roswitha and Sylvia." It would appear that the sole purpose of this is to show that Roswitha's actions were completely ineffectual. A third instance is the ironic, patronizing voice-over: "Having found no better way of experiencing reality, Roswitha and Sylvia learn a Brecht song by heart." Ibid., 32–33.

76. Liebman, "Why Kluge?" 22.

Chapter 6: Kluge on Television

1. As is often the case with Kluge's public statements, fragments of similar thoughts surface in different interviews. The first sentence is quoted in Christian Schröder, "Das etwas andere Autoren-Fernsehen," *Der Tagesspiegel*, 1 November 1991.

The second quote occurs in Bettina Huhndorf, "'Parasit mit Steinfernsehen,'" *Wiesbaden Kurier,* 13 September 1994.

2. The announcer actually says the name of the program twice, first in German ("Zehn vor eif") and then in English ("Ten to Eleven"). The program's logo also is bilingual: *10 vor 11, Ten to Eleven.*

3. Liebman, "On New German Cinema, Art, Enlightenment, and the Public Sphere," 29.

4. Klaus von Bismarck, Günter Gaus, Alexander Kluge, and Ferdinand Sieger, *Industrialisierung des Bewußtseins* (Munich and Zurich: Piper, 1985).

5. Alexander Kluge quoted in Wolfgang Michal, "Scheinheilige Unterschiede," *Vorwärts,* 12 March 1984.

6. Substantial declines in viewership might make it more difficult to justify the user license fees from which the public networks derive most of their revenues. Moreover, their advertising revenues could be adversely affected by the competition.

7. In 1987, Albert Scharf, president of the European Broadcasting Union, argued: "With DBS satellites, however, there can be no national control." Scharf called for cooperation among European nations to set minimum standards for program content and advertising. *Variety,* 14 January 1987, 154.

8. The first cable television experiment began in Ludwigshafen in January 1984, followed by others in Dortmund, Munich, and Berlin later in 1984 and 1985.

9. Most of Kluge's feature films received television funding in exchange for posttheatrical broadcast rights, under the Television Framework Accord. Unlike Fassbinder, Schlöndorff, Reitz, and other New German directors, however, Kluge was not interested in commissioned projects directly for the small screen.

10. Alexander Kluge quoted in Michal, "Scheinheilige Unterschiede." Kluge goes on to say: "When ZDF for example buys DM 250 million [of programs] from Leo Kirch [BETA-Taurus Films] it's easy to see [the similarities]. I believe that this is the way that jobs are lost for television producers. I believe that ZDF has here carried out a one-sided subsidization policy for the firm BETA-film." He does not mean to suggest that there are no differences between public and private, but he insists that these differences should not be exaggerated.

11. The two major forces in founding SAT 1 were Axel Springer and Leo Kirch. The two largest entities involved were PKS (Programmgesellschaft für Kabel und Satellitenrundfunk), which Kirch controls, and APF (Aktuelle Presse Fernsehen), comprised of 165 newspaper publishers, the most powerful of whom was Springer, with a 35 percent share. *Variety,* 13 February 1985, 65. Other publishers involved in SAT 1 include Burda, Holzbrink, Bauer, Otto Maier, and the *Frankfurter Allgemeine Zeitung.* Ibid., 74.

12. Unlike Kluge's films, most of his television work has never been shown outside of German speaking countries. Paradoxically, however, Kluge's television programs, much more so than his films, seem more international or cosmopolitan, in part because they utilize a great many English words and phrases. The name of Kluge's umbrella television production organization discussed below is a good example: DCTP, which stands for the English phrase, Development Corporation for Television Programs.

13. *Der Spiegel* has its own DCTP news magazine show (*Spiegel-TV*) as do *stern* magazine (*stern-tv*) and *Die Zeit* (*Die Zeit TV Magazine*). Dentsu, a Japanese firm, regarded DCTP as a foothold in the German television market.

14. This breaks down as follows: Kluge (50%), Dentsu (37.5%), and Spiegel

Publishing (12.5%). Kluge's 50 percent interest is the entity Arbeitsgemeinschaft Kabel-Satellit, an umbrella organization of film directors, theaters, book publishers, and musical institutions, but controlled by Kluge. Martin Peters, "Auch ein Quoten-killer versteht das Geschäft," *Rheinischer Merkur,* 27 May 1994, and Mark Siemons, "Die Welt zerspringt in tausend Stücke," *Frankfurter Allgemeine Zeitung,* 11 June 1994.

15. Wolfgang Timpe, "Kulturartist auf dem TV-Sat," *Neue Medien* (November 1987): 96. Most articles describing the program identify it as a "Kultursendung," or a "Kulturprogramm." Television listings also usually identify it as "Kultur."

16. It seems strange that Kluge has not, for the most part, attempted to use these programs to showcase new and radical works from unestablished film- and video-makers. Already completed films could be reviewed and selected by Kluge, and then repackaged for broadcast. Most young filmmakers or video artists would be delighted to have their films shown to a large television audience and would view any payment at all as a windfall, since they had already paid their production costs. Not only would this provide inexpensive and interesting programming without the risks of commissioning, it would also provide funding to that segment of the film production sphere that needs it most: unestablished young directors. Such a policy would also constitute a more effective implementation of the diversity of programming for which Kluge has argued. One can only speculate that at this stage of his career, Kluge is less interested in experimental work or younger artists. Perhaps such programming does not seem as appropriate to a targeted audience that is older and more affluent. Or perhaps he is simply reluctant to relinquish control at this critical stage of the venture.

17. In a newspaper interview, Kluge announced DCTP's goal as the creation of "cultural multiplicity" in private television and a "concern for classical forms of expression from book, film and music theater." Arno Makowsky, "Der Pate als Quoten-killer," *Süddeutsche Zeitung,* 16 October 1993.

18. Kluge quoted in Günther Wolf, "Roßkur für die Künste," *Hamburger Abendblatt,* 3 June 1991.

19. Kluge quoted in Manfred Lügenhorst, "Wir werden uns rächen," *Abendzeitung,* 13–14 July 1968.

20. Alexander Kluge, "On Film and the Public Sphere," *New German Critique,* nos. 24–25 (fall–winter 1981–82): 210–11.

21. Eder and Kluge, *Ulmer Dramaturgien,* 139.

22. Kilb, "Der lange Abschied des Herrn K."

23. Gertrude Koch and Heide Schlüpmann, "'Nur Trümmern trau ich . . .': Ein Gespräch mit Alexander Kluge," in *Kanalarbeit: Medienstratagien im Kulturwandel,* ed. Hans Ulrich Reck (Basel, Frankfurt am Main: Strömfeld/Roter Stern, 1988), 23.

24. Marcus Hertneck, "Die Unterwanderung des Bildes," *Süddeutsche Zeitung,* 11 May 1992.

25. The inclusion of English in Kluge's program titles not only is consonant with current trends in German media, but is prominent evidence of the international composition and aspirations of DCTP. Kluge has sought production participation from foreign entities (Paper Tiger TV in New York, Great Britain's Channel 4 and BBC, and the *International Herald Tribune*) and envisions the possibility of a European or possibly global cultural channel. Spiegel-TV has already achieved Europe-wide exposure through Britain's Superchannel. Birgit Weidinger, "Der Partisan aus Deutschland: Alexander Kluge wirbt in London für mehr Programmaustausch," *Süddeutsche Zeitung,* 13 December 1992.

26. According to one source, RTL viewership drops from 3 million to .6 million,

and SAT 1 numbers fall from 3 million to .2 million. Even this figure, the private channels claim, is probably too high, because a lot of people forget to turn off their televisions or fall asleep while they are still on. Tilmann P. Gangloff, "Saboteur im Zirkus," *Deutsches Allgemeines Sonntagsblatt,* 21 January 1994. Other sources suggest that the viewership for Kluge's RTL programs are closer to 1 million viewers per show. Kluge himself claims that 280 million viewers have watched the 250 *10 vor 11* programs he has produced. Siemons, "Die Welt zerspringt in tausend Stücke."

27. Bettina Huhndorf, "Inseln im bunten Einerlei," *Der Tagesspiegel,* 13 September 1994.

28. Kluge, however, opposes works with a smooth surface: "For a long time I haven't put enough scrap material into my broadcasts." Siemons, "Die Welt zerspringt in tausend Stücke."

29. Gangloff, "Saboteur im Zirkus."

30. Tilman Baumgärtel, "'Wir sind keine Untermieter': dctp-Chef Alexander Kluge zu erneuten Vorwürfen, seine Programme seien 'Quotenkiller,'" *die tageszeitung,* 23 October 1993, and Astrid Deubner-Mankowsky and Giaco Schiesser, "Die Schrift an der Wand," *WochenZeitung,* 21 January 1994.

31. For example, one critic compares Kluge's media techniques to the authoritarianism of the ostensibly anti-authoritarian German schoolteachers of the 1970s. Kluge, he argues, baffles the viewers and thereby holds them in thrall. Jessen, "Vom Elend der Denkanstöße."

32. Helmut Thoma claims that the media laws have simply granted Kluge "a license to collect money." Peters, "Auch ein Quotenkiller versteht das Geschäft."

33. Schröder, "Das etwas andere Autoren-Fernsehen."

34. Klaus Kreimeier, "Ten to Eleven oder: Kann man Zeit abbilden?" *Die Zeit,* 27 November 1992.

35. Marcus Hertneck, "Die unterschiedliche Wirkung einer Gartenschere," *Süddeutsche Zeitung,* 30 March 1992. Kluge discussed the situation in some depth in an interview, "Persönlich prüde," *epd/Kirche und Rundfunk,* no. 65, 21 August 1991.

36. "Kluge-Dentsu TV," *die tageszeitung,* 25 November 1986. Kluge has also explained why advertisers are interested in more up-scale cultural programming: "One cannot advertise the new generation of quality computers or a champagne in the commercial ghetto from six to eight p.m. among laundry detergent and junk food commercials." "Eine 'Spielwiese' im privaten Fernsehen: Alexander Kluges Kulturprogramm bei RTL plus," *Neue Zürcher Zeitung,* 2 June 1988.

37. A major setback to these plans occurred with the 1994 demise of Vox, a channel in which DCTP held an 11 percent interest and which Kluge hoped would expand throughout Europe. After single-handedly trying to save the channel, he finally sold his share to the U.S. bank Goldman-Sachs. Huhndorf, "Inseln in bunten Einerlei."

38. Quoted in an interview by Ingrid Scheib-Rotbart, "Alexander Kluge in New York," *Prisma Akzente,* no. 1 (1989): 61.

39. "'Spiegel' und Kluge mit RTL-plus," *die tageszeitung,* 19 May 1987. "Kluge-Dentsu-TV."

Chapter 7: Recollecting the Fragments

1. Quoted in Liebman, "On New German Cinema, Art, Enlightenment, and the Public Sphere," 58.

2. Lyotard, *The Postmodern Condition,* 78.

3. Eder and Kluge, *Ulmer Dramaturgien,* 98.

4. Recall Liebman's comments cited in chapter 1: "Your practice seems closer to what we call postmodernism than to that highly refined purism that we have come to call—unfortunately and certainly incorrectly—modernism." Liebman, "On New German Cinema, Art, Enlightenment, and the Public Sphere," 57.

5. Jim Collins, *Uncommon Cultures* (Routledge: New York and London, 1989), 136.

6. Ibid.

7. Ibid., 138.

8. Ibid., 144.

9. "According to Jencks, the collapse of Modernist architecture as a whole was inevitable, because from its inception it was a movement that demonstrated its indifference—if not downright contempt—for the context and eventual inhabitants of its designs." Ibid., 129.

10. Adorno, *Aesthetic Theory,* 20. Adorno blames the bourgeoisie for the corruption of art into philistine pleasure, while certain modern critiques would blame the same group for turning traditional arts into high-brow pleasures from which other classes were excluded.

11. Eder and Kluge, *Ulmer Dramaturgien,* 139.

12. Alexander Kluge quoted in Liebman, "On New German Cinema, Art, Enlightenment, and the Public Sphere," 42.

13. Alexander Kluge quoted in ibid., 40.

14. The roles that women have been traditionally allowed to play—such as actress, novelist, critic, and filmmaker—are amply represented on Kluge's program. Partly this represents a bias toward literary and filmic art—the primary spheres of Kluge's own activity—but partly it represents a bias toward established figures of authority. Given Kluge's theoretical notions, one might expect instead to see a student or housewife interviewed about her strategies from below.

15. Collins, *Uncommon Cultures,* 136.

16. "For in the course of a day he [Kluge] often goes twice to the cinema. And his 'home theaters' are the Schiller, the Sun and the Atlantic Theater, that is all those houses in which sharp shooting and hard hitting goes on." According to the reporter, "he believes that one can take what occurs on the screen as an instigation of one's own thoughts and associations." Lügenhorst, "Wir werden uns rächen," 16.

17. Ibid.

Filmography

The filmography and bibliography were compiled from many sources. I am particularly indebted, however, to the careful and extensive bibliographical work of Stuart Liebman, published in *October* 46. Other very useful compilations include Bernward Urbanowski's, which appeared in *Text + Kritik 85/86*, Thomas Böhm-Christl's in his collection of essays entitled *Alexander Kluge,* and Hans Helmut Prinzler's in *Herzog/ Kluge/Straub,* edited by Peter W. Jansen and Wolfram Shütte.

Feature Films

Abschied von gestern: (Anita G.) (*Yesterday Girl*), 1965–1966.
Director: Alexander Kluge. Screenplay: Alexander Kluge, from his story "Anita G." Cast: Alexandra Kluge, Günther Mack, Hans Korte, Alfred Edel. Voiceover: Alexander Kluge. Cinematography: Edgar Reitz, Thomas Mauch. Sound: Hans-Jörg Wicha, Klaus Eckelt, Heinz Pusel. Editing: Beate Mainka. Production: Kairos Film and Independent Film. Premiere: September 5, 1966. Format: 35mm, b&w, 88 mins.

Die Artisten in der Zirkuskuppel: ratlos (*Artistes at the Top of the Big Top: Disoriented*), 1967.
Director: Alexander Kluge. Screenplay: Alexander Kluge. Cast: Hannelore Hoger, Alfred Edel, Siegfried Graue, Bernd Hoeltz, Kurt Jürgens. Voiceover: Alexandra Kluge, Hannelore Hoger, Herr Hollenbeck. Cinematography: Günter Hörmann, Thomas Mauch. Sound: Bernd Hoeltz. Editing: Beate Mainka-Jellinghaus. Production: Kairos Film. Premiere: August 30, 1968. Format: 35mm, b&w and color, 103 mins.

Der grosse Verhau (*The Big Mess*), 1969–1970.
Director: Alexander Kluge. Screenplay: Alexander Kluge. Cast: Maris Sterr, Vinzenz Sterr, Hannelore Hoger, Hark Bohm. Cinematography: Thomas Mauch, Alfred Tichawski. Special Effects: Günter Hörmann, Hannelore Hoger, Joachim Heimbucher. Sound: Bernd Hoeltz. Editing: Maximiliane Mainka, Beate Mainka-Jellinghaus. Production: Kairos Film. Premiere: June 30, 1971. Format: 35mm, b&w and color, 86 mins.

245

Willi Tobler und der Untergang der 6. Flotte (*Willi Tobler and the Wreck of the Sixth Fleet*), 1969–1971.
Director: Alexander Kluge. Screenplay: Alexander Kluge. Cast: Alfred Edel, Hark Bohm, Hannelore Hoger, Kurt Jürgens, Helga Skalla. Cinematography: Dietrich Lohmann, Alfred Tichawski, Thomas Mauch. Sound: Bernd Hoeltz. Editing: Maximiliane Mainka, Beate Mainka-Jellinghaus. Production: Kairos Film. Premiere: Broadcast over Zweites Deutsches Fernsehen on January 19, 1972. Format: 35mm, b&w and color, 96 mins.

Gelegenheitsarbeit einer Sklavin (*Occasional Work of a Female Slave*), 1973.
Director: Alexander Kluge. Screenplay: Alexander Kluge, Hans Drawe, Alexandra Kluge. Cast: Alexandra Kluge, Franz Bronski (Bion Steinborn), Sylvia Gartmann, Traugott Buhre, Alfred Edel, Ursula Dirichs, Ortrud Teichart. Cinematography: Thomas Mauch. Sound: Gunter Kortwich. Editing: Beate Mainka-Jellinghaus. Production: Kairos Film. Premiere: December 7, 1973. Format: 35mm, b&w, 91 mins.

In Gefahr und größer Not bringt der Mittelweg den Tod (*The Middle of the Road Is a Very Dead End*), 1974.
Directors: Alexander Kluge, Edgar Reitz. Screenplay: Alexander Kluge, Edgar Reitz. Cast: Dagmar Bödderich, Jutta Winkelmann, Norbert Kentrup, Alfred Edel, Kurt Jürgens. Cinematography: Edgar Reitz, Alfred Hürmer, Günter Hörmann. Sound: Burkhard Tauschwitz, Dietmar Lange. Music: Richard Wagner, Giuseppe Verdi, among others, selected and edited by Kluge and Reitz. Editing: Beate Mainka-Jellinghaus. Production: RK-Film [Reitz Film, Kairos Film]. Premiere: December 18, 1974. Format: 35 mm, b&w, 90 mins.

Der starke Ferdinand (*Strongman Ferdinand*), 1975–1976.
Director: Alexander Kluge. Screenplay: Alexander Kluge, from his story "A Bolshevik of Capital." Cast: Heinz Schubert, Vérénice Rudolph, Heinz Schimmelpfennig, Siegfried Wischnewski, Hark Bohm, Joachim Hackethal, Gert Günther Hoffmann. Voiceover: Alexander Kluge. Cinematography: Thomas Mauch, Martin Schäfer. Sound: Heiko Hinderks, Reiner Wiehr. Editing: Heidi Genée, Agape von Dorstewitz. Production: Kairos Film in conjunction with Reitz Film. Premiere: April 4, 1976. Format: 35mm, color, 97 mins.
    A reedited version of this film was rereleased to theaters in 1977. The initial release of the film had been impeded by a newspaper strike.

"Zu böser Schlacht schleich ich heut nacht so bang—." ("Into This Evil Fight Tonight I Am Afraid to Creep . . . "), 1977.
Director: Alexander Kluge. Screenplay: Alexander Kluge, Maximiliane Mainka. Cast: Alfred Edel, Helga Skalla, Hark Bohm, Kurt Jürgens, Hannelore Hoger. Cinematography: Dietrich Lohmann, Alfred Tichawsky, Thomas Mauch. Sound: Bernd Hoeltz. Editing: Maximiliane Mainka. Production: Kairos-Film. Premiere: July 1977. Format: 35mm, color, 81 mins.
    Maximiliane Mainka reedited Kluge's *Willi Tobler und der Untergang der 6. Flotte* (1969), adding some new footage to produce this film.

Deutschland im Herbst (Germany in Autumn), 1977–1978.
Directors: Alf Brustellin, Rainer Werner Fassbinder, Alexander Kluge, Beate Mainka-Jellinghaus, Maximiliane Mainka, Edgar Reitz, Katja Ruppé, Peter Schubert, Hans Peter Cloos, Berhnard Sinkel, Volker Schlöndorff. Screenplay: Heinrich Böll, Peter Steinbach, and the directors. Cast: Rainer Werner Fassbinder, Hannelore Hoger, Katja Ruppé, Angela Winkler, Heinz Bennent, Helmut Griem, Vadim Glowna, Enno Patalas, Horst Mahler, Mario Adorf, Wolf Biermann. Voiceover: Alexander Kluge. Cinematography: Michael Ballhaus, Günter Hörmann, Jürgen Jürges, Bodo Kessler, Dietrich Lohmann, Werner Lüring, Colin Mounier, Jörg Schmidt-Reitwein. Sound: Klaus Eckelt. Editing: Heidi Genée, Mulle Götz-Dickopp, Juliane Lorenz, Beate Mainka-Jellinghaus, Tanja Schmidbauer, Christine Warnck. Production: Pro-Ject Filmproduktion im Filmverlag der Autoren in conjunction with Hallelujah Film and Kairos Film. Premiere: March 3, 1978. Format: 35mm, b&w and color, 123 mins.

Filmproduktion is owned by Theo Hinz, head of the important distribution company Film Verlag der Autoren, whom Kluge credits with the original idea for the collective film project.

At the film's premiere at the Berlin Film Festival, a 134 minute version was projected; this was shortened for the film's theatrical release on March 17, 1978.

Die Patriotin (The Patriot), 1977–79.
Director: Alexander Kluge. Screenplay: Alexander Kluge. Cast: Hannelore Hoger, Dieter Mainka, Alfred Edel, Alexander von Eschwege, Beate Holle, Kurt Jürgens, Willi Münch, Marius Müller-Westernhagen. Voiceover: Alexander Kluge. Cinematography: Jörg Schmidt-Reitwein, Petra Hiller, Charlie Scheydt, Thomas Mauch, Werner Lüring, Reinhard Oefle, Günter Hörmann. Sound: Peter Dick, Siegfried Moraweck, Kurt Graupner, O. Karla. Mix: Willi Schwadorf. Editing: Beate Mainka-Jellinghaus. Production: Kairos-Film. Premiere: September 20, 1979. Format: 35mm, b&w and color, 121 mins.

The "Bundeswehrlied" section of this film was directed by Margarethe von Trotta. An 89 minute version was shown in June, 1979 in Berlin.

Der Kandidat (The Candidate), 1979–1980.
Directors: Alexander Kluge, Stefan Aust, Alexander von Eschwege, Volker Schlöndorff. Screenplay: Stefan Aust, Alexander von Eschwege, Alexander Kluge, Volker Schlöndorff. Cast: Franz Josef Straus, Marianne Strauss. Voiceover: Stefan Aust. Cinematography: Igor Luther, Werner Lüring, Jörg Schmidt-Reitwein, Thomas Mauch, Bodo Kessler. Sound: Manfred Meyer, Vladimir Vizner, Anke Appelt, Martin Müller. Editing: Inge Behrens, Beate Mainka-Jellinghaus, Jane Sperr, Mulle Goetz Dickopp. Production: Pro-Ject Filmproduktion im Filmverlag der Autoren with Bioskop Film and Kairos Film. Premiere: April 18, 1980. Format: 35mm, b&w and color, 129 mins.

Krieg und Frieden (War and Peace), 1982–1983.
Directors: Alexander Kluge, Stefan Aust, Axel Engstfeld, Volker Schlöndorff. Screenplay: Heinrich Böll and the directors. Cast: Jürgen Prochnow, Gunther Kaufman, Manfred Zapatka, Bruno Gans, Hans-Michael Rehberg, Michael Gahr. Cinematography: Igor Luther, Werner Lüring, Thomas Mauch, Bernd Mosblech, Franz Rath. Sound: Christian Moldt, Edward Porente, Olaf Reinke, Manfred von Rintelen, Karl-Walter

Tietze, Vladimir Vizner. Editing: Dagmar Hirtz, Beate Mainka-Jellinghaus, Carola Mai, Barbara von Weitershausen. Production: Pro-ject Filmproduktion im Filmverlag der Autoren with Bioskop Film and Kairos Film. Premiere: October 1982. Format: 35mm, color, 120 mins.

Kluge has made several different versions of this film, although the materials and general strategy remain essentially the same. A partly reedited and shortened version was premiered on February 1, 1983.

Die Macht der Gefühle (*The Power of Emotion*), 1983.
Director: Alexander Kluge. Screenplay: Alexander Kluge. Cast: Hannelore Hoger, Alexandra Kluge, Edgar Boehlke, Klaus Wennemann. Cinematography: Werner Lüring, Thomas Mauch. Sound: Olaf Reinke, Karl-Walter Tietze. Editing: Beate Mainka-Jellinghaus, Carola Mai. Production: Kairos Film. Premiere: September 16, 1983. Format: 35mm, b&w and color, 115 mins.

Der Angriff der Gegenwart auf die übrige Zeit (*The Blind Director*), 1985.
Director: Alexander Kluge. Screenplay: Alexander Kluge. Cast: Jutta Hoffmann, Armin Mueller-Stahl, Michael Rehberg, Rosel Zech. Cinematography: Thomas Mauch, Werner Lüring, Hermann Fahr, Judith Kaufmann. Sound: Josef Dillinger, Olaf Reinke, Georg Otto. Editing: Jane Seitz. Production: Kairos Film in conjunction with Zweites Deutsches Fernsehen and the Frankfurt State Opera Theater. Premiere: October 1985. Format: 35mm, color, 113 mins.

Vermischte Nachrichten (*Odds and Ends*), 1986.
Director: Alexander Kluge. Screenplay: Alexander Kluge. Cast: Mariata Breuer, Rosel Zeck, Sabine Wegner, André Jung, Sabine Trooger. Voiceover: Alexander Kluge. Cinematography: Werner Lüring, Thomas Mauch, Michael Christ, Hermann Fahr. Sound: Willi Schwadorf. Editing: Beate Mainka-Jellinghaus. Production: Kairos Film in conjunction with Zweites Deutsches Fernsehen. Premiere: September 25, 1986. Format: 35mm, b&w and color, 103 mins.

The documentary material of Helmut Schmidt's visit to the DDR was filmed by Franz Rath and directed by Volker Schlöndorff.

Short Films

Brutalität in Stein (Brutality in Stone; since 1963, a slightly altered version has circulated under the title *Die Ewigkeit von gestern* [The Eternity of Yesterday]), 1960.
Directors: Alexander Kluge, Peter Schamoni. Script: Peter Schamoni, Alexander Kluge. Voiceover: Christian Marschall, Hans Clarin. Cinematography: Wolf Wirth. Music: Hans Posegga. Editing: Alexander Kluge, Peter Schamoni. Production: Alexander Kluge, Peter Schamoni. Premiere: February 8, 1961. Format: 35mm, b&w, 12 mins.

Rennen (Racing), 1961.
Directors: Alexander Kluge, Paul Kruntorad. Script: Hans von Neuffer, Paul Kruntorad. Voiceover: Mario Adorf. Cinematography: archival material. Editing: Bessi Lemmer, Alexander Kluge. Production: Rolf A. Klug, Alexander Kluge. Premiere: 1961. Format: 35mm, b&w, 9 mins.

Lehrer im Wandel (Teachers through Change), 1962–1963.
Director: Alexander Kluge. Script: Alexander and Karen [aka Alexandra] Kluge. Cinematography: Alfred Tichawsky. Sound: Hans-Jörg Wicha. Editing: Alexander Kluge. Production: Alexander Kluge. Premiere: February 20, 1963. Format: 35mm, b&w, 11 mins.

Protokoll einer Revolution (Protocol of a Revolution), 1963.
Director: Alexander Kluge. Script: Alexander Kluge, Peter Berling. Cast: Uschi Glass. Voiceover: Sammy Drechsel, Rolf Illig. Cinematography: Günter Lemmer. Format: 35mm, b&w, 12 mins.

Porträt einer Bewährung (Proven Competence Portrayed), 1964.
Director: Alexander Kluge. Script: Alexander Kluge. Cast: Police Inspector Müller-Seegeberg. Cinematography: Wilfried E. Reinke, Günter Hörmann. Sound: Peter Schubert. Editing: Beate Mainka. Production: Kairos Film. Premiere: February 24, 1965. Format: 35mm, b&w, 13 mins.

Pokerspiel (Poker Game; a reedited version of Mack Sennett's *Nip and Tuck,* 1923), 1966.
Director: Alexander Kluge. Editing: Alexander Kluge. Production: Kairos Film. Premiere: October 14, 1966. Format: 35mm, b&w, 14 mins.

Frau Blackburn, geb. 5 Jan. 1872, wird gefilmt (Frau Blackburn, Born January 5, 1872, Is Filmed), 1967.
Director: Alexander Kluge. Script: Alexander Kluge. Cast: Martha Blackburn (Kluge's grandmother), Herr Guhl. Voiceover: Alexander Kluge, Hannelore Hoger. Cinematography: Thomas Mauch. Sound: Bernd Hoeltz. Editing: Beate Mainka-Jellinghaus. Production: Kairos Film. Premiere: June 28, 1967. Format: 35mm, b&w, 14 mins.

Die unbezähmbare Leni Peickert (The Indomitable Leni Peickert), 1966–1969.
Director: Alexander Kluge. Script: Alexander Kluge. Cast: Hannelore Hoger, Bernd Hoeltz, Nils von der Heyde. Cinematography Günter Hörmann, Thomas Mauch. Sound: Bernd Hoeltz. Editing: Beate Mainka-Jellinghaus. Production: Kairos Film. Premiere: Broadcast over West Deutsche Rundfunk on March 29, 1920. Format: 35mm, b&w, 60 mins.
   Kluge and Maximiliane Mainka prepared a 35 minute version of this film for a special exhibition of the Freunde der Kinemathek. It premiered in October 1976.

Feuerlöscher E. A. Winterstein (Fireman E. A. Winterstein), 1968.
Director: Alexander Kluge. Script: Alexander Kluge. Cast: Alexandra Kluge, Hans Korte, Peter Staimmer, Bernd Hoeltz. Cinematography: Edgar Reitz, Thomas Mauch. Sound: Hans-Jörg Wicha. Editing: Beate Mainka-Jellinghaus. Production: Kairos Film. Premiere: Not released. Format: 35mm, b&w, 11 mins.

Ein Arzt aus Halberstadt (A Doctor from Halberstadt), 1969–1970.
Director: Alexander Kluge. Script: Alexander Kluge. Voiceover: Alexandra Kluge. Cast: Dr. Ernst Kluge (Kluge's father). Cinematography: Alfred Tichawski, Günter Hör-

mann. Sound: Bernd Hoeltz. Editing: Maximiliane Mainka. Production: Kairos Film. Premiere: October 1976. Format: 35mm, b&w, 29 mins.

In 1987, Kluge reedited the film for television broadcast over SAT 1 (it aired on December 21, 1987). This version, which he prefers, is 14 minutes long.

Wir verbauen 3 X 27 Milliarden Dollar in einen Angriffschlachter (We Are Expending 3 X 27 Billion Dollars on an Attack Ship), 1970.
Director: Alexander Kluge. Script: Alexander Kluge, from his story "Angriffschlachter En Cascade." Cast: Hannelore Hoger, Hark Bohm, Kurt Jürgens, Ian Bodenham. Cinematography: Alfred Tichawski, Günter Hörmann, Hannelore Hoger, Thomas Mauch. Sound: Bernd Hoeltz. Editing: Maximiliane Mainka, Beate Mainka-Jellinghaus. Production: Kairos Film. Premiere: March 1970. Format: 35mm, b&w and color, 18 mins.

This film is also known by the titles *Der Angriffschlachter* and *Angriffsschlachter En Cascade.*

Besitzbürgerin, Jahrgang 1908 (A Woman of Means, Class of 1908), 1973.
Director: Alexander Kluge. Script: Alexander Kluge. Cast: Alice Schneider (Kluge's mother), Herr Guhl. Cinematography: Thomas Mauch. Sound: Francesco Joan-Escubano. Editing: Beate Mainka-Jellinghaus. Production: Kairos Film. Premiere: not released. Format: 35mm, b&w, 11 mins.

Die Menschen, die das Staufer-Jahr vorbereiten (The People Putting Together the Hohenstaufen Commemorative Year), 1977.
Director: Alexander Kluge. Script: Alexander Kluge, Maximiliane Mainka. Cast: Staff of the Württemberg State Museum, Stuttgart. Cinematography: Jörg Schmidt-Reitwein, Alfred Tichawsky. Editing: Maximiliane Mainka. Production: Kairos Film in conjunction with the Ulm Institut für Filmgestaltung. Premiere: April 1977. Format: 35mm, b&w and color, 41 mins.

Nachrichten von den Staufern (News from the Hohenstaufens), 1977.
Director: Alexander Kluge, Maximiliane Mainka. Script: Alexander Kluge, Maximiliane Mainka. Cast: Staff of the Würtemberg State Museum, Stuttgart. Cinematography: Jörg Schmidt-Reitwein, Alfred Tichawsky. Editing: Maximiliane Mainka. Production: Kairos-Film in conjunction with the Ulm Institut für Filmgestaltung. Premiere: April 1977. Format: 35mm, b&w and color, first part: 13 mins; second part: 11 mins.

Biermann-Film (Biermann Film), 1974–1983.
Director: Alexander Kluge, Edgar Reitz. Cinematography: Edgar Reitz, Vit Martinek (footage taken from *In Gefahr und grösster Not . . .*). Music: Wolf Biermann. Editing: Beate Mainka-Jellinghaus. Production: Kairos Film. Premiere: October 1, 1983. Format: 35mm, b&w, 3 mins.

Auf der Suche nach einer praktisch-realistichen Haltung (In Search of a Practical and Realistic Method), 1983.
Director: Alexander Kluge. Script: Alexander Kluge. Cinematography: Thomas Mauch. Editing: Beate Mainka-Jellinghaus. Production: Kairos Film. Premiere: October 2, 1983. Format: 35mm, b&w, 13 mins.

Other Film Work

Kluge collaborated on but did not direct the following films:

Unendliche Fahrt—aber begrenzt (The Never-Ending but Finite Journey), 1965.
Director: Edgar Reitz. Screenplay: Edgar Reitz, from a story idea by Alexander Kluge. Cinematography: Thomas Mauch, Gerhard Peters. Production: Insel Film. Premiere: June 1965. Format: 35mm, b&w and color, 60 hours; 60 sections of different durations.

Mahlzeiten (*Meals*), 1966.
Director: Edgar Reitz. Screenplay: Edgar Reitz. Advisors: Alexander Kluge, Hans-Dieter Müller. Cinematography: Thomas Mauch. Production: Edgar Reitz Filmproduktion through the Kuratorium Junger Deutscher Film. Premiere: March 21, 1967. Format: 35mm, b&w, 94 mins.

Die Reise nach Wien (The Journey to Vienna), 1973.
Director: Edgar Reitz. Screenplay: Edgar Reitz, Alexander Kluge. Cast: Elke Sommer, Hannelore Elsner, Mario Adorf. Cinematography: Robby Müller, Martin Schäfer. Production: Edgar Reitz Filmproduktion. Premiere: September 26, 1973. Format: 35mm, color, 102 mins.

Zwischen den Bildern. 3. Teil: Über die Trägheit der Wahrnehmung (Between the Images. Third Part: On the Laziness of Perception), 1981.
Directors: Klaus Feddermann, Helmut Herbst. Script: Alexander Kluge. Cast: Alexander Kluge. Cinematography: Helmut Herbst. Production: Stiftung Deutsche Kinemathek in conjunction with Zweites Deutches Fernsehen. Premiere: April 22, 1982. Format: 35mm, color, 12 mins.

Videography

Stunde der Filmemacher: Filmgeschichte(n) (Hour of the Filmmakers: Film History (Stories))

Kluge served as executive producer for these television shows, which were produced by Kluge under the aegis of Neue Medien Ulm and broadcast over SAT 1. Individual programs were produced by different individuals (such as Schlöndorff, Reitz or Sander) and credit was given to their own production companies. Some were credited to the Ulm Institute. These biweekly broadcasts were fifty-five minutes in length in 1985 and were shortened to thirty minutes and then fifteen minutes in 1987. Viewers ranged from 10,000 viewers per program (less than 1 percent share) to 400,000 (almost 30 percent share). The latter figure was highly unusual, with most programs averaging about 100,000 (or about 7 percent). In general, the figures fell as more diverse programming became available throughout Germany via cable and satellite.

1985 Twenty-two programs. In addition, the feature film *Der starke Ferdinand* was broadcast in 1984, and *Die Macht der Gefühle* was broadcast in 1985.
1986 Twenty-three programs.
1987 Fifteen programs.
1988 Twenty programs.
1989 Twenty-four programs.
1990 Twenty-five programs.
1991 Twenty-six programs.
1992 Twenty-six programs with an average audience of 112,000.
1993 Twenty-six programs with an average audience of 77,000.

Selected Programs

"Die armen Leute von Kombach, I" ("The Poor People of Kombach"), 55 min., 8 January 1985.
"Zwei Generationen des neuen deutschen Films" ("Two Generations of the New German Cinema"), 55 min., 23 April 1985.

"Die Entdeckung der Langsamkeit" ("The Discovery of Slowness"), 55 min., 10 September 1985.

"Ein Vormittag mit Christa Wolf, I" ("A Morning with Christa Wolf"), 30 min., 6 July 1986.

"' . . . Null Verständnis': Die schönste Szenen aus Filmen mit A. Edel (I)" ("'Zero Understanding': The Most Beautiful Scenes from Films Starring A. Edel"), 30 min., 20 July 1986.

"Der imaginäre Opernführer, 1. Folge" ("The Imaginary Opera Guide, First Series"), 30 min., 5 March 1987.

"Heiner Müller über Tacitus" ("Heiner Müller on Tacitus"), 30 min., 2 July 1987.

"Das Laszive im Gaumen Römer" ("The Lascivious in the Roman Palate"), 30 min., 11 October 1987.

"Ein Film namens Hemingway" ("A Film Called Hemingway"), 15 min., 10 April 1988.

"Objekte der Reklame" ("Advertising Objects"), 15 min., 8 May 1988.

"Kino, Glasnost und die DDR" ("Cinema, Glasnost and the GDR"), 15 min., 18 June 1989.

"Topographie der ernsthaften Musik im 20. Jahrhundert" ("Topography of Serious Music in the Twentieth Century"), 15 min., 9 July 1989.

10 vor 11 (10 to 11)

Produced by Kluge under the aegis of DCTP and broadcast on RTL. These weekly broadcasts began on May 2, 1988 and continue through the present (1997). They began as thirty-minute programs but within a few weeks were shortened to twenty-five minutes. Despite the program name, its starting time has varied from 22:50 to 23:30 on Monday nights. In 1988, some of these programs were also broadcast on SAT 1 on Monday nights at about the same time as other 10 vor 11 programs were on RTL. This practice was discontinued when SAT 1 began broadcasting News and Stories in 1989.

1988   Thirty-five programs.
1989   Fifty-two programs.
1990   Fifty-three programs with an average audience of 443,000 (7.2 percent).
1991   Forty-eight programs with an average audience of 529,800 (6.2 percent).
1992   Fifty programs with an average audience of 495,800.
1993   Fifty programs with an average audience of 662,400 (6.5 percent).
1994   Forty-six programs with an average audience of 649,000 (5.3 percent).
1995   Fifty programs with an average audience of 591,000 (5.3 percent).

Selected Programs

"Die Afrikanerin oder Liebe mit tödlichem Ausgang" ("The African Woman or Love with Fatal Consequences"), 2 May 1988.

"Die Guillotine. Karl-Heinz Bohrer berichtet" ("The Guillotine: Karl-Heinz Bohrer Reports"), 30 May 1988.

"Die Walküre in Warschau./Eine Begegnung mit dem Regisseur August Everding" ("The Valkyrie in Warsaw: An Encounter with the Director August Everding"), 4 July 1988.

"Japan-Clips," 10 October 1988.

"Karl-Heinz Stockhausen: 'Montag aus Licht'" ("Karl-Heinz Stockhausen: 'Monday out of Light'"), 12 December 1988.

"Das ferne Stalingrad" ("The Distant Stalingrad"), 27 February 1989.

"Heute: Walzer" ("Today: Waltzes"), 1 May 1989.

"Der gläubige Thomas—einer der Brüder Schamoni" ("The Doubt-less Thomas—One of the Schamoni Brothers"), 25 September 1989.

"'Blauäugig'/Portrait des Schauspielers Götz George bei den Dreharbeiten in Argentinien zu Reinhard Hauffs neuem Film" ("'Blue-eyed': Portrait of the Actor Götz George during the Filming in Argentina of Reinhard Hauff's New Film"), 23 October 1989.

"Edisons Kinder/Portrait der Budapester Filmemacherin Enyedi Ildikò und ihres neuen Films 'Mein 20. Jahrhundert'" ("Edison's Children: Portrait of the Budapest Filmmaker Enyedi Ildikò and Her New Film 'My Twentieth Century'"), 15 January 1990.

"Heiner Müller über Rechtsfragen/Zum Kleist-Preis 1990" ("Heiner Müller on Legal Questions: For the Kleist Prize 1990"), 22 October 1990.

"'Ganz wie in der Liebe: keine Erklärungen'/Unser Programm zu Jean-Luc Godards 60. Geburtstag" ("Just Like in Love, No Explanations: Our Program for Jean-Luc Godard's Sixtieth Birthday"), 3 December 1990.

"Das Goldene Vlies und die Catchpenny-Drucke—Anselm Kiefer gewidmet—" ("The Golden Fleece—Dedicated to Anselm Kiefer"), 21 January 1991.

"Frauen, Privileg, Rasse, Sprachverwirrung und 'Flash back'" ("Women, Privilege, Race, Linguistic Confusion and 'Flashback'"), 17 June 1991.

"Oper mit großem Scheißhaufen" ("Opera with Large Manure Piles"), 23 September 1991.

"Dreharbeiten zur 'Hexenpassion'/Edgar Reitz und sein neuer Film 'Heimat, 2'" ("The Filming of 'Witches' Passion': Edgar Reitz and His New Film 'Heimat, 2'"), 13 January 1992.

"Mozart als Fremder" ("Mozart as Stranger"), 10 February 1992.

"Die deutsche Punk- und New Wave-Szene von 1980" ("The German Punk and New Wave Scene of 1980"), 17 February 1992.

"Zum Rosenmontag: Johann Strauss" ("For Rose Monday: Johann Strauss"), 2 March 1992.

"Alfred Edel und die Postmoderne" ("Alfred Edel and the Postmodern"), 30 March 1992.

"Knopf-Akkordeon und Avantgarde" ("Button Accordion and the Avantgarde"), 23 November 1992.

"'Die Linke nach dem Sieg des Westens'" ("'The Left after the Victory of the West'"), 7 December 1992.

"Portrait von Dennis Hopper" ("Portrait of Dennis Hopper"), 4 January 1993.

"'Annie's Shooting'/Annie Leibowitz fotografiert Gertrud Höhler" ("Annie Liebowitz Photographs Gertrud Höhler"), 22 February 1993.

"Tod des Seneca" ("Death of Seneca"), 26 April 1993.

"Navaho Talking Picture/Sprechende Bilder in der Navaho-Sprache," 2 August 1993.

"Texas Polka," 25 October 1993.

"Gesang aus dem Walzwerk/Portrait der Sopranistin Maria Panner" ("Song from the Waltz Work: Portrait of the Soprano Maria Panner"), 7 February 1994.

"Die verblüffende Simplizität des Chinesischen" ("The Amazing Simplicity of the Chinese"), 14 March 1994.

"Unwahrscheinlichkeit des Bösen/Das Geheimnis der Wissenschaft nach Descartes"

("The Improbability of Evil: The Secret of Knowledge according to Descartes"),
23 May 1994.

"Sägezahn und 'La Paloma'/Besondere mechanische und elektronische Musikspeicher"
("Sawtooth and 'La Paloma': Special Mechanical and Electronic Music Storage"),
10 October 1994.

"'Die Welt ist nicht schlecht, sondern voll'/Gespräch mit Heiner Müller" ("'The World
is not Bad, But Full': Conversation with Heiner Müller"), 21 November 1994.

"Die 8. Kunst: Zündeln/Brilliantfeuerwerk mit Tschaikowsky 1812" ("The Eighth Art:
Playing with Fire/Brilliant Fireworks with Tschaikovsky's '1812'"), 5 December 1994.

Prime Time Spät Ausgabe (Prime Time Late Edition)

Also produced by Kluge under the DCTP standard and broadcast on RTL. These
weekly broadcasts began in 1989 and continue to the present (1997). They are twenty-
minute programs broadcast at approximately 23:00 on Sunday nights.

1990 Forty-six programs with an average audience of 698,000 (5.9 percent).

1991 Forty-seven programs with an average audience of 578,000 (5.1 percent).

1992 Thirty programs with an average audience of 493,000.

1993 Forty-six programs with an average audience of 860,000 (10.1 percent).

1994 Forty-five programs with an average audience of 721,000 (5.4 percent).

1995 Forty-four programs with an average audience of 662,800 (5.4 percent).

Selected Programs

"Pitbull Apollo—Portrait eines Kampfhundes und seines Herrn" ("Pitbull Apollo—
Portrait of a Fighting Dog and Its Master"), 4 February 1990.

"Besuch aus New York/Monty Cantsin, Pop-hard-art-singer" ("Visit From New York/
Monty Cantsin, Pop-hard-art-singer"), 18 March 1990.

"Zum 100. Geburtstag des Filmregisseurs Fritz Lang" ("On the Hundredth Birthday of
the Film Director Fritz Lang"), 8 April 1990.

"Die neue Laurie Anderson Show" ("The New Laurie Anderson Show"), 23 December
1990.

"Wolke in Hosen/Der berühmte Dichter Jewgenij Jewtuschenko über Pasternak, Ma-
jakowski und Osip Mandelstam" ("Clouds in Pants: The Famous Poet Yevgeny
Yevtushenko"), 13 January 1991.

"Paper Tiger TV und Golfkrise" ("Paper Tiger TV and the Gulf Crisis"), 7 April 1991.

"Schwert und Schild/Die Polarität von Bewegung und Feuerkraft im modernen Krieg"
("Sword and Shield: The Polarity of Mobility and Firepower in Modern Warfare"), 5 May 1991.

"'Die Liebe is eine Himmelsmacht'/Verdi Melodien" ("Love is a Heavenly Power: Verdi
Melodies"), 27 October 1991.

"'Pommerland ist abgebrannt'/Unterhaltungsmagazin für Pyromanen" ("Pommerania
is Incinerated: Entertainment Magazine for Pyromaniacs"), 23 February 1992.

"900 Sekunde mit Chantal Ackerman/Chansons aus ihren Spielfilmen" ("900 Seconds
with Chantal Ackerman: Songs from her Films"), 1 March 1992.

"Gorbatschow und der neue Spielfilm von Wim Wenders" ("Gorbachev and the New
Film by Wim Wenders"), 3 May 1992.

"Szenen aus dem Eisenzeitalter/Walter Benjamin zum 100. Geburtstag" ("Scenes from the Iron Age: On Walter Benjamin's Hundredth Birthday"), 10 May 1992.

"Der Tod des Admiral Yamamoto" ("The Death of Admiral Yamamoto"), 4 October 1992.

"Portrait einer Wurstfabrik in Sachsen-Anhalt" ("Portrait of a Sausage Factory in Saxon-Anhalt"), 3 January 1993.

"Bunte Blätter/non sequitur/Ein Musikmagazin" ("Colorful Leaves: non sequitur: A Music Magazine"), 14 February 1993.

"'Der Letzte Mohikaner'/Fidel Castro und seine Republik" ("'The Last of the Mohicans': Fidel Castro and His Republic"), 21 March 1993.

"Der Anfang der öffentlich Oper/Monteverdis vorletzte Oper" ("The Beginning of Public Opera: Monteverdi's Penultimate Opera"), 23 May 1993.

"Das Wetter in Stalingrad" ("The Weather in Stalingrad"), 15 August 1993.

"Berlin Baustelle Friedrichstraße" ("Berlin Construction Site: Friedrich Street"), 6 March 1994.

"'Wir sind ein Volk'/Audiotour mit Nahverkehrsmittel in den neuen Bundesländern" ("'We Are One People': Audio Tour via Local Transport through the New Federal States"), 17 April 1994.

"Konzert zum 25. Todestag von Th. W. Adorno" ("Concert on the Twenty-fifth Anniversary of the Death of T. W. Adorno"), 7 August 1994.

"Kill Normality before it kills you!" 30 October 1994.

"'Im Zweifel für den Angeklagten'/Peter Satorius über den Mordprozess gegen O.J. Simpson" ("'In Doubt for the Accused': Peter Satorius on the Murder Trial of O.J. Simpson"), 6 November 1994.

"Lenins kalte Knochen" ("Lenin's Cold Bones"), 4 December 1994.

"Im Garten der Reichskanzlei/Wie wurde Hitlers Leiche gefunden?" ("In the Garden of the Reich's Chancellory: How Was Hitler's Corpse Found?"), 30 April 1995.

"Hitler gegen Dada/Dada gegen Hitler" ("Hitler Versus Dada: Dada Versus Hitler"), 23 July 1995.

"'Ich bin Reporter und das ist mein Beruf'/Igor Kostin als erster in Tschernobyl" ("'I'm a Reporter and That's My Job': Igor Kostin, the First into Chernobyl"), 3 December 1995.

News and Stories

Kluge has served as executive producer for these programs which are broadcast on SAT 1, also under the DCTP aegis. Although he has produced the majority of these programs himself, a substantial number have been produced by Günter Gaus. These weekly programs run fifty minutes and are aired on Monday nights at about 23 : 00 — opposite Kluge's *10 vor 11*.

1989   Fifty-one programs.

1990   Fifty-two programs (fourteen interviews by Gaus) with an average audience of 275,000.

1991   Fifty-three programs (ten interviews by Gaus) with an average audience of 202,000.

1992   Fifty-one programs (nine interviews by Gaus) with an average audience of 231,000.

1993   Fifty-one programs (eight interviews by Gaus) with an average audience of 209,000.

1994   Fifty-one programs (nine interviews by Gaus) with an average audience of 325, 300 (3.5 percent).

1995   Fifty-one programs (nine interviews by Gaus) with an average audience of 376,000 (4.1 percent).

Selected Programs

"Der Eiffelturm, King Kong und die weiße Frau" ("The Eiffel Tower, King Kong and the White Woman"), 2 January 1989.

"Antiquitaten der Reklame" ("Antiquities of Advertising"), 20 February 1989.

"Thomas Manns Operentwürfe" ("Thomas Mann's Opera Drafts"), 4 September 1989.

"'Jan, Ken, Poi'/Schere, Stein, Papier" ("'Jan, Ken, Poi': Rock, Paper, Scissors"), 2 October 1989.

"Minuten-Opern von Darius Milhaud" ("Minute Operas by Darius Milhaud"), 27 November 1989.

"Goldlocky, President Th. Roosevelt und die Teddybärs" ("Goldilocks, President T. Roosevelt and the Teddy Bears"), 23 April 1990.

"Deutschland, Selbstvertrauen und Musik" ("Germany, Self-Confidence and Music"), 12 November 1990.

"Bilder aus dem Leben Rußlands" ("Pictures of Russian Life"), 19 November 1990.

"Werner Herzog im Jahr 1990, Teil 1" ("Werner Herzog in 1990, Part 1"), 18 February 1991.

"Revolution, Sport, Unterhaltung und rätselhaftes Verhalten der Massen" ("Revolution, Sport, Entertainment and the Puzzling Behavior of the Masses"), 10 June 1991.

"Kaiser Friedrich, II," 17 June 1991.

"China, das unbekannte Wesen" ("China, the Unknown Essence"), 5 August 1991.

"'Das Gesicht meines Vaters'/Nagisa Oshima, geb. 1932" ("'The Face of My Father': Nagisa Oshima, Born 1932"), 9 December 1991.

"Der lange March in die Marktwirtschaft—" ("The Long March into the Market Economy"), 30 March 1992.

"'Spiegelbild des Herzens'/Aus der Frühzeit der Fotographie" ("'Mirror of the Heart': From the Early Period of Photography"), 6 April 1992.

"Japan und der Tod" ("Japan and Death"), 9 November 1992.

"Günter Gaus: Zur Person/Albert Hetterle, Intendant des Maxim Gorki Theaters" ("Günter Gaus Interviews Albert Hetterle, Artistic Director of the Maxim Gorki Theater"), 16 November 1992.

"Vergewaltigung von Frauen im Krieg/Ein Bericht von Helke Sander" ("The Rape of Women in War: A Report by Helke Sander"), 7 December 1992.

"Lamento auf den Tod des Minotaurus" ("Laments on the Death of the Minotaur"), 15 March 1993.

"Günter Gaus: Zur Person/Rolf Hochhuth" ("Günter Gaus Interviews Rolf Hochhuth"), 29 March 1993.

"Konzert im August/Minimal Music," 2 August 1993.

"'Kristallnacht'/Zum Vorabend des 9. November" ("'Crystal Night': On the Eve of the Ninth of November"), 8 November 1993.

"Der Mann der Zeitgeschichte/Valentin Falin zu seinem neuen Buch 'Politische Erinnerungen'" ("The Man of Contemporary History: Valentin Falin on His New Book, 'Political Memoirs'"), 29 November 1993.

"Early Black Cinema," 10 January 1994.

"350 Jahre Oper" ("350 Years of Opera"), 25 July 1994.

"Organisiertes Glück/Siegfried Kracauer und die Attraktionen der Moderne" ("Organized Happiness: Siegfried Kracauer and the Attractions of the Modern"), 19 September 1994.

"Alexander von Humboldts Gesammelte Reisen" ("Alexander von Humboldt's Collected Travels"), 10 October 1994.

"Der Fall Lindemann—ein General im Widerstand und seine Helfer" ("The Case of Lindemann—A General in Resistance and His Helpers"), 28 November 1994.

"Eine Kämpfernatur/Armand Gatti, dramatischer Anarchist" ("A Warrior's Nature: Armand Gatti, Dramatic Anarchist"), 15 May 1995.

"Eine Haut so zart wie Radiergummi/Die Elefantenherde des Zoo Zürich" ("Skin as Delicate as a Rubber Eraser: The Elephant Herd of the Zurich Zoo"), 17 July 1995.

"Einladung zum Münchner Oktoberfest" ("Invitation to Munich's Oktoberfest"), 25 October 1995.

"Gitta Sereny: Albert Speer/Kritische Biografie eines mächtigen Mannes" ("Critical Biography of a Powerful Man"), 20 November 1995.

Bibliography

Books by Kluge

Die Universitäts-Selbstverwaltung: Ihre Geschichte und gegenwärtige Rechtsform. Frankfurt am Main: Klostermann, 1958. Reprint (in German), New York: Arno Press, 1977.

With Hellmut Becker. *Kulturpolitik und Ausgabenkontrolle.* Frankfurt am Main: Klostermann, 1961.

Lebensläufe. Stuttgart: Goverts, 1962. The English translation by Leila Vennewitz, *Attendance List for a Funeral: Eleven Stories by Alexander Kluge* (New York: McGraw-Hill, 1966), deleted one story and added three others. This translation was republished with a new introduction by Hans-Bernhard Moeller as *Case Histories* (New York: Holmes & Meier, 1988). Other German editions include: the paperback edition, *Lebensläufe* (Frankfurt am Main: 1964); a revised and enlarged edition, *Lebensläufe: Anwesenheitsliste für eine Beerdigung* (Frankfurt am Main: Suhrkamp, 1974); and a new paperback edition, based on the 1974 edition, that includes a new afterword by Kluge, *Lebensläufe* (Frankfurt am Main: Bibliothek Suhrkamp, 1986).

Schlachtbeschreibung. Olten: Walter, 1964. Translated by Leila Vennewitz under the title *The Battle* (New York: McGraw-Hill, 1967). Other German editions include: the revised paperback edition, *Schlachtbeschreibung* (Frankfurt am Main: Fischer, 1968); a reprint of the 1964 edition with a new title, *Der Untergang der Sechsten Armee (Schlachtbeschreibung)* (Munich: Piper, 1969); a newly typeset version (by a different publisher) of the 1964 edition with the new title, *Der Untergang der Sechsten Armee (Schlachtbeschreibung)* (Stuttgart: 1969); and an expanded version of the 1964 edition with a new title, *Schlachtbeschreibung: Der organisatorische Aufbau eines Unglücks* (Munich: Goldmann, 1978).

Die Artisten in der Zirkuskuppel: ratlos: Die Ungläubige. Projekt Z. Sprüche der Leni Peickert. Munich: Piper, 1968. Selections from this work were translated into English by Thomas Y. Levin and Miriam B. Hansen. These selections comprise a section ("The Spectator as Entrepreneur") of a larger article that presents selected translations from a number of Kluge's writings, "On Film and the Public Sphere," *New German Critique,* nos. 24–25 (fall–winter 1981–1982): 210–11.

With Oskar Negt. *Öffentlichkeit und Erfahrung: Zur Organisationsanalyse von bürger-licher und proletarischer Öffentlichkeit*. Frankfurt am Main: Suhrkamp, 1972. Translated by Peter Labanyi, with an introduction by Miriam Hansen, under the title *The Public Sphere and Experience* (Minneapolis: University of Minnesota Press, 1993). Excerpts from this English edition were published as "*The Public Sphere and Experience:* Selections" in *October*, no. 46 (fall 1988): 60–82. An English translation of chapter five, "The Context of Life as Object of Production of the Media Conglomerate," was also published in *Media, Culture and Society* 5 (1983): 65–74.

With Michael Dost and Florian Hopf. *Filmwirtschaft in der BRD und in Europa: Götter-dämmerung in Raten*. Munich: Hanser, 1973.

Lernprozesse mit tödlichem Ausgang. Frankfurt am Main: Suhrkamp, 1973. Translated by Christopher Pavsek under the title *Learning Processes with a Deadly Outcome* (Durham, N.C.: Duke University Press, 1996). Prior to this full translation, se-lections had been translated in various periodicals: "Big Business Bolshevik," translated by Skip Acuff and Hans-Bernard Moeller, *Wide Angle* 3, no. 4 (1980): 32; "Excerpts from 'Big Business Bolshevik,'" translated by Skip Acuff, *Quar-terly Review of Film Studies* 5, no. 2 (spring 1980): 195–203; and "Mass Death in Venice," translated by Jeffrey S. Librett, *New German Critique*, no. 30 (fall 1983): 61–63.

Kritische Theorie and Marxismus: Radikalität ist keine Sache des Willens sondern der Erfahrung. Giessen: prolit-Buchvertrieb, 1974. This volume includes an essay by Oskar Negt.

Gelegenheitsarbeit einer Sklavin: Zur realistischen Methode. Frankfurt am Main: Suhr-kamp, 1975. English translations of selections from this work include: "The Occasional Work of a Female Slave," translated by Jan Dawson in her *Alexander Kluge and "The Occasional Work of a Female Slave"* (New York: Zoetrope, 1977); "Roswitha's Programme," translated by Stephen Elford, in ibid.; "Selected Writ-ings by Alexander Kluge," translated by Skip Acuff and Hans-Bernard Moeller, *Wide Angle* 3, no. 4 (1980): 26–28.

Neue Geschichten, Hefte 1–18: Unheimlichkeit der Zeit. Frankfurt am Main: Suhr-kamp, 1977. Several of the stories in this work have been translated in vari-ous periodicals: "Military Training Films," translated by Skip Acuff and Hans-Bernard Moeller, *Wide Angle* 3, no. 4 (1980): 33; "The Air Raid on Halberstadt, 8 April 1945," translated by Reinhard Mayer, *Semiotext* 4, no. 2 (1982): 306–15; "Foreword," "The Concrete Tomb," and "An Episode from the Age of En-lightenment," translated by Joyce Rheuban, *October*, no. 46 (fall 1988): 103–16.

Die Patriotin. Texte/Bilder 1–6. Frankfurt am Main: Zweitausendeins, 1979. Selections from this work were translated by Thomas Y. Levin and Miriam B. Hansen and appear in "On Film and the Public Sphere," *New German Critique*, nos. 24–25 (fall–winter 1981–1982): 206–10.

Edited with Klaus Eder. *Ulmer Dramaturgien: Reibungsverluste*. Munich: Hanser, 1980. Selections from this work were translated by Levin and Hansen in "On Film and the Public Sphere," *New German Critique*, 24–25 (fall–winter): 211–20.

With Oskar Negt. *Geschichte und Eigensinn*. Frankfurt am Main: Zweitausendeins, 1981.

Editor. *Bestandsaufnahme: Utopie Film*. Frankfurt am Main: Zweitausendeins, 1983.

Die Macht der Gefühle. Frankfurt am Main: Zweitausendeins, 1984.

Der Angriff der Gegenwart auf die übrige Zeit: Abendfüllender Spielfilm, 35 mm, Farbe mit s/w-Teilen, Format: 1:1,37; Drehbuch. Frankfurt am Main: Syndikat, 1985.

With Klaus von Bismarck, Günter Gaus, and Ferdinand Sieger. *Industrialisierung des Bewußtseins: Eine kritische Auseinandersetzung mit den "neuen" Medien.* München, Zürich: Piper, 1985.

Theodor Fontane, Heinrich von Kleist und Anna Wilde: Zur Grammatik der Zeit. Berlin: Klaus Wagenbach, 1987.

With Oskar Negt. *Maßverhältnisse des Politischen: 15 Vorschläge zum Unterscheidungs-vermögen.* Frankfurt am Main: Fischer, 1992.

With Heiner Müller. *"Ich schulde der Welt einen Toten": Gespräche.* Hamburg, Rotbuch, 1995.

With Valentin Falin. *Interview mit dem Jahrhundert.* Hamburg: Rotbuch, 1995.

Die Wächter des Sarkophags: 10 Jahre Tschernobyl. Hamburg: Rotbuch, 1996.

With Heiner Müller. *"Ich bin ein Landvermesser": Gespräche mit Heiner Müller, neue Folge.* Hamburg: Rotbuch, 1996.

Articles by Kluge

"Was wollen die 'Oberhausener?'" *Kirche und Film* (November 1962): 2–4.

"Instrumentarium Verratsbegriff." *Merkur,* no. 179 (January 1963): 107–12.

"Mandorf: Erzählung." *Merkur,* no. 187 (September 1963): 864–76.

"An einen Kritiker der 'Oberhausener.'" *Kirche und Film* (October 1963): 5–7.

"Hauptfeldwebel Hans Peickert." *Akzente* 20, no. 2 (1963): 265–79.

"Wissensschaft in Wandel." *Merkur,* no. 192 (February 1964): 197–200.

"Totenkapelle für Bechtolds." *Der Spiegel,* 30 September 1964.

"Die Utopie Film." *Merkur,* no. 201 (December 1964): 1135–46.

With Edgar Rietz and Wilfried Reinke. "Wort und Film." *Sprache im technischen Zeit-alter,* no. 13 (January–March 1965): 1015–30. Translated by Miriam Hansen under the title "Word and Film," *October,* no. 46 (fall 1988): 83–96.

"Film ist eine Intelligenzform." *Die Andere Zeitung* (Hamburg), 15 September 1966.

"Ungeduld hilft nicht, aber Geduld auch nicht." Parts 1 and 2. *Film,* (March 1967): 7; (April 1967): 7.

"'Traurig, traurig, sieht man hin, sieht man hin, traurig, traurig!' (Anita G.)." *Film* (July 1967): 7.

"Schnulzen-Kartel versperrt die Zukunft." *Die Welt,* 22 September 1967.

"*Die Artisten in der Zirkuskuppel: ratlos:* Alexander Kluge über seinen Film." *Film* 6, no. 10 (October 1968): 41–52.

"Informationen zu *Der grosse Verhau.*" In *1. Internationales Forum des Jungen Films 1971.* West Berlin, 1971.

"Medienproduktion." In *Perspektiven der kommunalen Kulturpolitik,* edited by Hilmar Hoffman. Frankfurt am Main: Suhrkamp, 1974.

"Wer immer hofft stirbt singend." *Frankfurter Rundschau,* 2 August 1974.

"Das ganze Maul voll Film." *Frankfurter Rundschau,* 21 November 1974.

With Edgar Rietz. "In Gefahr und grösster Not bringt der Mittelweg den Tod: Was heisst Parteilichkeit im Kino. Zum Autorenfilm—dreizehn Jahre nach Ober-hausen." Parts 1 and 2. *Kirche und Film* (January 1975): 1–5; (February 1975): 6–9.

With Edgar Reitz. "In Gefahr und grösster Not bringt der Mittelweg den Tod." *Kurs-buch* 41 (1975): 41–84. Selections from this essay were translated by Skip Acuff and Hans-Bernard Moeller under the title "Exposé and Notes of 'In Times of Danger and Greatest Peril, the Path of Compromise Leads to Death,'" *Wide Angle* 3, no. 4 (1980): 28–31.

"Das Besondere an Traven." *Frankfurter Rundschau,* 26 July 1976.

"Wer alternative Schulprojekte ausschliesst, bricht das Recht." *päd, extra* (June 1977).

"Die Hexenjagd auf die Intellektuellen produziert eine Antwort." In *Nicht heimlich und nicht kühl. Entgegnungen an Dienst- und andere Herren.* Berlin: Ästhetik und Kommunikation, 1977.

With Alf Brustellin, Rainer Werner Fassbinder, Volker Schlöndorff, and Bernhard Sinkel. "Worin liegt die Parteilichkeit des Films?" *Ästhetik und Kommunikation* 9, no. 32 (June 1978): 24–25.

"Ach ja, die Deutschen und die Lust." *Lui* (February 1979).

"Ein lebhaftes Kontaktbedürfnis. Alte schlafsüchtige Frau. Das Rennpferd." *Zeitmagazin* 11 (9 March 1979): 24–25.

"Eine neue Tonart von Politik: Alexander Kluge über Peter Glotz: Die Innenausstattung der Macht." *Der Spiegel,* 30 April 1979.

"Das politische als Intensität alltäglicher Gefühle." *Freibeuter* 1 (September 1979): 56–62. Translated by Andrew Bowie under the title "The Political as Intensity of Everyday Feelings," *Cultural Critique* 4 (fall 1986): 119–28.

"Ein Liebesversuch." *Freibeuter* 1 (September 1979): 88–90.

"Das Knie des Obergefreiten Wieland spricht." *Frankfurter Rundschau,* 2 December 1979.

With Oskar Negt. "Tödliche Logik, deutsch." *Frankfurter Rundschau,* 29 December 1979.

With Oskar Negt. "Der antike Seeheld als Metapher der Aufklärung; die deutschen Grübelgegenbilder: Aufklärung als Verschanzung; 'Eigensinn.'" In *Stichworte zur 'Geistigen Situation der Zeit,'* edited by Jürgen Habermas. Frankfurt am Main: Suhrkamp, 1979.

"Alexander Kluge 1980: Auf Lorbeeren kann man schlecht sitzen." In *Deutscher Filmpreis 1951–1980,* edited by Manfred Hohnstock and Alfons Bettermann. Bonn: Bundesministerium des Innern, 1980.

"Ein Hauptansatz des Ulmer Instituts." *Baden-Württembergischen Filmwoche 80* (June 1980).

"Die Gefühle fest im Griff des Verstandes." *Kursbuch* 68 (June 1982): 138–49.

"Vier Geschichten für Herbert Achternbusch: 'Arch Zeit.' 'Das Gefühl besteht aus Unverbrauchtem.' 'Reden, um die anderen zum lachen zu bringen.' 'Totmachen der Täufer.'" In *Herbert Achternbusch,* edited by Jörg Drews. Frankfurt am Main: Suhrkamp, 1982.

"Instrumentarium unseres Verratsbegriffs." *Merkur* 17, no. 179 (January 1983): 107–12.

"Geschichte, Bilder, Notizen zur 'Macht der Gefühle.'" *Frankfurter Rundschau,* 3 September 1983.

"Die Macht der Gefühle: Geschichten, Gespräche und Materialien von und über Alexander Kluge." *Ästhetik und Kommunikation* 14, nos. 53–54 (December 1983): 168–201.

"Die Befähigung zum Richteramt." *Ästhetik und Kommunikation* 14, nos. 53–54 (December 1983): 203–10.

"Übergabe des Kindes." *Ästhetik und Kommunikation* 14, nos. 53–54 (December 1983): 211–15.

"Über Gefühle." *Ästhetik und Kommunikation* 14, nos. 53–54 (December 1983): 216–18.

"Filmzitate und Musiken zu 'Macht der Gefühle.'" *Ästhetik und Kommunikation* 14, nos. 53–54 (December 1983): 219–23.

"Anmerkungen zu Jutta Brückner." *Ästhetik und Kommunikation* 14, nos. 53–54 (December 1983): 233–35.

"Antwort auf zwei Opernzitate." In *Oper in Hamburg 1983/84,* edited by Peter Dannenberg, Angelus Seipt, and Wolfgang Willaschek. Hamburg: Hans Christians, 1984.

"Das Politische als Intensität alltäglicher Gefühle." In *Die Linke neu denken,* 150–58. Berlin: Klaus Wagenbach, 1984.

"Mangel an Deutschland." *Merkur* 423 (January 1984): 102–6.

"Zum Unterschied von machbar and gewalttätig." *Merkur* 425 (April 1984): 243–53.

"Das Schicksal und seine Gegengeschichten. Zu zwei Textstellen aus Opern." *Merkur* 428 (September 1984): 639–50.

"Feuerlöscherkommandant W. Schönecke berichtet," "Mit allen Sinnen sannen wir auf Rettung," "Die Pferde," "Ein blauer Montag," "Der Taucher," and "Wetteifer (émulation)." *Text + Kritik* 85–86 (January 1985): 33–7, 78–81, and 103–10.

"Wächter der Differenz: Rede zur Verleihung des Kleist-Preis." In *Kleist-Jahrbuch 1986,* edited by Hans Joachim Kreutzer, 25–37. Erich Schmidt, 1986.

"5 Minuten für ein Bild." *Tages-Anzeiger Magazin* (Zurich) 51–52 (1986): 50.

With Heinz Ungureit, Günter Rohrbach, and Gunther Witte. "Erklärung anlässlich der Mainzer Tage der Fernseh-Kritik 1983." In *Neue Medien contra Film-kultur?* edited by Kraft Wetzel. Berlin: Speiss, 1987.

"Warum Kooperation zwischen Film and Fernsehen? Zur Mainzer Erklärung." In *Neue Medien contra Filmkultur?* edited by Kraft Wetzel. Berlin: Spiess, 1987. Translated by Stuart Liebman under the title "Why Should Film and Television Cooperate? On the Mainz Manifesto," *October,* no. 46 (fall 1988): 96–103.

"Die näheren Umstände der moralischen Kraft." *die tageszeitung,* 19 May 1989.

"The Assault of the Present on the Rest of Time." *New German Critique,* no. 49 (winter 1990): 11–22.

"On Opera, Film and Feelings." *New German Critique,* no. 49 (winter 1990): 89–138.

"Das Waldhaus in Sils-Maria." *Zeitmagazin* (28 September 1990): 58–59.

"Öffentlichkeit 1990." In *Verleihung des Lessingspreises 1989 an Alexander Kluge,* 15–27. Hamburg: Hans Schmidt, 1991. Also published as "Augenblick tragisch-glücklicher Wiedererkennung." *Frankfurter Rundschau,* 24 November 1990.

With Oskar Negt. "Die Menschheit als Zwangszusammenhang." *Frankfurter Rundschau,* 21 March 1992.

"Was ich als Autor im Fernsehen treibe." *Funk-Korrespondenz,* no. 48 (3 December 1993): 21–23.

"Schriften an der Wand." *Die Woche,* 9 December 1993.

"Es ist ein Irrtum, daß die Toten tot sind." *Berliner Zeitung,* 17 January 1996.

Interviews with Kluge

"Wir wollen den neuen deutschen Film machen." *Süddeutsche Zeitung,* 10 March 1962.

Schöler, Franz. "Das Publikum soll zufrieden sein." *Die Welt,* 19 March 1966.

———. "Man muß zärtlich sein." Parts 1 and 2. *Handelsblatt,* 23–24 September 1966.

Grafe, Friede and Enno Patalas. "Tribune des Jungen Deutschen Films: Alexander Kluge." *Filmkritik* 10, no. 9 (September 1966): 487–91.

Peters, Karsten. "Filme zum Träumen: Gespräch mit Alexander und Alexandra Kluge." *Abendzeitung* (Munich), 5 October 1966.

Schöler, Franz. "Das Repräsentative und das Individuelle." *Echo der Zeit,* 16 October 1966.

———. "Mit Phantasie die Welt beflügeln." *Die Welt,* 14 September 1968.

Hopf, Florian. "Wie man Kluges Film versteht: Ein Gespräch über 'Die Artisten in der Zirkuskuppel: ratlos.'" *Filmreport,* no. 19 (18 October 1968): 1–5.

Gmür, Leonhard H. "Wie ein Fisch in Winter." *Filmblätter,* 1 November 1968.

Lackschéwitz, Klaus. "Gewisse Positionen der Liebe zur Kunst." *konkret,* 4 November 1968.

Schöler, Franz. *"Die Artisten in der Zirkuskuppel: ratlos."* *Film und Ton* 14, no. 12 (December 1968): 32.

Hopf, Florian. "Das All-Kramladen des Kapitalismus." *Filmreport,* no. 12 (1 July 1971): 15–9.

Gregor, Ulrich. "Zwei Bayern im Weltraum." *Kirche und Film* 24, no. 10 (October 1971): 8–10.

Hopf, Florian. "Fürsorge und was weitere?" *Filmreport,* nos. 23–24 (31 December 1973): 1–5.

Kerr, Charlotte. "'Das Drehbuch ist kein Evangelium': Gespräch mit dem Filmemacher Alexander Kluge." *Süddeutsche Zeitung,* 7 May 1974.

Meyer, Andreas. "KINO-Gespräch mit Alexander Kluge—Filmförderung, Fernsehen, Kino—und das Trivialinteresse des Menschen." *KINO,* no. 14 (15 May 1974): 37–46.

Theurig, Gerhard, et al. "Gelegenheitsarbeit einer Sklavin: Gespräch mit Alexander Kluge." *Filmkritik* 18, no. 6 (June 1974): 279–83.

Dawson, Jan. "Interview with Alexander Kluge." *Film Comment* (November–December 1974): 51–57.

Eder, Klaus. "Gespräch mit Alexander Kluge und Edgar Reitz." *Kirche und Film* 28, no. 4 (1975): 8–13.

Boehncke, Heiner. "Die Rebellion des Stoffs gegen die Form und der Form gegen den Stoff." In *Das B. Traven Buch,* edited by Johannes Beck, Klaus Bergmann, and Heiner Boehncke, 338–47. Reinbek: Rowohlt, 1976.

Gregor, Ulrich. "Interview mit Alexander Kluge." In *Herzog/Kluge/Straub,* edited by Peter W. Jansen and Wolfram Schütte. Munich: Hanser, 1976.

Hopf, Florian. "Ein Fall für die Öffentlichkeit." *Frankfurter Rundschau,* 27 April 1976.

Zimmer, Dieter E. "Schicksale des guten Willens." *Die Zeit,* 30 April 1976.

Hopf, Florian. "Zäh weiterarbeiten." *Filmdienst,* 14 June 1976.

Blumenberg, Hans C. "Der Film ist Öffentlichkeit." *Kölner Stadt-Anzeiger,* 16 June 1976.

Simonoviescz, Andre. "Das *tip*-Interview." *tip,* 25 June 1976.

Buschmann, Christel. "Ein Film für die Blindenanstalt." *konkret,* no. 8 (August 1976): 49–50.

Gansera, Rainer, et al. "Gespräch mit Alexander Kluge." *Filmkritik* 20, no. 12 (December 1976): 562–600.

Pflaum, Hans Günther. "Wir müssen gewissermaßen unterm Eis wegtauchen." *Frankfurter Rundschau,* 22 December 1976.

Buchka, Peter. "Es ist Zeit, nein zu sagen." *Süddeutsche Zeitung,* 5 May 1977.

Buschmann, Christel. "Realismus ist anstrengend." *konkret,* no. 8 (28 July 1977): 39.

Kluge, Alexandra and Bion Steinborn. "Film ist das natürliche Tauschverhältnis der Arbeit." *Filmfaust* 1, no. 6 (December 1977): 93–105.

Lewandowski, Rainer and Rainer Vasel. "'Zeit der Rache'—Gespräch über Terrorismus und Dokumentarliteratur." *Die Zeit,* 16 December 1977.

Arnold, Frank. "Den bloßen Individualismus des Autorenfilms überwinden." *Film-Korrespondenz* 24, no. 2 (8 February 1978): 5–8.

Steinborn, Bion. "'Deutschland im Herbst' oder 'Modell Deutschland.'" *Filmfaust* 3, no. 7 (1978): 3–17.

Wiedemann, Horst. "Filmpolitik und 'Der starke Ferdinand.'" *Film und Ton* 24, no. 1 (1978): 54–58.

Bitomsky, Hartmut, Harun Farocki, and Klaus Henrichs. "Gespräch mit Alexander Kluge: Über 'Die Patriotin,' Geschichte und Filmarbeit." *Filmkritik* 23, no. 11 (November 1979): 505–20.

Bevers, Jürgen, Klaus Kreimeier, Jutta Müller. "Der Film in unserem Kopf." *Zitty* (28 December 1979): 38–39.

Lewandowski, Rainer. "Interview." In his book *Die Filme von Alexander Kluge*, 29–59. Hildesheim: Olms, 1980.

"Eine realistische Haltung müsste der Zuschauer haben, müsste ich haben, müsste der Film haben." *Filmfaust*, 20 (November 1980): 19–26.

Lewandowski, Rainer. "Gespräch mit Alexander Kluge." In his book *Die Oberhausener: Rekonstruktion einer Gruppe 1962–1982*, 83–93. Diekholzen: Verlag für Bühne und Film, 1982.

Steinborn, Bion. "Cinema Pure, Cinema Impure." *Filmfaust* 7, no. 26 (February–March 1982): 32–64.

Eder, Klaus and Peter Hamm. "Reise in die Wirklichkeit: Ein Gespräch mit Alexander Kluge und Volker Schlöndorff über das Projekt eines Krieg- und Frieden-Films." *Kirche und Film* 35, no. 3 (March 1982): 6–9.

Knödler-Bunte, Eberhard, et al. "Die Geschichte der Lebendigen Arbeitskraft: Ein Gespräch mit Oskar Negt und Alexander Kluge." *Ästhetik und Kommunikation* 13, no. 48 (1982): 78–109.

Steinborn, Bion. "Unser Herrgott ist der erste Kernaggressor." *Filmfaust* 8, no. 32 (February–March 1983): 2–24.

Hank, Fraucke. "Von grossen und kleinen Gefühlen." *Frankfurter Rundschau*, 16 September 1983.

Fründt, Bodo. "Happy End und die Lüge, Lust auf das Unwahrscheinliche." *Kölner Stadtanzeiger*, 8 December 1983.

Karrmann, Uwe. "Ein Schaufenster gegen Teilveröffentlichungen. Interview mit Alexander Kluge über die Beteiligung des Filmverlags der Autoren am Satellitenfernsehen." *die tageszeitung*, 6 April 1984.

Barth, Achim. "Deutsche TV-Filme in Gefahr? Regisseur Alexander Kluge: Wir brauchen eine 80-Prozent-Quote." *Münchner Merkur*, 21 August 1984.

Michal, Wolfgang. "Scheinheilige Unterschiede." *Vorwärts*, 4 December 1984.

Hopf, Florian. "Flaschenpost von Musil." *Stuttgarter Zeitung*, 9 January 1985.

Gliewe, Gert. "Der Angriff der Gegenwart auf die übrige Zeit." *Abendzeitung* (Munich), 21 September 1985.

Zucker, Renee. "Die Verschwörung der Dinge." *die tageszeitung*, 30 October 1985.

Rotthaler, Viktor. "Wir müssen einsehen, daß uns nicht viel Zeit bleibt." *Mittelbayerische Zeitung*, 4 December 1986.

"Begegnung mit Alexander Kluge." In *Filmwerkschau Alexander Kluge, Cinéaste Allemand*, edited by Robert Richter and Hans Wysseier, 1–7. Lausanne: Cinémathèque Suisse, 1987.

Schlüpmann, Heide and Gertrud Koch. "Gespräch mit Alexander Kluge: 'Nur Trümmern trau ich. . . .'" *Frauen und Film* 42 (August 1987): 83–93.

Liebman, Stuart. "On New German Cinema, Art, Enlightenment, and the Public Sphere: An Interview with Alexander Kluge." *October*, no. 46 (fall 1988): 23–59.

Indiana, Gary. "The Demolition Artist: Alexander Kluge." *Village Voice*, 25 October 1988.

Rötzer, Florian. "Die Rettung der Bilder durch ihre Zerstörung." *Frankfurter Rundschau*, 3 December 1988.

Rainer, Yvonne and Ernest Larsen. "We are Demolition Artists: An Interview with Alexander Kluge." *The Independent* (June 1989): 18–25.

Scheib-Rotbart, Ingrid. "Alexander Kluge in New York." *Prisma Akzenta*, no. 1 (1989): 61–65.

Kümmel, Peter. "Es werden viele Abenteuer freigesetzt in dieser Zeit." *Stuttgarter Nachrichten*, 5 January 1990.

————. "Auf der Kippe zum Irrationalen." *Stuttgarter Nachrichten*, 15 January 1991.

"Kluges Kultursendungen unter Pornographie-Verdacht." *Funk-Korrespondenz*, no. 34 (22 March 1991): 9–10.

Lilienthal, Volker. "Persönlich prüde." *Kirche und Rundfunk*, no. 65 (21 August 1991): 4–8.

"Grimme-'Gold' für Kluge-Film. Die Preisträger beim 28. Marler Fernsehwettbewerb." *Frankfurter Rundschau*, 3 January 1992.

"'Die Welt ist Babylon.' Ein Gespräch mit Alexander Kluge." *NZZ-Folio*, April 1993.

Niroumand, Mariam. "Plüsch für das Auge." *die tageszeitung*, 15 July 1993.

Baumgärtel, Tilman. "Wir sind keine Untermieter." *die tageszeitung*, 23 October 1993.

Deuber-Mankowsky, Astrid, and Giaco Schiesser. "Die Schrift an der Wand." *Freitag*, 21 January 1994.

"Hecht mit Ambitionen im Karpfenteich der Privaten. Das von RTL, bis SAT 1 reichende Fernsehreich des Alexander Kluge und seiner Gesellschaft DCTP." *Rheinische Post*, 23 September 1994.

Eder, Klaus. "Einführung: Begriff ohne Anschauung ist leer. Anschauung ohne Begriff ist blind." In *Anschauung und Begriff: Die Arbeit des Institüt für Filmgestaltung Ulm 1962 bis 1995*, edited by Klaus Eder et al., 7–14. Frankfurt am Main: Stroemfeld/Roter Stern, 1995.

"Gespräch mit Alexander Kluge." In *Bilder in Bewegung: Essays. Gespräche zum Kino*, edited by Edgar Reitz. Reinbek bei Hamburg: Rowohlt, 1995.

Binzegger, Lilli and Andreas Heller. "Kolonisatoren, die in die Schwäche eindringen." *Neue Rundschau*, no. 106 (1995): 22–27.

Publications about Kluge

Adelson, Leslie A. "Contemporary Critical Consciousness: Peter Sloterdijk, Oskar Negt/Alexander Kluge, and the 'New Subjectivity.'" *German Studies Review*, 10, no. 1 (February 1987): 57–68.

Ahrends, Martin. "Feuersturm, ausgebrannt." *Die Zeit*, 26 October 1990.

Albig, Jorg-Uwe. "Abschied von Gestern." *Stern* (21 November 1985): 235.

Arnold, Heinz Ludwig, ed. *Text + Kritik*, nos. 85–86 (January 1985). Kluge issue.

Baumgärtel, Karl-Friedrich, et al. "Associativ montiert: Materialien zur 'Patriotin.'" *Zelluloid*, no. 9 (February 1980): 54–65.

Baumgärtel, Tilman. "Die kleine Unbekannte." *die tageszeitung*, 6 January 1993.

————. "'Wir sind keine Untermieter': dctp-Chef Alexander Kluge zu erneuten Vorwürfen, seine Programme seien 'Quotenkiller.'" *die tageszeitung*, 23 October 1993.

————. "Und redet. Und redet. Und redet: 'Hunger nach Sinn': Ein TV-Portrait über den dctp-Gründer Alexander Kluge (23 Uhr, West 3)." *die tageszeitung,* 26 June 1995.

Bayer, Eva-Susanne. "Menetekel der weltweiten Zerstörung." *Stuttgarter Zeitung,* 23 July 1982.

Bechtold, Gerhard. *Sinnliche Wahrnehmung von sozialer Wirklichkeit.* Tübingen: Gunter Narr, 1983.

Berg-Ganschow, Uta, Claudia Lenssen, and Sigried Vagt. "Kein Dunkel hat Seinesgleichen." *Frauen und Film,* no. 23 (1980): 4–13.

Bichsel, Peter, et al. "'Abschied von gestern': Fünf Stimmen zu Alexander Kluge erstem Film." *Die Weltwoche* (Zurich), 18 November 1966.

Biller, Maxim. "Im Dunkel der Köpfe." *Der Spiegel* (28 October 1985): 268–69.

Bitala, Michael. "Uns kann niemand mehr aufgepfropft werden." *Süddeutsche Zeitung,* 12 July 1996.

Blumenberg, Hans C. "Deutschland im Herbst." *Die Zeit,* 10 March 1978.

———. "Lage der Nation." *Die Zeit,* 24 March 1978.

———. "Kino der Freibeuter." *Die Zeit,* 21 September 1979.

———. "Deutsche Ängste, deutsche Bilder." *Die Zeit,* 25 April 1980.

———. "Ferdinand-zum zweiten." *Die Zeit,* 16 December 1997.

Böhm-Christl, Thomas, ed. *Alexander Kluge.* Frankfurt: Suhrkamp, 1983.

Bolz, Norbert. "Eigensinn zur politisch-theologisch Poetik Hans Magnus Enzensbergers und Alexander Kluges." In *Das schnelle Altern des neuesten Literatur,* edited by Jochen Hörisch and Hubert Winkels, 40–59. Düsseldorf: Claassen, 1985.

Bosse, Ulrike. "Kluges Nachforschungen zu Geschichte und Gegenwart." *Mittelbayrische Zeitung,* 3 October 1986.

———. *Alexander Kluge: Formen literarischer Darstellung von Geschichte.* Frankfurt am Main: Peter Lang, 1989.

Bowie, Andrew. "Problems of Historical Understanding in the Modern Novel." Ph.D. diss., University of East Anglia, 1980.

———. "'Sich rächen ist eine komplizierte Arbeitsleistung.' Überlegungen zur Vergangenheitsbewältigung am Biespiel Alexander Kluges." *Literatur und Erfahrung,* no. 6 (1981): 69–84.

———. "New Histories: Aspects of the Prose of Alexander Kluge." *Journal of European Studies,* no. 12 (1982): 180–208.

———. "Geschichte und Eigensinn." *Ideas & Production,* no. 1 (1983): 44–45.

———. "Individuality and Difference." *Oxford Literary Review* 7, nos. 1–2 (1985): 117–30.

———. "Geschichte und Eigensinn." *Telos,* 66 (winter 1985–1986): 183–90.

———. "Alexander Kluge: An Introduction." *Cultural Critique,* no. 4 (fall 1986): 111–18.

Bronnen, Barbara. "Roswitha ist so listig." *Abendzeitung* (Munich), 7 December 1973.

Bruck, Jan. "Brecht's and Kluge's Aesthetics of Realism." *Poetics* 17, nos. 1–2 (April 1988): 57–68.

Brunow, Jochen. "Suchen nach Geschichte." *tip* 8, no. 26 (3 January 1980): 16–7.

Brustellin, Alf. "Elefanten und andere Zeitgenössische Utopien." *Süddeutsche Zeitung,* 30 October 1968.

Buchka, Peter. "Das Gesamtkunstwerk Alexander Kluge." *Süddeutsche Zeitung,* 31 October 1985.

———. "Die Augen bleiben nämlich nicht stehen." *Süddeutsche Zeitung,* 27 September 1986.

Bürger, Rudolf. "Die Mikrophysik des Widerstandes." *Ästhetik und Kommunikation* 13, no. 48 (June 1982): 110–24.

Burmeister, Hans-Peter. *Kunst als Protest und Widerstand.* Frankfurt am Main: Peter Lang, 1985.

Buselmeier, Michael. "Operativität bei Alexander Kluge." In *Arbeitskreis Linker Germanisten,* 1–38. Heidelberg: Arbeitskreis Linker Germanisten, 1975.

Canby, Vincent. "'The Blind Director' From West Germany's Alexander Kluge." *New York Times,* 21 September 1986.

Carp, Stefanie. *Kriegsgeschichten: Zum Werk Alexander Kluges.* Munich: Wm. Fink, 1987.

Cook, Roger F. "Film Images and Reality: Alexander Kluge's Aesthetics of Cinema." *Colloquia Germanica* 18, no. 4 (1985): 281–99.

Cornelius, Hanns-Peter. "Ein passionierter Aufklärer mit seiner 'Strategie von unten.'" *Main Echo,* 25 September 1990.

Corrigan, Timothy. *New German Film: The Displaced Image,* 95–119. Austin: University of Texas Press, 1983.

———. "The Commerce of Auteurism: A Voice without Authority." *New German Critique,* no. 49 (winter 1990): 43–58.

Cramer, Sibylle. "Unsere ptolemäische Gefühle." *Süddeutsche Zeitung,* 20 February 1988.

Curtiss, Thomas Quinn. "'The Arp Statue' Shown at Venice." *New York Times,* 4 September 1971.

Dattenberger, Simone. "Liebe Sehgewohnheiten wurden hart erschüttert." *Münchner Merkur,* 12 July 1986.

Dawson, Jan. "The Sacred Terror." *Sight and Sound* 48, no. 4 (autumn 1979): 242–45.

Delling, Manfred. "Ein Wunschtraum wird wahr: RTL-plus: Alexander Kluge und sein neues Kurzfilmmagazin '10 vor 11.'" *Deutsches Allgemeine Sonntagsblatt,* 15 May 1988.

Desalm, Brigitte. "Als Grenzganger einflußreich." *Kölner Stadt-Anzeiger,* 27 November 1993.

Donner, Wolf. "'Gelegenheitsarbeit einer Sklavin': Alexander Kluges Neubeginn." *Die Zeit,* 4 January 1974.

———. "Profi der Gewalt in Panik." *Die Zeit,* 30 April 1976.

———. "Herrlicher Quatsch." *Der Spiegel,* 17 December 1979.

Drews, Jörg. "Leseprozesse mit paradoxem Ausgang." *Süddeutsche Zeitung,* 25 March 1979.

———. "Arbeit am Mythos: Zu Alexander Kluges Film 'Die Patriotin.'" *Merkur,* no. 4 (April 1980): 393–97.

"Durch die Sonne." *Der Spiegel,* 17 January 1972.

Durgnat, Raymond. "Yesterday Girl." *Films and Filming* 13, no. 8 (May 1967): 27–28.

Eder, Klaus. "Lebenslauf eines Perfektionisten." *Deutsche Volkszeitung,* 15 July 1976.

———, et al. *Anschauung und Begriff: Die Arbeiten des Instituts für Filmgestaltung Ulm 1962 bis 1995.* Frankfurt am Main: Stroemfeld/Red Stern, 1995.

Enzensberger, Hans Magnus. "Ein herzloser Schriftsteller: Hans Magnus Enzensberger über Alexander Kluge: 'Neue Geschichten.'" *Der Spiegel,* 2 January 1978.

Esslinger, Detlef. "RTL bindet sich weiter an Alexander Kluge." *Süddeutsche Zeitung,* 18 December 1996.

Felix, Jurgen et al., eds. *Augenblick,* no. 23 (1996). Special issue on Kluge's television titled "Fernsehen ohne Ermäßigung: Alexander Kluges Kulturmagazine."

Fiedler, Theodore. "Alexander Kluge: Mediating History and Conciousness." In *New German Filmmakers*, edited by Klaus Phillips, 195–229. New York: Frederick Ungar, 1984.

Franklin, James C. "Alienation and the Retention of the Self: The Heroines in *Der gute Mensch von Sezuan, Abschied von Gestern*, and *Die verlorene Ehe der Katharina Blum*." *Mosaic* 12, no. 4 (summer 1979): 87–98.

———. *New German Cinema: From Oberhausen to Hamburg*, 59–74. Boston: Twayne, 1983.

Frundt, Bodo. "Die Karriere des 'Kandidaten.'" *Stern*, 24 April 1980.

Gallasch, Peter F. "Nun ist Papas Kino wirklich tot." *Neue Ruhr Zeitung*, 29 October 1966.

Gangloff, Tilmann P. "Genial verpackter Kultur-Bluff?" *Stuttgarter Zeitung*, 12 June 1990.

———. "Kuckuckseier im privaten Lotternest." *Rheinischer Merkur*, 5 October 1990.

———. "Saboteur im Zirkus." *Deutsches Allgemeines Sonntagsblatt*, 21 January 1994.

Geldner, Wilfried. "Gaumengenuß-Dozentur. 'News & Stories' (SAT 1)." *Süddeutsche Zeitung*, 15 January 1992.

Gnam, Andrea. *Positionen der Wunschökonomie: Das ästhetische Textmodell Alexander Kluges und seine philosophischen Voraussetzungen*. Frankfurt: Peter Lang, 1989.

Gräber, Gerhard. "Über das Elend der Theorie: Zu Negt/Kluges 'Geschichte und Eigensinn.'" *Anachronistische Hefte*, 3 (1982): 5–13.

Gregor, Ulrich. "Renaissance des deutschen Films." *Die Welt*, 12 September 1966.

———. "Alexander Kluge: Kommentierte Filmographie." In *Herzog/Kluge/Straub*, edited by Peter W. Jansen and Wolfram Schütte, 131–52. Munich: Hanser, 1976.

von Grote, Alexandra. "Das Wetter bleibt trübe." *Ästhetik und Kommunikation* 9, no. 32 (1978): 128–32.

Grüneis, Olaf. *Schauspielerische Darstellung in Filmen Alexander Kluges: Zur Ideologiekritik des Schauspielens im Film*. Essen: Die Blaue Eule, 1994.

Habermas, Jürgen. "Nützlicher Maulwurf, der den schönen Rasen zerstört." *Frankfurter Rundschau*, 29 September 1990.

Habernoll, Kurt. "Wer versagt wird bestraft." *Abendzeitung* (Munich), 2 September 1968.

Hachmeister, Lutz. "'Herr Kluge kann das nicht allein entscheiden': Ein Gespräch mit dem Landesmedien-direktor Hans Hege." *Der Tagesspiegel*, 29 October 1988.

Handke, Peter. "Augsburg im August: trostlos." *Film* 7, no. 1 (1969): 30–32.

Handwerk, Michael. "Kluges Fernsehen, dummer Streit. Mit seinem Intellektuellen-TV a la '10 vor 11' bringt Alexander Kluge RTL-chef Helmut Thoma zur Weißglut." *TV Spielfilm*, September 1996.

Hansen, Miriam. "Cooperative Auteur Cinema and Oppositional Public Sphere." *New German Critique*, nos. 24–25 (fall–winter 1981–1982): 36–56.

———. "Introduction to Adorno, 'Transparencies on Film' (1966)." *New German Critique*, nos. 24–25 (fall–winter 1981–1982): 186–98.

———. "Alexander Kluge, Cinema and the Public Sphere: The Construction Site of History." *Discourse*, no. 6 (fall 1983): 53–74.

———. "Alexander Kluge: Crossings between Film, Literature, Critical Theory." In *Film und Literatur: Literarische Texte und der neue deutsche Film*, edited by Sigrid Bauschinger, Susan L. Cocalis, and Henry A. Lea, 169–96. Bern: Francke, 1984.

———. "The Stubborn Discourse: History and Story-Telling in the Films of Alexander Kluge." *Persistence of Vision*, no. 2 (fall 1985): 19–29.

————. "Space of history, language of time: Kluge's *Yesterday Girl* (1966)." In *German Film and Literature: Adaptations and Transformations,* edited by Eric Rentschler, 193–216. New York: Methuen, 1985.

————. "Reinventing the Nickelodeon: Notes on Kluge and Early Cinema." *October,* no. 46 (fall 1988): 179–98.

————, ed. *New German Critique,* no. 49 (fall 1990). Special issue devoted to Kluge that contains Hansen's introduction (3–10).

————. "Unstable Mixtures, Dilated Spheres: Negt and Kluge's *The Public Sphere and Experience,* Twenty Years Later." *Public Culture,* no. 2 (winter 1993): 179–212.

Hegedo, Herbert. "'Oberhausener' im Winterschlaf." *Hamburger Abendblatt,* 13 April 1963.

Heinrich, Frank. "Teil einer Hetzkampagne." *Medien Bulletin,* 20 September 1993.

Heißenbüttel, Helmut. "Story contra Montage." *Film* 4, no. 11 (1966): 16–17.

Herrgesell, Oliver. "'Verquere Ideen': Helmut Thoma." *Die Woche,* 22 July 1993.

Hertneck, Marcus. "Die unterschiedliche Wirkung einer Gartenschere." *Süddeutsche Zeitung,* 30 March 1992.

————. "Die Unterwanderung des Bildes." *Süddeutsche Zeitung,* 11 May 1992.

Hohlweg, Rudolf. "Musik für den Film—Film für Musik: Annäherung an Herzog, Kluge, Straub." In *Herzog/Kluge/Straub,* edited by Peter W. Jansen and Wolfram Schütte, 52–61. Munich: Hanser, 1976.

Höhne, Petra. "Weibliches von Sinnlichkeit und Abstraktion." *Medium* 9, no. 11 (November 1979): 32–33.

Hopf, Florian. "Die Lehrerin und das Knie." *Stern,* 13 December 79.

Huber, Jörg, et al. "Mit Film auf verordnetes Schweigen reagieren." *Cinema* (Zurich) 24, no. 2 (May 1978): 3–32.

Huhndorf, Bettina. "Inseln im bunten Einerlei." *Der Tagesspiegel,* 13 September 1994.

————. "'Parasit mit Steinfernsehen.'" *Wiesbaden Kurier,* 13 September 1994.

————. "Einsamer Streiter für intelligente Quotenkiller." *Deutsche Tagespost* (Hamburg), 24 September 1994.

————. "Kluger Fernseh-Mann für das wenig geliebte Programm mit Niveau." *Main Echo,* 28 December 1994.

Hummel, Christoph, ed. *Kinemathek,* no. 63 (September 1983). Kluge issue.

Hurst, Heike. "Vom großen Verhau zum großen Verschnitt." *Frauen und Film,* no. 16 (1978): 15–23.

Huyssen, Andreas. "An Analytic Storyteller in the Course of Time." *October,* no. 46 (fall 1988): 117–28.

Indiana, Gary. "Alexander Kluge." *BOMB* 27 (spring 1997): 46–51.

"Inflation des Angebots: Junges Forum in Berlin." *Die Welt,* 2 July 1971.

Jakobs, Hans-Jürgen. "Alexander Kluges Tanz auf vielen Hochzeiten." *Capital* (December 1989): 31–32.

Jameson, Fredric. "On Negt and Kluge." *October,* no. 46 (fall 1988): 151–77.

Jansen, Peter W. "*Die Artisten in der Zirkuskuppel: ratlos.*" *Filmkritik* 12, no. 11 (November 1968): 775–77.

————. "Ein Jahr Kinorebellion." *Merkur* 22, no. 248 (December 1968): 1135–47.

————. "Wildes Denken, kontrolliert." *Der Tagesspiegel,* 14 February 1992.

———— and Wolfram Schütte, eds. *Herzog/Kluge/Straub.* Munich: Hanser, 1976.

Jenny, Urs. "Anita G. macht von sich reden." *Süddeutsche Zeitung,* 6 September 1966.

————. "Wiedersehen mit Anita G." *Süddeutsche Zeitung,* 20 October 1966.

————. "Alle Macht den Elefanten." *Süddeutsche Zeitung,* 2 September 1968.

Jeremias, Brigitte. "Alexander und Alexandra." *Frankfurter Allgemeine Zeitung*, 14 November 1966.

———. "Mündig ist der Elefant." *Frankfurter Allgemeine Zeitung*, 2 September 1968.

———. "Die Geschichte als Raubgrabung und Wintermärchen." *Frankfurter Allgemeine Zeitung*, 8 December 1979.

Jessen, Jens. "Vom Elend der Denkanstöße." *Frankfurter Allgemeine Zeitung*, 31 October 1990.

Jeuck, Dieter and Guntram Vogt. "Fernsehen ohne Ermäßigung." *Frankfurter Rundschau*, 16 December 1989.

Jochum, Norbert. "Alexander-Schlacht." *Die Zeit*, 23 August 1985.

Kaes, Anton. *Deutschlandbilder. Die Wiederkehr der Geschichte als Film*, 43–73. Munich: Text + Kritik, 1987. The corresponding section in the revised English edition, *From Hitler to Heimat: The Return of History as Film* (Cambridge, MA: Harvard University, 1989), is chapter four, "In Search of Germany: Alexander Kluge's *The Patriot*," 105–35.

———. "Über den nomadischen Umgang mit Geschichte." *Text + Kritik*, nos. 85–86 (January 1985): 132–44.

Kaiser, Moritz. "Thomas Kampf gegen den Trittbrettfahrer." *Die Welt*, 21 December 1993.

Kallweit, Marlies, Helke Sander, and Mädi Kemper. "'Gelegenheitsarbeit einer Sklavin.'" *Frauen und Film*, no. 11 (1974): 12–25.

Karasek, Hellmuth. "Ein Mann sieht braun." *Der Spiegel*, 26 April 1976.

Kay, Karyn. "*Part-Time Work of a Domestic Slave.*" *Film Quarterly* (fall 1975): 52–57.

Keller, Harald. "Jetzt kommt 'Bäckerblume TV.'" *die tageszeitung*, 18 July 1995.

Kilb, Andreas. "Der lange Abschied von Herrn K." *Die Zeit*, 24 June 1988.

"Kluge-Dentsu TV." *die tageszeitung*, 25 November 1986.

Knödler-Bunte, Eberhard. "The Proletarian Public Sphere and Political Organization." *New German Critique*, no. 4 (winter 1975): 51–75.

Knott-Wolf, Brigitte. "Ein Exot schreibt Fernsehgeschichte." *Funk-Korrespondenz*, no. 27 (8 July 1988): 1–2.

Koch, Gerhard. "Frankfurt zwischen Verdi und Valentin." *Frankfurter Allgemeine Zeitung*, 3 October 1983.

Koch, Gertrund. "Alexander Kluge's Phantom of the Opera." *New German Critique*, no. 49. (winter 1990): 79–88.

Koch, Krischan. *Die Bedeutung des "Oberhausener Manifestes" für die Filmentwicklung in der BRD*. Frankfurt am Main: Peter Lang, 1985.

Kohl, Andreas. "Unsichtbare Bilder eines Blinden." *Rheinischer Merkur*, 12 October 1985.

Korn, Karl. "Aktennotizen über Anita G." *Frankfurter Allgemeine Zeitung*, 7 September 1966.

———. "Frei schwebend in der Zirkuskuppel." *Frankfurter Allgemeine Zeitung*, 5 November 1968.

Kötz, Michael. "Kluge: Anstatt einer Filmkritik." *Medium* 13, no.11 (November 1980): 36–37.

———. " . . . und möchten noch nicht sterben." *Deutsches Allgemeine Sonntagsblatt*, 20 February 1983.

———. "Der Film im eigenen Kopf." *Deutsches Allgemeine Sonntagsblatt*, 17 November 1985.

———. "Die Wirklichkeit ist gar nicht wirklich." *Deutsches Allgemeine Sonntagsblatt*, 2 November 1990.

Kötz, Michael, and Petra Höhne. *Sinnlichkeit des Zusammenhangs: Zur Filmarbeit von Alexander Kluge.* Cologne: Prometh, 1981.

Kreimeier, Klaus. "Werner Holt und Anita G.: Zweimal Abschied von gestern." *Kirche und Film,* no. 11 (November 1966): 2–9.

———. "Film-Montage und Montage-Film." *Spuren* 3, no. 3 (June–July 1980): 28–30.

———. "'Zweitausend Jahre Hoffnung, Wünsche, Arbeit . . .' Über Alexander Kluges Film 'Die Patriotin.'" *Spuren* 3, no. 1 (1980): 15–16.

———. "Hermetisch und transparent: Alexander Kluge zum Sechzigsten." *Film,* no. 2 (February 1992): 17–19.

———. "Ten to Eleven oder: Kann man Zeit abbilden?" *Die Zeit,* 27 November 1992.

Kremski, Peter. "Geschichten zur Geschichte." *Filmbulletin* 29, no. 5 (October–November 1987): 47–48.

Kriewitz, Günther. "Reisender in Sachen Film." *Stuttgarter Zeitung,* 8 February 1980.

Kummer, Elke. "Die leisen Töne der Zeit aufzeichnen." *epd Film,* no. 11 (1985): 24–26.

"Kunstfreiheit und Menschenwürde. 'Diese Drombuschs' und '10 vor 11': Streit um die Fersehwirklichkeit." *Süddeutsche Zeitung,* 15 January 1992.

Künzel, Uwe. "Der Zusammenhang im Kopf des Zuschauers." *Basler Zeitung,* 26 September 1987.

———. "Der Aufklärer als Realist." *Zoom,* 5 November 1987.

Kurnitzky, Horst. "Wenn das Leben sich nicht für die Wirklichkeit interessiert, ist Wirklichkeitsliebe nur von den Toten zu erwarten." *Freibeuter,* no. 3 (1980): 153–60.

Kursell, Gregor. "Alexander Kluges Wundertüte." *Münchner Merkur,* 3 October 1986.

Labanyi, Peter. "The Texts of Alexander Kluge." Ph.D. diss., Trinity College, 1982.

Lackschéwitz, Klaus. "Junger Deutscher Film: Porträt eines Autors und Regisseurs." *Film-Telegramm* 19, no. 4 (24 January 1967): 9.

Land, Bodo. "Der Quotenkiller." *TV Today,* 21 January 1995.

Lambert, Lothar. "Vergleichende Analyse der Filme 'Abschied von gestern' (Alexander Kluge) und 'Mahlzeiten' (Edgar Reitz)." Master's thesis, Freie Universität, 1968.

Langford, Michelle. "Film Figures: Rainer Werner Fassbinder's 'The Marriage of Maria Braun' and Alexander Kluge's 'The Female Patriot.'" In *Kiss Me Deadly: Feminism and Cinema for the Moment,* edited by Laleen Jayamanne, 147–79. Sydney: Power, 1995.

Lau, Jörg. "Heilige Krieger." Parts 1 and 2. *die tageszeitung,* 20–21 April 1996.

Leder, Dietrich. "Schmuggelgut im Privat-TV." *Stern,* 8 August 1991.

———. "Der stille Machthaber." *Die Woche,* 22 April 1993.

———. "Leben nach dem Tod. Der TV-Sender Vox, den es gar nicht mehr geben sollte, hat Erfolg mit billigen Notprogrammen." *Die Woche,* 25 June 1994.

Leicht, Robert. "Der Mythos eines deutschen Wesens." *Süddeutsche Zeitung,* 21 April 1980.

Lepthien, Carsten. "Der Quotenkiller: Wenig Zuschauer für die Sender—aber viel Geld für Alexander Kluge." *Bild am Sonntag,* 3 December 1995.

Le Viseur, Raimund. "Alle schwärmen von Alexandra." *Der Abend* (Berlin), 2 November 1966.

———. "Der Film in unseren Köpfen." *Der Abend* (Berlin), 2 November 1966.

Lewandowski, Rainer. *Alexander Kluge.* Munich: C. H. Beck, 1980.

———. *Die Filme von Alexander Kluge.* Hildesheim: Olms, 1980.

————. *Die Oberhausener: Rekonstruktion einer Gruppe.* Diekholzen: Verlag für Bühne und Film, 1982.

————. "Der Wunsch etwas zu verändern." *Medium,* no. 4 (April 1982): 13.

Liebman, Stuart, ed. *October,* no. 46 (fall 1988). This special issue devoted to Kluge also contains Liebman's "Why Kluge?" (2–22) and "On New German Cinema, Art, Enlightenment, and the Public Sphere: An Interview with Alexander Kluge" (23–59).

Lillienthal, Volker. "Freie Fahrt für freie Sender." *Die Zeit,* 12 July 1996.

————. "Das eine soll zum anderen passen." *Frankfurter Allgemeine Zeitung,* 16 August 1996.

Limmer, Wolfgang. "Bilder aus der Wirklichkeit." *Der Spiegel,* 6 March 1978.

Linder, Christian. *Die Traume der Wunschmaschine.* Reinbek bei Hamburg: Rowohlt, 1981.

"Lob in Venedig." *Der Spiegel,* 12 September 1966.

Lütgenhorst, Manfred. "Wir werden uns rächen." Parts 1 and 2. *Abendzeitung,* 13–14 July 1968.

Makowsky, Arno. "Der Pate als Quotenkiller." *Süddeutsche Zeitung,* 16 October 1993.

McCormick, Ruth. "Germany in Autumn." *Cineaste* 9, no. 3 (spring 79): 53–54.

Messias, Hans. "'Wenn man sich etwas ganz fest wünscht . . .' Alexander Kluges Kulturmagazin '10 vor 11' bei RTL plus." *Film-Korrespondenz,* no. 12 (7 June 1998): 7–9.

Meyer, Klaus. "Die Balance halten: Alexander Kluges Fernsehimperium trotzt den großen Privatsendern." *Der Tagesspiegel* (Berlin), 1 June 1993.

Moeller, Hans-Bernard and C. Springer. "Directed Change in the Young German Film: Alexander Kluge and 'Artists under the Big Top: Perplexed.'" *Wide Angle* 2, no. 1 (1978): 14–21.

Naefe, Vivian. "Wir müssen uns Nebenbuhler suchen." *Abendzeitung* (Munich), 3 January 1979.

Nagel, Ivan. "Triumph der Angst." *Der Spiegel,* 21 April 1980.

Nemeczek, Alfred. "Der Schuß auf den Minister." *Stern,* 20 May 1976.

Nettelbeck, Uwe. "Reformzirkusvorbereitungspolitik." *Die Zeit,* 8 November 1968.

————. "Die Verwirrungen der Anita G." *Die Zeit,* 2 September 1966.

O'Kane, John. "History, Performance, Counter-Cinema: Alexander Kluge's *Die Patriotin.*" *Screen* 26, no. 6 (November–December 1985): 2–17.

Ott, Klaus. "Schlechte Karten für den Untermieter: Die geplante Mediengesetznovelle bedroht Alexander Kluges DCTP-Programme." *Süddeutsche Zeitung,* 1 December 1995.

————. "Auferstanden aus Ruinen." *Süddeutsche Zeitung,* 14 March 1996.

Patalas, Enno. "'Abschied von Gestern (Anita G.)' von Alexander Kluge." *Filmkritik* 10, no. 11 (November 1966): 623–25.

————. "Die Toten Augen." In *Im Off. Filmartikel,* edited by Frieda Grafe and Enno Patalas, 131–41. Munich: Hanser, 1974.

————, ed. *Abschied von Gestern: Protokoll.* Frankfurt am Main: Verlag Filmkritik, n.d.

Pavsek, Christopher. "The Storyteller in the Age of Mechanical Reproduction: Alexander Kluge's Reworking of Walter Benjamin." *Found Object* 2 (fall 1993): 83–92.

————. "History and Obstinacy: Negt and Kluge's Redemption of Labor." *New German Critique* 68 (spring–summer 1996): 137–63.

Perl, Ilona. "Reflexionen über die Mittel des Kinos." *Film* 4, no. 10 (October 1966): 9–13.

Peters, Karsten. "Der beste Godard." *Abendzeitung* (Munich), 14 October 1966.

Peters, Martin. "Auch ein Quotenkiller versteht das Geschäft." *Rheinischer Merkur*, 27 May 1994.

Peuckert, Tom. "Der Doktor der das Leben jagt: Fragmentarische Gedanken zum Werk Alexander Kluges." *Der Tagesspiegel* (Berlin), 15 March 1992.

Pflaum, Hans Günther. "Das Knie des Obergefreiten Wieland." *Süddeutsche Zeitung*, 15 December 1979.

———. "Ein vergebliches Suchen." *Süddeutsche Zeitung*, 12 February 1983.

———. "Vom Abbau der Katastrophen." *Süddeutsche Zeitung*, 17 September 1983.

———. "Hortus conclusus oder Spielwiese?" *epd Film*, no. 9 (1985): 7.

Prinzler, Hans Helmut. "Gegeninformation: Notizen zu neuen Dokumentarfilmen aus der Bundesrepublik und zu 'Deutschland im Herbst.'" In *Jahrbuch Film 78/79*, edited by Hans Günther Pflaum, 48–61. Munich: Hanser, 1978.

Rausch, Mechthild. "Nachtrag zu Abschied von gestern." *Kino*, no. 5 (June 1967): 9–11.

Rentschler, Eric. "Kluge, Film History and *Eigensinn*." *New German Critique*, no. 31 (winter 1984): 109–24.

———. "Remembering Not to Forget: A Retrospective Reading of Kluge's *Brutality in Stone*." *New German Critique*, no. 49 (winter 1990): 23–42.

Reuther, Hanno. "Schwierigkeiten, sich anzupassen." *Frankfurter Rundschau*, 14 October 1966.

Rich, B. Ruby. "She Says, He Says: The Power of the Narrator in Modernist Film Politics." *Discourse*, no. 6 (fall 1983): 31–46.

Riepe, Manfred. "Faszinierend. 'News & Stories'." *Frankfurter Rundschau*, 7 October 1992.

———. "Banale Monotonie." *Frankfurter Rundschau*, 15 November 1995.

Roberts, David. "Die Formenwelt des Zusammenhangs: Zur Theorie und Funktion der Montage bei Alexander Kluge." *Zeitschrift für Literatur und Linguistik*, no. 46 (1982): 104–19.

Röhl, Wolfgang. "Professor Sandmann." *Stern*, 15 May 1997.

"RTL plus wird 'mehr und mehr' zu einem Gefährdungspotential: Niedersächsiger Landesrundfunkausschuß rügt Kastrationsszene in Kluges '10 vor 11.'" *Kirche und Rundfunk*, no. 4 (18 January 1992): 13.

Rumler, Fritz. "Ratlose Artisten in der Pulvermühle." *Der Spiegel*, 9 September 1968.

Sander, Helke. "'You Can't Always Get What You Want': The Films of Alexander Kluge." *New German Critique*, no. 49 (winter 1990): 59–68.

Sanders-Brahms, Helma. ". . . desto ferner sieht es zurück." *Film und Fernsehen*, no. 1 (January 1992): 10–13.

Sandford, John. *The New German Cinema*, 17–26. London: Oswald Wolff, 1980.

"SAT-1 verteidigt Alexander Kluge gegen Pornographie-Vorwurf." *Kirche und Rundfunk*, no. 70 (7 September 1991): 13.

Sauvaget, Daniel. *Alexander Kluge*. Paris: Goethe Institut and La Cinémathèque Française, 1984.

Schirmacher, Wolfgang. "Der Spröde ist bunt: ein Symposium über Alexander Kluge in den USA." *Nürnberger Zeitung*, 23 November 1968.

———. "Ein nachdenklicher Affe im Medienschungel." *Berliner Zeitung*, 14 February 1992.

Schirrmacher, Frank. "Angriff der Gegenwart auf die Zeit: Der Schriftsteller und Filmemacher Alexander Kluge wird sechzig." *Frankfurter Allgemeine Zeitung*, 14 February 1992.

Schlicht, Burghard. "Gefühle glauben an einen glücklichen Ausgang." *Der Spiegel,* 26 September 1983.

Schlüpmann, Heide. "What is Different is Good: Women and Femininity in the Films of Alexander Kluge." *October,* no. 46 (fall 1988): 129–50.

———. "Femininity as Productive Force: Kluge and Critical Theory." *New German Critique,* no. 49 (winter 1990): 69–78.

Schmerber, Helmut. "Doch noch deutscher Film? Anmerkungen zu Alexander Kluges 'Abschied von Gestern.'" *Frankfurter Hefte,* no. 12 (1966): 882–85.

Schmidt, Eckhardt. "Alexander Kluges 'Lebensläufe.'" Parts 1 and 2. *Süddeutsche Zeitung,* 11–12 June 1966.

Schödel, Helmut. "Endspiel." *Die Zeit,* 18 February 1983.

———. "Schrottintensive Zeiten." *Die Zeit,* 8 November 1985.

Schramm, Renate. "Oft geht Kluge zweimal pro Tag ins Kino." Parts 1 and 2. *Abendzeitung* (Munich), 14–15 September 1968.

Schröck, Rudolf. "Fernsehkrach um Alexnder Kluge—Bußgeld für Pornofilm." *Abendzeitung* (Munich), 23 August 1991.

Schröder, Christian. "Das etwas andere Autoren-Fernsehen." *Der Tagesspiegel,* 1 November 1991.

Schulte, Christian. "Kluges Interview—Technik." *Medien & Erziehung,* no. 6 (December 1995): 374–75.

Schulze-Reimpell. "Die Zuschauer vor dem Bildschirm: ratlos." *Die Welt,* 4 April 1970.

Schütte, Wolfram. "Auf der Mittelweg." *Frankfurter Rundschau,* 5 May 1976.

———. "Lichte Tiefen auf Bohrgelände." *Frankfurter Rundschau,* 8 December 1979.

———. "Porträt mit Blindstellen." *Frankfurter Allgemeine Zeitung,* 23 April 1980.

———. "Kälte & Wärmestrom: Alexander Kluges 'Ur' and Kino- 'Patriotin.'" *Frankfurter Rundschau,* 9 January 1981.

———. "Trapezakt: Das kontroverse Gemeinschaftsprojekt 'Krieg und Frieden.'" *Frankfurter Rundschau,* 12 February 1983.

———. "Abrüstung der V. Akte oder die Bewaffnung der Gefühle." *Frankfurter Rundschau,* 21 September 83.

———. "Verweigerte Übergabe." *Frankfurter Rundschau,* 8 November 1985.

Seidel, Hans-Dieter. "Der Angriff der Gegenwart auf die übrige Zeit." *Frankfurter Allgemeine Zeitung,* 2 November 1985.

———. "Die Assoziationswut des Herrn K." *Frankfurter Allgemeine Zeitung,* 15 November 1986.

Siemons, Mark. "Die Welt zerspringt in tausend Stücke." *Frankfurter Allgemeine Zeitung,* 11 June 1994.

———. "Zwölftonmusik im Zirkus. Das Fernsehen Alexander Kluges." In *Fernsehen, Medien, Macht und Märkte,* edited by Helmut Monkenbusch. Reinbek bei Hamburg, 1994.

———. "Das Idol ist immer der Gärtner: Hinter Kluge steckt Kluge: Ein Porträt (WDR 3)." *Frankfurter Allgemeine Zeitung,* 28 June 1995.

Silberman, Marc. "Introduction to *Germany in Autumn.*" *Discourse,* no. 6 (fall 1983): 48–52.

Simon-Zülch, Sybille. "Sammler und Zerleger. Alexander Kluges '10 vor 11,' montags, RTL plus." *epd/Kirche und Rundfunk,* no. 67 (28 August 1991): 3–5.

Skasa-Wieß, Ruprecht. "Leitpartikel aus aller Welt." *Stuttgarter Zeitung,* 6 March 1987.

"'Spiegel' und Kluge mit RTL-plus." *die tageszeitung,* 19 May 1987.

"Eine 'Spielwiese' im privaten Fernsehen: Alexander Kluges Kulturprogramm bei RTL plus." *Neue Zürcher Zeitung,* 2 June 1988.

Steinborn, Bion. "Ferdinand le Radical." *Filmfaust* 1, no. 6 (1977): 86–92.

———. "Eine Patriotin der Phantasie." *Filmfaust* 3–4, no. 15 (1979): 29–36.

Stollmann, Rainer. "Reading Kluge's 'Mass Death in Venice.'" *New German Critique,* no. 30 (fall 1980): 65–95.

Theweleit, Klaus. "Artisten im Fernsehstudio, unbekümmert." *Die Zeit,* 18 August 1995.

Thompson, Howard. "Yesterday Girl." *New York Times,* 22 September 1967.

Timpe, Wolfgang. "Kulturartist auf dem TV-Sat." *Neue Medien* (November 1987): 96.

Tittelbach, Rainer. "Intellektuelle Explosionen im Dazwischen." *Die Welt,* 23 January 1989.

"Die Verantwortung der Filmwirtschaft." *Medium,* no. 4 (April 1982): 2.

Viertel, Wolfram. "Das große Himmelswagen." *Filmkritik,* no. 4 (1972): 204–9.

Vogt, Guntram, "Zum Zusammenhang von Ästhetik und Ethik im Essayismus Alexander Kluges." In *Versuche über den Essayfilm,* edited by Hanno Möbius, 83–106. Marburg: Augenblick 10, 1991.

Weidinger, Birgit. "Der Partisan aus Deutschland: Alexander Kluge wirbt in London für mehr Programmaustausch." *Süddeutsche Zeitung,* 13 December 1992.

Wendt, Ernst. "Fluchtbeschreibung." *Film* 4, no. 11 (November 1966): 12–16.

———. "Die Fähigkeit zu trauern." *Film* 6, no. 10 (October 1968): 25–26.

Wiegenstein, Roland H. "Alexander Kluges Katastrophen-Kataster." *Merkur* 27, no. 306 (November 1973): 1081–83.

Willemsen, Roger. "Kluge, der Magier." *Die Woche,* 18 November 1996.

Wilson, David. "Yesterday Girl." *Sight and Sound* 36, no. 2 (spring 1967): 95.

———. "Artists at the Top of the Big Top: Disoriented." *Sight and Sound* 39, no. 1 (winter 1969–1970): 46–47.

Winterstein, Axel. "Zu böser Schlacht schleich ich heut nacht so bang." *Filmbeobachter,* 7 April 1979.

Witt, M. "Die klugen Geschäfte des Herrn Kluge." *TV Spielfilm,* 19 September–1 October 1993.

Witte, Karsten. "Subjektivität als Aneignung von Wirklichkeit." *Medium* 8, no. 5 (May 1978): 25–27.

Wolf, Günther. "Roßkur für die Künste." *Hamburger Abendblatt,* 3 June 1991.

———. "Kopf-Kino für den Bildschirm: '10 vor 11.'" *Berliner Morgenpost,* 6 June 1991.

Zimmer, Dieter E. "Kraftwerk für Babylon." *Die Zeit,* 7 October 1983.

General Bibliography

Adorno, Theodor W. "Transparencies on Film." *New German Critique,* nos. 24–25 (fall–winter 1982): 199–206.

———. *Aesthetic Theory.* Translated by C. Lenhardt. Edited by Gretel Adorno and Rolf Tiedemann. London and Boston: Routledge and Kegan Paul, 1984.

ARD-Jahrbuch 75. Hamburg: Hans Bredow Institut, 1975.

Benjamin, Walter. *Charles Baudelaire: A Lyric Poet in the Era of High Capitalism.* London: Verso, 1983.

———. *Understanding Brecht.* Translated by Anna Bostock. London: Verso, 1983.

Berman, Marshall. *All That Is Solid Melts into Air: The Experience of Modernity.* New York: Simon and Schuster, 1982.

Berman, Russell. *Modern Culture and Critical Theory: Art, Politics and the Legacy of the Frankfurt School.* Madison: University of Wisconsin Press, 1989.

Bordwell, David. "Eisenstein's Epistemological Shift." *Screen* 15, no.4 (winter 1974–1975): 32–46.

Bradbury, Malcolm, and James McFarlane, eds. *Modernism: 1890–1930.* London: Penguin, 1976.

Brecht, Bertolt. "The Modern Theater Is the Epic Theater" and "Short Description of a New Technique of Acting which Produces an Alienation Effect." In *Brecht on Theatre: The Development of an Aesthetic,* edited and translated by John Willett. New York: Hill and Wang, 1978.

Brewster, Ben. "Editorial Note." *Screen* 15, no. 4 (winter 1974–1975): 29–32.

Bürger, Peter. *Theory of the Avant-Guarde.* Minneapolis: University of Minnesota Press, 1984.

Calinescu, Matei. *Five Faces of Modernity.* Durham, N.C.: Duke University Press, 1987.

Carroll, Noël. "Film." In *The Postmodern Moment: A Handbook of Contemporary Innovation in the Arts,* edited by Stanley Trachtenberg, 101–34. Westport, Connecticut: Greenwood Press, 1985.

Chefdor, Monique, Ricardo Quinones, and Albert Wachtel, eds. *Modernism, Challenges and Perspectives.* Urbana and Chicago: University of Illinois Press, 1986.

Collins, Jim. *Uncommon Cultures.* New York and London: Routledge, 1989.

Collins, Richard, and Vincent Porter. *WDR and the Arbeiterfilm: Fassbinder, Ziewer and Others.* London: British Film Institute, 1981.

Corrigan, Timothy. *New German Film: The Displaced Image.* Austin: University of Texas Press, 1983.

Dawson, Jan. "A Labyrinth of Subsidies: The Origins of New German Cinema." *Sight and Sound,* nos. 50–51 (winter 1980–1981): 14–20.

"Der deutsche Film hat 1967 eine Chance." *Starpress* (Hamburg) 14, nos. 80–81 (20 December 1966): 6.

Dyson, Kenneth and Peter Humphreys. *Broadcasting and New Media Policies in Western Europe.* London: Routledge, 1988.

Elsaesser, Thomas. *New German Cinema: A History.* New Brunswick, New Jersey: Rutgers University Press, 1989.

Emery, Walter B. *National and International Systems of Broadcasting.* East Lansing: Michigan State University, 1969.

Fassbinder, Rainer Werner. *Filme befreien den Kopf.* Frankfurt am Main: Fischer, 1984.

Filmförderung 1974–1979: Der deutsche Film und das Fernsehen. Frankfurt: ZDF, 1980.

Foster, Hal, ed. "Discourse of Others: Feminism and Postmodernism." *The Anti-Aesthetic: Essays on Post-Modern Culture,* 57–77. Port Townsend, Washington: Bay Press, 1983.

Geduld, Harry M., ed. *Filmmakers on Filmmaking.* Bloomington: Indiana University Press, 1967.

Gitlin, Todd. "Postmodernism defined, at last." *Utne Reader* (July–August 1989): 52–61. This article first appeared in *Dissent.*

Greenberg, Clement. *Art and Culture.* Boston: Beacon Press, 1961.

Habermas, Jürgen. "Modernity versus Postmodernity." *New German Critique,* no. 22 (winter 1981): 3–14.

———. *Habermas and Modernity.* Edited with an introduction by Richard J. Bernstein. Cambridge, Massachusetts: M.I.T. Press, 1985.

————. *Autonomy and Solidarity: Interviews*. Edited with an introduction by Peter Dews. London: Verso, 1986.

Harvey, David. *The Condition of Postmodernity*. Oxford: Blackwell, 1989.

Harvey, Sylvia. "Whose Brecht? Memories for the Eighties." *Screen* 23, no. 1 (May–June 1982): 45–59.

Hauser, Arnold. *Sociology of Art*. Translated by Kenneth J. Northcott. Chicago and London: University of Chicago Press, 1982.

Hembus, Joe. *Der deutsche Film kann gar nicht besser sein: Ein Pamphlet von gestern, eine Abrechnung von heute*. 2d ed. Munich: Rogner and Bernhard, 1981.

Hillier, Jim, ed. *Cahiers du Cinéma, The 1950s: Neo-Realism, Hollywood, New Wave*. Cambridge, Massachusetts: Harvard University Press, 1985.

Hoberman, J. "After Avant-Garde Film." In *Art After Modernism: Rethinking Representation*, edited by Brian Wallis. New York: The Museum of Contemporary Art, 1984.

Horkheimer, Max, and Theodor W. Adorno. *Dialectic of Enlightenment*. Translated by John Cumming. New York: Continuum, 1987.

Huyssen, Andreas. *After the Great Divide*. Bloomington and Indianapolis: Indiana University Press, 1986.

Jameson, Fredric. "Reflections in Conclusion." In *Aesthetics and Politics*, 206–8. London: NLB, 1977.

————. "Postmodernism and Consumer Society." In *Postmodernism and its Discontents*, edited by E. Ann Kaplan, 13–29. London and New York: Verso, 1988.

Jay, Martin. *Adorno*. Cambridge: Harvard University Press, 1984.

Johnston, Sheila. "The Author as Public Institution." *Screen Education*, nos. 32–33 (autumn/winter 1979–80): 67–78.

Kaes, Anton. *From Hitler to Heimat: The Return of History as Film*. Cambridge, Massachusetts: Harvard University Press, 1989.

Kaplan, E. Ann, ed. *Postmodernism and its Discontents*. London and New York: Verso, 1988.

Karl, Frederick R. *Modern and Modernism: The Sovereignty of the Artist 1885–1925*. New York: Atheneum, 1985.

Lindinger, Herbert, ed. *Die Moral der Gegenstände*. Berlin: Internationales Design Zentrum Berlin, 1987.

Lucie-Smith, Edward. *Art in the Seventies*. Ithaca, New York: Cornell University Press, 1980.

Lunn, Eugene. *Marxism and Modernism: An Historical Study of Lukács, Brecht, Benjamin and Adorno*. Berkeley: University of California Press, 1982.

Lyotard, Jean-François. *The Postmodern Condition*. Minneapolis: University of Minnesota Press, 1984.

Moeller, Hans-Bernhard. "New German Cinema and Its Precarious Subsidy and Finance System." *Quarterly Review of Film Studies* (spring 1980): 157–68.

Owens, Craig. "The Discourse of Others: Feminists and Postmodernism." In *The Anti-Aesthetic: Essays on Postmodern Culture*, edited by Hal Foster, 57–79. Port Townsend, Washington: Bay Press, 1983.

Rentschler, Eric. *West German Film in the Course of Time: Reflections on Twenty Years since Oberhausen*. Bedford Hills, New York: Redgrave, 1984.

————, ed. *West German Filmmakers on Film: Visions and Voices*. New York: Holmes and Meier, 1987.

Rodowick, D. N. *The Crisis of Political Modernism: Criticism and Ideology in Contemporary Film Theory.* Berkeley: University of California, 1984.

Sandford, John. *Mass Media of the German Speaking Countries.* London: Oswald Wolff, 1976.

————. *The New German Cinema.* New York: DaCapo, 1982.

Sannwald, Daniela. *Von der Filmkrise zum Neuen Deutschen Film: Filmausbildung an der Hochschule für Gestaltung Ulm 1958–1968.* Berlin: Spiess, 1997.

Schmieding, Walther. *Kunst oder Kasse: Der Ärger mit dem deutschen Film.* Hamburg: Rütten und Loening, 1961.

Simmel, Georg. *The Sociology of Georg Simmel.* Translated and edited by Kurt H. Wolff. Glencoe, Ilinois: Free Press, 1950.

Stam, Robert. "Bakhtin and Left Cultural Critique." In *Postmodernism and its Discontents,* edited by E. Ann Kaplan, 116–45. London and New York: Verso, 1988.

Strobel, Hans Rolf. "Kein fröhlicher Rückblick—kein trauriger Ausblick." *Medium* 12, no. 4 (April 1982): 3–5.

Taylor, Ronald, ed. *Aesthetics and Politics.* London: NLB, 1977.

Trilling, Lionel. *Beyond Culture.* New York: Viking, 1965.

Wallis, Brian, ed. *Art After Modernism: Rethinking Representation.* New York: New Museum of Contemporary Art, 1984.

Wellbery, David E. "Postmodernism in Europe: On Recent German Writing." In *The Postmodern Moment: A Handbook of Contemporary Innovation in the Arts,* edited by Stanley Trachtenberg, 229–50. Westport, Connecticut: Greenwood Press, 1985.

Williams, Raymond. *The Politics of Modernism.* London and New York: Verso, 1989.

Index

109, 197. —*Willi Tobler und der Untergang der 6. Flotte* (*Willi Tobler and the Wreck of the Sixth Fleet*), 84, 91, 225 n.9, 226 n.13, 230 n.34; structure, 65, 68, 72–76, 225 n.9. —*"Zu böser Schlacht schleich ich heut nacht so bang—."* ("Into this Evil Fight Tonight I Am Afraid to Creep . . ."), 223 n.80, 225 n.9, 229 n.23
short films: *Besitzbürgerin, Jahrgang 1908* (Woman of Means, Class of 1908, A), 218 n.8; *Brutalität in Stein* (Brutality in Stone), 39, 223 n.80; *Feuerlöscher E. A. Winterstein* (Fireman E. A. Winterstein), 219 n.26; *Frau Blackburn, geb. 5 Jan. 1872, wird gefilmt* (Frau Blackburn, Born January 5, 1872, Is filmed), 218 n.8, 219 n.26; *Lehrer im Wandel* (Teachers through Change), 219 n.24; *Porträt einer Bewährung* (Proven Competence Portrayed), 219 n.26, 223 n.80; *Rennen* (Racing), 219 n.26
television programs: *Stunde der Filmemacher, Die* (Hour of the Filmmakers), 183, 185; *News & Stories*, 195; *Prime Time Spät Ausgabe* (Prime Time Late Edition), 195; *10 vor 11* (10 to 11), 179, 197, 207, 240 n.2, 242 n.26
Kluge, Alexandra Karen, 37–38, 174, 218 n.8, 238 n.62, 238 n.70
Kluge, Alice Hausdorf, 37, 218 n.8
Kluge, Ernst, 37–38, 218 n.8
Kluge, Leonard, 38
Kluge, Sophie Alexandra, 38
Kluge film theory, 11, 29, 161–62
Koch, Gertrude, 147
Kohl, Helmut, 120
Kotulla, Theodor, 221 n.56
Kremski, Peter, 99
Krieg und Frieden (War and Peace) (Kluge), 144, 167–68, 216 n.41, 230 n.27; style, 104, 111, 230 n.24
Kriemhilds Rache (Kriemhild's Revenge) (Lang), 116, 118–19, 122, 125, 126, 127
Kristl, Vlado, 221 nn.52, 54

Kückelmann, Norbert, 221 n.51
Kulturpolitik und Ausgabenkontrolle (Cultural Politics and Financial Control) (Kluge and Becker), 38
Kuratorium junger deutscher Film (Board of Young German Film), 49, 55, 56, 61, 221 n.52

Lacan, Jacques, 29
Lang, Fritz, 200, 202; *indische Grabmal, Das* (Journey to the Lost City), 38; *Kriemhilds Rache* (Kriemhild's Revenge), 116, 118–19, 122, 125, 126, 127; *M*, 114
Last Year at Marienbad, 25
Lautréamont, 214 n.15
Lebensläufe (Attendance List for a Funeral) (Kluge), 39, 41–42, 223 n.80, 224 n.95
LeGrice, Malcolm, 99
Lehrer im Wandel (Teachers through Change) (Kluge), 219 n.24
Lernprozesse mit tödlichem Ausgang (Learning Processes with a Deadly Outcome) (Kluge), 42
Lewandowski, Rainer, 222 n.69
Liebman, Stuart: avant-garde, 16, 26; Kluge characters, 93; modernism, 15–16, 26, 99, 243 n.4; postmodernism, 15–16, 164–65, 243 n.4; spectators, 176
Lucie-Smith, Edward, 215 n.24
Lumière, Auguste and Louis, 152, 180, 186
Lyotard, Jean-Francois, 135, 136, 204

M (Lang), 114
Macht der Gefühle, Die (Power of Emotion, The) (Kluge), 116–27, 231 nn.47–54; actors, 38, 92, 93, 238 n.62; awards, 223 n.80; city, 148; humor, 170–71, 238 n.62; structure, 65, 80, 87–88, 226 n.19; opera, 25, 87–88; sexuality, 235 n.14; stylistic devices, 99, 102, 105, 109–11, 115, 231 n.42
Mainka, Maximiliane, 51, 226 n.15, 229 n.23
Mainka-Jellinghaus, Beate, 221 n.54, 226 n.15, 229 n.23
Malkovich, John, 185

Books in the Contemporary Film and Television Series